BLUE BLOOD
II

ALSO BY ART CHANSKY

BLUE BLOOD II

*Duke-Carolina: The Latest on the Never-Ending
and Greatest Rivalry in College Hoops*

Art Chansky

ST. MARTIN'S PRESS ☙ NEW YORK

BLUE BLOOD II. Copyright © 2018 by Art Chansky. All rights reserved. Printed in the United States of America. For information, address St. Martin's Press, 175 Fifth Avenue, New York, NY 10010.

www.stmartins.com

The Library of Congress Cataloging-in-Publication Data is available upon request.

ISBN 978-1-250-19327-8 (hardcover)
ISBN 978-1-250-19329-2 (ebook)

Our books may be purchased in bulk for promotional, educational, or business use. Please contact your local bookseller or the Macmillan Corporate and Premium Sales Department at 1-800- 221-7945, extension 5442, or by email at MacmillanSpecialMarkets@macmillan.com.

First Edition: October 2018

10 9 8 7 6 5 4 3 2 1

To the millions of college basketball fans who can't wait for the next Duke-Carolina game, and to the thousands who have read these Blue Blood books. And, of course, to the Blue Devils and Tar Heels—past, present, and future!

CONTENTS

ACKNOWLEDGMENTS

Mortality of a Rivalry

In early 2017, I sent a picture to Pete Wolverton, my editor at St. Martin's Press in New York City. It showed a shelf at the Bull's Head Bookshop at UNC with copies of the original *Blue Blood*, which was published in 2005!

Pete texted me back: "Still selling, great!"

Yes, it was, through five printings of the hardback edition and two of the paperback. And twelve years had passed in the rivalry!

So I pitched Pete on the idea of *Blue Blood II*—but not because it would be more of the same anecdotal history of the greatest college basketball rivalry on Earth.

As the Blue Devils and Tar Heels kept winning ACC championships and NCAA titles, the rivalry changed along with the rolling landscape of the college game. Duke was taking players it *knew* wouldn't stay all four years, and Carolina was still winning the Dean Smith, old-fashioned way.

ACKNOWLEDGMENTS

The players on both campuses no longer knew each other from squaring off in eight to ten games during their college careers; if they knew each other at all, it was from competing in the same AAU leagues, playing in the same prep all-star games, or making the same international youth teams. High school recruits had become stars long before they chose a college.

The race for these players was now even more intense, although college coaches knew what they were getting and for how long. Building a successful college basketball program in the twenty-first century became more complicated than ever.

Still, the Blue Bloods down on Tobacco Road kept putting great players and teams out there, producing sensational game after sensational game. It was the true embodiment of the name on the front of the jersey being more important than whatever names graced the back of the unies.

Thus, Pete Wolverton agreed to publish *Blue Blood II*, which would be different from the first. Maybe kinder and gentler than when Smith was protecting his turf and Mike Krzyzewski was trying to claim his piece of it. Or maybe it would be about two programs with still-fiery coaches in their sixties and seventies, respectful of each other, sensing the end of their tenures and vowing to go out strong, whenever that day came.

That's what *Blue Blood II* is about more than anything. The mortality of a rivalry.

It begins with two of the greatest four-year players in the history of college hoops—J. J. Redick playing his last season at Duke and Tyler Hansbrough his first at Carolina. And it runs through a dozen more years of powerhouse programs defending their own backyards while trying to reach the last week of the season at the Final Four. Along the way, some history of the rivalry is woven in for context and comparison.

ACKNOWLEDGMENTS

Wolverton and his assistant, Jennifer Donovan, organized the project and set firm deadlines so the book would come out at the start of another season. Photographer Robert Crawford, who played freshman basketball at UNC in 1967, compiled a colorful file of pictures covering every season since 2005. And colleagues like Al Featherston and Barry Jacobs, still fixtures at every Duke-Carolina game, led the legion of sources who provided their insights, stories, and statistics about the rivalry in the twenty-first century. Hansbrough sat for a candid one-hour interview before heading off to China and his latest pro gig.

Content came from other former players, the *Chronicle* at Duke and *Daily Tar Heel* at UNC, regional newspapers, blogs tied to both schools, video and YouTube clips of game highlights and press conferences, and even an occasional Facebook or Twitter post of interest—nothing from the back-and-forth trolling of fans.

Clearly, Duke-Carolina basketball gets more coverage than any other rivalry in sports because it is truly a national treasure. Editing the manuscript fell to Owen Davis, my longtime newsroom brother since our days at the *DTH* and Atlanta *Constitution*. Now retired in Clemmons, North Carolina, Davis remains the best editor and researcher on the planet. If this book is a damn good read, Owen Davis deserves a lot of the credit.

Much of the overlying theme of *Blue Blood II* is the changes that have occurred in the rivalry and the changes that are, inevitably, coming. The current Hall of Fame coaches personify that theme because they combine for more than fifty years as caretakers and have remained in synch with their players even as that age gap has grown to fifty years as well.

The coaches may be graying and limping and the fans who grew up with them perhaps slower and heavier. But what has stayed exactly the same is the age and excellence of the players and the students who

ACKNOWLEDGMENTS

paint their bodies and crowd courtside each season. Their collective heartbeat is still the soul of the Blue Blood rivalry.

When their turn comes, they compete and cheer with the same gusto as their predecessors from any era. No matter what has gone out of style, they are still all in.

THE RIVALRY IN THEIR OWN WORDS

Mike Krzyzewski:

I don't wake up with a different feeling on game day for Duke-UNC, but it's a different day. It's a day that has more opportunities to be distracted; in other words, there are more people who pay attention to it. There are more people who want to be a part of it. And I have to make sure the people that I'm charged with are themselves on that day—that they're not trying to be somebody different, that they're not too anxious or nervous.

You know because the people around them on that day have a different vibe. And I want to make sure that my team has its normal good vibe. And then the event itself will lift them. But if they're lifted throughout the day or distracted, they won't be the same team that night.

Roy Williams:

I've been involved with this rivalry in about every stage you can be— as a student, an assistant coach, a head coach eleven hundred miles away, and now the head coach at North Carolina. We try to say that it's just a game, and in truth it really is. It's one game on the schedule, but there's a different feeling about it.

You don't have to motivate the team quite as much because they're already motivated. It's the greatest rivalry in all of college basketball, and I've been involved in Kansas-Missouri and the border wars with Oklahoma and Oklahoma State, but this is the best. It does give you as a coach, and I think also as a player, a different feeling in the preparation. For those last couple of days of practice, you have everybody's attention.

Coach K:

There are loud crowds at both places. Obviously, I like it at Cameron because the crowd is cheering for us. I don't look at playing at another place as pressure. I look at it as a great opportunity. One of the best things that can happen as a competitor is to win on an opposing team's home court. And when it's North Carolina's home court, you are playing against one of the great programs of all time. I try not to look at the crowd whether I'm home or away and just concentrate on the people who are out on the court. Over the years, I've been able to do that fairly well.

It's just two good teams, so you can beat each other whether it's home or away. Both programs are not afraid to play on the road. You can look at the overall record over the past twenty-five years of who is best on the road in the ACC, and it would probably be our two programs. It has a life that day that can't be copied because of the intensity. And it just brings something out from the fans you can't copy.

Roy:

Playing the game in either location is different. Here, playing at the Smith Center, you have that excitement from the crowd. The fans are there early and in their seats. They're not waiting till tip-off. They're involved in warm-ups. They're watching. You can tell the apprehension and the anticipation of hopefully a great night. When you go to Cameron, you're the villain. You walk in and everybody's against you. When the guys go out for early warm-ups, they're just shooting around, and when they come back in they're talking. There's not a lot of space there in the locker room, and we see all the guys going out and coming back in, going up the stairs and going back down.

It's a different feeling. You're out there on an island by yourself at Cameron Indoor. When you're over there and they're making a big run and you're trying to slow them down, the crowd just gets louder and louder. The fans can take the noise to a level I've never heard anywhere else. We had it here with Marvin's three-point play in 2005.

Coach K:

I could tell you a lot of stories where it has had a negative influence on my family, and people have done some bad things as a result of the rivalry, but we've been able to handle it. The thing I've tried to do is live my life normally and I'm proud to be the Duke coach, and if you don't like that then it's too bad.

I always tell my teams to respect the rivalry whether we are winning or we're getting killed. In other words, play this out and remember you're in the moment that every kid would like to be in and every coach would like to be in. So, if we win or lose, handle it properly because you should respect the game, especially the game that is played between Duke and North Carolina.

Roy:

The community involvement in both places, and the pride that people have in their own team is as good as it gets. I don't know if it hurts when you lose as much as wanting to brag the next day if you win, but I hope that getting to brag is more important than the hurt you feel. There is no question about it, the signs in my yard and walking around campus and people beeping their horns the day after we win. If we lose, I don't step out to cross the street without looking in both directions completely. If we win, I feel more confident that nobody's going to run me over. It's a total involvement on both campuses and I think in both communities, too.

Coach K:

An NCAA tournament game has more pressure because it's one and done. You know there's a game after you play UNC, whether it's in the middle of the season or in the ACC tournament. You know there's life after that game, but you have to be careful that the one game doesn't become an end-all because sometimes when you lose in a Duke-Carolina game, it's multiple losses. You know you can take it on to the next game. But an NCAA game is always more pressure because if you lose, that's the end of your season.

Roy:

Would Carolina fans rather beat Duke than win anything else? I can give you a great example. In 2007, we played Duke at home in the last regular-season game. It was a day game and we won, so that night Wanda and I went to Squid's for dinner. We walk in and there's a standing ovation. The ACC tournament is the next week in Tampa; we win three games and our first ACC championship and get a No. 1 NCAA seed. After we chartered back, Wanda and I went back to Squid's. Not one person stood up, not one person clapped. Someone said, "Hi, Coach," and went right back to eating. The fans, I think, would rather beat Duke twice and not worry about the Final Fours.

THE RIVALRY IN THEIR OWN WORDS

Coach K:

Roy and I have always been friends because we've been on the board of directors of the coaches' association. We've probably been in a hundred meetings together. We haven't played against each other hundreds of times, so there's that familiarity and a certain level of respect when you see someone in a meeting giving back to the game where we both understand that the game is bigger than either of us.

And my relationship with him as a head coach comes after I've been a head coach for a while. I'm not just trying to build a program here at Duke and fighting for everything. So I have a greater level of respect for who he is and what they do. We'd still like to beat them, nonetheless.

Roy:

When Mike first came to Duke as a young head coach, I was an assistant here. Then I left for fifteen years. We made some very difficult decisions as NABC board members. We were very close together on most issues, what we thought was best for college basketball. And then I came back to North Carolina and it's still a big-time rivalry for everyone, but we have that foundation of a very good relationship.

That doesn't mean I have to like him during the game. It's important, in my mind, for both of us to be very good for the rivalry on the national stage. Now I don't want him to be good on game night. No question, during that game, I want them to stink it up. But there is a very good relationship.

Coach K:

Both coaches, the players and the programs, North Carolina and Duke, are very lucky that we're eight miles apart, and everyone who has been a part of the rivalry has benefited greatly. It's an honor for me. You have two of the storied programs in the history of college basketball right here together. Two great schools, coaches who have tried to do it the right way, players who have handled themselves in a magnificent manner, on and off the court. The standard of college basketball has been set at a higher level as a result of this rivalry.

I'm very lucky to have been at Duke for more than three decades and even luckier that I'm in the ACC and that the ACC has produced the Duke–North Carolina rivalry. To be involved in at least two, sometimes three, games a year has helped me immensely. It has helped Duke University immensely and I think it's helped the University of North Carolina. And it really celebrates the game. And to be a part of that is a pretty cool thing.

Roy:

I feel flattered to be the caretaker on this side, and I like the success that Mike has had because it sets the standard for the current-day coaches to try to live up to that. Coach Smith set that standard for many, many years. In recruiting, I don't talk about any other school, just ours, but one thing I do say is that it's the biggest stage, and why would you not want to play on the biggest stage? If it gets down to our two schools, we've got to make sure that a player understands how important the Duke-Carolina rivalry is, that he wants to play here, that he wants to play against Duke and wants to beat Duke.

And it's not like, "Well, I'm going to North Carolina but I'm going to still like Duke." When you choose to come to North Carolina, you're going to try to beat Duke. And I would say it's the same way for the Duke kids, too.

Coach K:

Dean Smith was one of the great coaches of any sport of all time. He was a masterful tactician, but he was a program builder. He built something that will be forever. And he did it the right way. Just being on the court, competing against him, he played solid basketball—offense, defense, team-wise. He always recruited really good guys, and we didn't want to copy anything he did, but we also understood that you needed character, you needed to be fundamentally sound, and you needed to be competitive. I thought Dean was as competitive as anyone I've gone against in coaching.

Roy:

So many lessons Roy Williams learned from Coach Smith. Complete preparation every single day. Don't leave anything to chance. Make sure you touch every area you can possibly touch on. And that was for every game, not just before playing Duke or N.C. State. And Coach Smith was about people, understanding your players are not machines. They're going to make mistakes. They're going to have good moments and bad, and you've got to be able to handle that. Move them off the bad spots and get them moving back in a positive direction. And make sure they don't get too big for themselves.

Coach K:

The most memorable game for me was when we won our first championship [in 1986]. It was in Cameron on Senior Day, and we won our first regular-season championship. Since then we've won a lot of championships, but you always remember the first one. And to have been able to beat a great North Carolina team that day made it even more worthwhile.

Roy:

The first game in the Smith Center [in 1986]. The fact that it was against Duke in the regular season made it off the charts. I was coaching the JV team, and when that game was over the building was almost packed. If I remember it right, Warren Martin scored the first basket for North Carolina. And it was a great, great win for us.

Coach K:

If we both played for the national championship, people would take it to the extreme. I wouldn't be worried about the competitors on the court, coaches would know how to handle it. I really shudder to think what might happen. I wouldn't want to see that, I would rather not have that. I'd rather have us alternate. You play for it one year, we play for it the next. I worry about the intensity of the rivalry spilling over into some bad stuff.

Roy:

It would mean we made the Final Four and had a chance to win the national championship.

(Excerpts from media interviews and transcripts of interviews for the video documentary Duke-Carolina: The Blue Blood Rivalry, *produced by Greatest Fan Films.)*

BLUE BLOOD
II

ALL-TIME WINS

North Carolina: 2,232*

Duke: 2,144*

Rivalry: UNC 137, Duke 111

- In Durham: Duke leads 52–48
- In Chapel Hill: UNC leads 63–36
- In ACC tournament: Duke leads 13–9
- In NIT: UNC leads 1–0
- In NCAA tournament: 0–0

Longest Duke winning streak vs. UNC: 8 (2/23/51–2/20/54)

Longest UNC winning streak vs. Duke: 16 (2/23/21–2/11/28)

Biggest Duke win: 104–69 at UNC (2/29/64)

Biggest UNC win: 55–18 in Raleigh (3/5/21)

Duke vs. UNC under Mike Krzyzewski: 46–42

- In Durham, 21
- In Chapel Hill, 16
- ACC tournament, 9

UNC vs. Duke under Dean Smith: 59–35

UNC vs. Duke under Roy Williams: 14–19

- In Chapel Hill, 7
- In Durham, 6
- ACC tournament, 1

(*) Kentucky has most wins of all time with 2,256; Kansas is second with 2,248; UNC is third; and Duke is fourth.

PROLOGUE

Their basketball rivalry morphed into one of the fiercest on Tobacco Road—from the days of two-sport Duke star Dick Groat to bitter battles between Blue Devils bad boy Art Heyman and feisty Tar Heels guard Larry Brown—and eventually into the best and most talent-laden college competition in America. National television covered every matchup since 1986, featuring Hall of Fame coaches Dean Smith, Mike Krzyzewski, and then Roy Williams, all of whom possessed tremendous power but ran their programs in unique ways and over time developed different personas.

All time, Duke has won five national championships, each under the commanding Krzyzewski, who passed his rival Smith and mentor Bob Knight for the most career college coaching victories (1,100 through the 2018 season). Final Four coaches Vic Bubas (3) and Bill Foster (1) have added to Duke's 2,144 total wins.

Carolina has six NCAA titles won by three different coaches, Frank McGuire (1), Smith (2), and Williams (3), who own 1,467 of the school's 2,232 all-time victories.

Which program is better can be a long debate, but no doubt these are the two best by any numbers used to measure them against all the rest. And the two sit beside each other, taking care of their own business while also collaborating in many ways. Robertson Scholars have matriculated on both campuses since 2000. The respective sports information offices plan their press conferences so they do not conflict and, in fact, maximize both their media coverage.

No rivalry in sports, college or professional, has this kind of prideful proximity while being so successfully competitive. Duke and Carolina fans have long pondered this question: What has made them happier, their school winning or the archrival losing?

Together, having won more Atlantic Coast Conference and NCAA championships than the rest of the ACC combined made the two schools true blue bloods of basketball. When the prequel to this book came out in 2005, few fans thought the passionate backyard battle could get any better. While the most cherished days of Duke-Carolina remain the mid-1980s through the late 1990s (before the advent of one-and-done players), the last thirteen years have added new wrinkles and different fabrics to the mosaic that has become the only remaining virtue of college basketball's regular season, which for everyone else is now a qualifying run to the NCAA tournament and March Madness.

"More than five thousand regular-season basketball games will be contested this year, but there are only two that need to be savored: North Carolina at Duke and Duke at North Carolina," Chris Dufresne wrote in the *Los Angeles Times* in 2009. The same still applies today.

But Duke-Carolina has since become a study into its own rival recruiting philosophies, disparate playing styles, classic game encounters, coaching milestones, All-Americans and NBA draft picks galore, plus off-the-court drama, and, most recently, the ultimate question of who will be the next caretakers of this national treasure. Krzyzewski turned seventy-one during his thirty-eighth season at Duke; Williams was sixty-eight after fifteen years back at his alma mater following fifteen at Kansas. They have grown older with the rivalry.

Since Williams rescued UNC from the controversy-marred Matt Doherty era in the spring of 2003, the programs combined for 20 ACC regular-season and tournament championships, eight trips to the Final Four, and five NCAA titles through 2018. This left the sky and royal blue bloods virtually dead even in most meaningful, as well as meaningless, metrics.

Williams, who was inducted into the Naismith Hall of Fame in 2007 (following Krzyzewski in 2001 and Smith in 1983), reached 800 career victories, only the eighth coach to do so and the second fastest (behind Kentucky legend Adolph Rupp) to be in that rarefied air. He went into the 2018–19 season, his thirty-first as a head coach, needing 37 victories to match Smith's 879 in thirty-six.

The Blue Devils won more ACC tourneys than Carolina (6–3) during this time and led in head-to-head matchups (19–14). But tellingly, they lost six of seven games against UNC that decided the conference championship on the last day of the regular season. This speaks to where Duke's true priorities settled after reaching seven Final Fours in the nine years from 1986 and 1994. Krzyzewski thought there was no fair way to decide the regular-season title after the ACC expanded and ended its full round-robin competition.

Thus, Williams' Tar Heels finished first in the ACC standings more times (8–3), an accomplishment usually rewarded with a first or second seed in the NCAA tournament; won three national championships to Duke's two since 2004; and they did it with only three one-and-done recruits compared to Duke's fifteen. Although Krzyzewski easily owns the most NCAA tournament coaching victories (94), Williams has a surprisingly better NCAA tourney record since he took over at UNC, 43–11, compared to Krzyzewski's 34–13 through the 2018 season, which has been lost on even some Tar Heels fans.

Carolina accomplished this while using an older style of developing three- and four-year players, necessitated, at least in part, by a

seemingly endless battle with the NCAA for alleged academic impro-
prieties dating back, some say, to the Smith era. That scandal and
the threat of going on probation cost Carolina several in-state marquee players the Tar Heels had traditionally signed, losing two of them
(Brandon Ingram and Harry Giles) to a Duke program that had
almost exclusively recruited out-of-state stars.

Even with these differences, the rivalry kept building after the
original *Blue Blood* was published in 2005. The blue bloods added six
more Final Four appearances and four NCAA championships to their
collective résumé through 2018. Their celebrated coaches did not retire or even wind down, despite health issues plaguing them both, and
signed new contracts that seemed to assure they would work well into
their seventies. The famous arenas in which their teams played looked
the same from inside, save digital upgrades of the age, but both skins
received additions and cosmetic face-lifts, which served mostly as
tributes to their gloried basketball pasts while promoting continued
success.

Duke still squeezed about 9,000 fans into seventy-eight-year-old
Cameron Indoor Stadium, which was expanded on its north and east
flanks to include new concourses with glass trophy cases and photos
of its greatest resident teams and stars, and more meeting rooms
where Iron Duke donors could schmooze before games. To help pay
for that, Duke raised all-inclusive Iron Duke ticket prices as high
as $225 for the UNC game and up to $200 for those against other
opponents.

A once cramped dressing room with wire-mesh lockers was turned
over to the women's volleyball team in favor of a new plush players
lounge and locker room underneath the expanded concourse. Also
erected next to Cameron was a practice facility in whose hallways
hung even more hardware of lore and where former players were always welcome to change and work out. This is what millions more in

television money and championships will buy in these abundant days of college athletics. The basketball offices had long since been relocated to an austere tower that overlooked the complex and a grassy area converted to a tent city named after Krzyzewski, where overzealous students camped out in dicey weather before the annual Carolina game, sometimes for two months if the regular-season finale was at Cameron.

The Dean Smith Center at UNC was now into its fourth decade, having hosted more seasons than were played at cozy Carmichael Auditorium, where Carolina's breakout teams of the 1960s, '70s, and early '80s rose to national fame. It seemed time for the Dean Dome to receive a multi-hundred-million-dollar renovation to correct its original foibles of a narrow, one-floor concourse and now too many seats to solve the supply-and-demand slippage caused by HD TV and 9 p.m. tip-off times. Or better yet, raze the octagon for a billion-dollar rebuild with fewer seats in favor of corporate boxes, which would end the two-generational seat licenses that kept season-ticket-holders from having to re-up to refinance the Dome over the last thirty years. Both ideas were tabled.

Instead, a basketball museum in an adjacent building was expanded, and creative use of space allowed for a Letterman's Lane donated by one of their most famous former stars (Vince Carter). It came along with Williams raising the money for a spectacular trophy-lined basketball suite above a lavish third locker room expansion that belied the Smith Center's cramped bowels.

Even with this continuing cadence of success for both Duke and Carolina Basketball, philosophical differences arose between the programs, caused mostly by the growth of the game and problems inherent within. After being among the last college teams to have players leave early for the NBA—Corey Maggette was Duke's first one-and-done, in 1999—the Blue Devils twelve years later began signing prep stars they knew would not stay for long. This seemed contradictory to the school's longtime and proud reputation of educational as well as athletic excellence.

From 2011 to 2018, Kyrie Irving, Austin Rivers, Jabari Parker, Rodney Hood, Jahlil Okafor, Justise Winslow, Tyus Jones, Ingram, Giles, Jayson Tatum, and Frank Jackson left after playing only one season at Duke. All were high NBA draft choices, multimillionaires before they could legally drink. After the 2018 season, four more one-and-dones—starters Marvin Bagley III, Wendell Carter Jr., Trevon Duval, and Gary Trent Jr.—helped the Blue Devils reach the NCAA Midwest Regional final and then declared for the NBA draft.

Krzyzewski has never been shy about playing freshmen, but his recruitment of one-and-done talents was reflected in their domination of Duke freshman records in minutes played, points scored, and rebounding. It underscored Coach K's viewpoint that the best players got the minutes, regardless of class.

The fast philosophy, which included coaxing several recruits to re-classify after their junior years in high school and jump right to college, was as much a fallacy as a success. The strategy worked better for the players, most of whom wound up drafted, than the schools using it. Duke and Kentucky combined for five Final Fours and two national championships over an eight-year period, when more was expected of both packed, high-profile programs.

One of those Duke seasons, 2015, delivered an NCAA title. The 2013 team that did not lose anyone early had Duke's second-best NCAA tournament run of that stretch, echoing its mostly veteran national championship teams of 1991, '92, 2001, and 2010. One of Krzyzewski's favorite cities was Las Vegas, where he became friends with hotel casino impresario Steve Wynn. While he knew that stockpiling one-year, NBA-bound players was a solid bet to keep the Blue Devils in the headlines and rankings, Coach K was rolling the dice on developing them into a true national championship contender in such a short period of time.

UNC, meanwhile, had two one-and-done players during the three seasons of 2005–07, but went without another for ten years. That was attributable mainly to an NCAA investigation that scared off most of the top high school prospects, who feared they would be on a team banned from postseason play.

In fact, both universities could not avoid controversies and scandals that threatened their very greatness and long-standing pristine images.

In March of 2006, the Duke men's lacrosse team held its annual rowdy house party. Three white players were accused of sexually assaulting an African American exotic dancer who was hired for fun, not felonious activities. The story made national news and attracted the usual opponents in a racially torn battle. The culprit turned out to be an overambitious Durham district attorney, a UNC law school graduate, no less, who ignored lack of evidence and proceeded with indictments that divided a campus and city.

The case was eventually thrown out by state attorney general Roy Cooper, whose swift decision cost the local DA his job and law license. It also catapulted Cooper toward the 2016 gubernatorial race, which he won in part because the incumbent supported a discriminatory statute aimed at the LGBTQ community. The backlash against the law—since repealed—cost North Carolina billions in revenues from sporting and entertainment events that were canceled or moved out of the state, and it dealt a blow to the name of a once progressive state considered among the top retirement and industry destinations in the country.

A year after Duke's dramatic 2010 NCAA basketball championship, one of the Blue Devils' senior starters on that team, Lance Thomas, was exposed for having purchased more than $100,000 of bling from a New York City jeweler early in the season, paying for about one-third of it and leaving an IOU for the balance. That could have been an impermissible benefit while Thomas was still a competing amateur athlete. Thomas was already in the NBA when the story broke and, shortly after, the jeweler who had called in the note said he was paid off in full. A potential NCAA investigation and penalty, which could have revoked Duke's fourth championship banner, was averted by the university. Its records not only were protected from the Freedom of Information Act, the private school could more easily shut down leaks and settle matters internally. Plus, the governing body of college athletics lacked subpoena power and the gumption to grill Krzyzewski, who by then was also the head of the USA Basketball men's team and about to win his country's second of three consecutive Olympic gold medals under his leadership.

Much the same non-outcome resulted in 2014 after two Duke coeds complained that a star basketball player named Rasheed Sulaimon had offended them with unwanted sexual advances, according to a report in *The Chronicle*, the student newspaper. Before the mainstream media could run any of that down, the participants and witnesses went silent, and the story died with no charges filed. Sulaimon, who had been booted from the team for undisclosed reasons, finished Duke in three years and transferred to Maryland. He played his final (2016) season as a graduate student for the Terrapins, who the year before had bolted the Atlantic Coast Conference for the Big Ten.

Without Sulaimon, the 2015 Blue Devils started three freshmen and beat veteran Michigan State and Wisconsin teams to win Duke's fifth NCAA championship. Three of the freshmen became poster children for the basketball program's shockingly sudden switch from signing true "student-athletes" to going after the most highly rated recruits who had the expressed intent to play one season and be gone, entering the NBA draft.

PROLOGUE

None of that compared to what happened eight miles down the road, where UNC spent most of seven years under NCAA scrutiny. The result was one probation and a 2012 postseason ban for its football team and a second investigation into academic irregularities that arose during the first probe. Having the NCAA stalk its campus for the first time in fifty years, the University of North Carolina found itself ill-equipped to manage the inquiry and school its athletes on not being tripped up by interrogators' trick questions. When one football player said too much about loving his college experience and all who had helped him, the name of a tutor surfaced, and the NCAA hit the tip of the iceberg that nearly proved Titanic to the Tar Heels' future.

It opened a Pandora's box at a highly rated university, and it hardly remained quiet. UNC already had the typical detractors toward big-time college athletics, including faculty members who wanted "less-qualified" students (i.e., athletes) to stay the hell away from their departments and classes. Then came the learning specialist who blew whistles about information that was supposed to be private.

With the first probation over and the NCAA sending a letter of finality, the Board of Governors that runs the state university system insisted on one more independent investigation into certain classes taken by athletes in the African and Afro-American Studies department, part of the School of Arts and Sciences.

The study was conducted by a former federal prosecutor who had moved into private practice, and the results compelled the NCAA to return for a second inquest. It lasted for three-plus years and produced thousands of public documents the media could, and did, sue to have released. That's one thing Duke had over UNC, the ability to bury its bodies wherever it chose while the state university was subject to public records requests and, in this case, botched its own attempted transparency in multiple ways.

The investigation found that the African and Afro-American Studies Department administrative assistant—and thirty-year live-in girlfriend of a former Dean Smith player (Warren Martin)—converted some cataloged lecture courses to independent studies. By doing that, she eliminated regular class time, and she leniently graded papers for athletes (and nonathletes) who needed help to either stay eligible or boost their grade point average. The NCAA called it lack of institutional control, but levied no more penalties because it was primarily an academic matter outside its own purview and bylaws.

Regardless of the final outcome, Carolina suffered damage to its public-Ivy image and served a probationary period with its accreditation agency, which cited substantial lack of administrative oversight. Meanwhile, Roy Williams, its renowned basketball coach who had signed twenty-six McDonald's All-Americans in the years before the scandal broke, could barely get a five-star prospect to visit campus. Most of them were spooked by rival recruiters who warned that they would never play in an NCAA tournament game while wearing a North Carolina uniform.

Fortunately, the program was already stocked with potentially good players who stayed three or four years. In spite of the ongoing saga, which featured three separate notices of allegations from the NCAA, three strong responses from the university and its legal team, and as many twists and turns as a John Grisham novel, the basketball team won an ACC regular-season race and reached consecutive national championship games. The first season, 2016, ended with a buzzer-beating loss to Villanova, the second with a redemptive victory over Gonzaga. The championship relieved the strain of being ridiculed by rival fans and chewed up by most of the media for problems that long preceded the players who eventually cut down the nets.

In the final irony of the ordeal, the NCAA Committee on Infractions reached a decision the same day a new championship banner was to be unfurled. Though it clearly wanted to impose punishment, the NCAA agreed with what UNC and informed pundits like lawyer/ESPN analyst Jay Bilas—a former Duke player—had argued for months. No matter what kinds of classes were offered, how they were taught and graded, and how many jocks took them, academics was not in the jurisdiction of the National Collegiate *Athletic* Association unless it could prove any athletes had cheated and were rendered, retroactively, as ineligible participants. Frankly, the classes in question appeared to be so easy, no enrollees needed to cheat to get a grade and move on.

That is most of what this book has to say about those, and other, off-court indignities at the two beloved schools because so much more infinitely interesting stuff about basketball is reported, including how long the current coaches would continue after combining for three knee replacements and five other surgeries in a four-year span. As they healed up both their bodies and rosters during the off-seasons, the games of the last thirteen years have been as close and intense as any in the rivalry's history, with upsets, improbable comebacks, and even more talented individual play.

So, enjoy *BLUE BLOOD II.*

RIVALRY BESTS

NCAA titles: UNC 6, Duke 5
- Mike Krzyzewski, 5
- Roy Williams, 3
- Dean Smith, 2

NCAA Final Fours: UNC 20 (1), Duke 16 (4)
- Mike Krzyzewski, 12 (tied with John Wooden for most)
- Dean Smith, 11
- Roy Williams, 9 (4 at Kansas)

NCAA Sweet 16s: UNC 33, Duke 30
- Mike Krzyzewski, 24 (all-time leader)
- Dean Smith, 21
- Roy Williams, 18 (9 at Kansas)

NCAA tournament wins: UNC 124, Duke 111
- Mike Krzyzewski, 94 (all-time leader)*
- Roy Williams, 77 (34 at Kansas)
- Dean Smith, 65

ACC regular-season championships: UNC 31, Duke 19
- Dean Smith, 17
- Mike Krzyzewski, 12
- Roy Williams, 8

ACC tournament championships: Duke 20, UNC 18
- Mike Krzyzewski, 14
- Dean Smith, 13
- Roy Williams, 3

(*) Coach K's NCAA winning percentage of .764 leads all active coaches

INTRODUCTION

CELEBRATIONS

For the second time in their storied basketball rivalry, Duke University and the University of North Carolina held NCAA championship celebrations in consecutive years.

The first came after Duke won back-to-back national titles in 1991 and 1992 and Carolina won in '93. Duke's championships were the first and second in a rich history that included eight previous trips to the Final Four. At the raucous reception at Cameron Indoor Stadium upon the team's arrival home from Minneapolis on April 7, 1992, a day after the Blue Devils defeated Michigan's Fab Five 71–51, students and fans began to chant, "Mike has two, Dean has one!"

Duke coach Mike Krzyzewski, at the beginning of his ascension toward the zenith of his profession, tried halfheartedly to stop the boisterous barb, saying into the microphone, "Let's be happy about what we have accomplished." The year before, after Duke had broken through and won the 1991 NCAA tournament by defeating Kansas in Indianapolis, the team bus chugged down Interstate 40 from Raleigh-Durham Airport when it approached the fork that had a left arrow pointing to Chapel Hill and the right arrow going to Durham. Now known widely as Coach K, he turned to his team and said loudly, "Hey, you want to go cruise Franklin Street?"—the main drag abutting the UNC campus. The players broke out in joyous laughter at their coach's dig.

By early in the 1992–93 season, coach Dean Smith's Tar Heels knew they had a team capable of not only winning his second national championship, they were determined to reclaim the ballyhoo they had lost to Duke. Smith's first title had come in the 1982 epic victory over Patrick Ewing and Georgetown in New Orleans on a swish shot by freshman Michael Jordan, but they had returned to the Final Four only once since then, in 1991, along with Duke. UNC lost to Roy Williams' third Kansas team in the national semifinals; the Blue Devils upset top-ranked and unbeaten UNLV and then defeated the Jayhawks for their first NCAA title.

The geographic area of North Carolina known as the Research Triangle is a hub for technology companies and home to three major universities within a twenty-five-mile radius, and the market is covered by the same media. The Raleigh *News & Observer* and Durham *Herald-Sun* both report on all three schools; television stations WRAL, WNCN, and WTVD, plus the sports talk shows, try to be fair and impartial to the giant athletic programs at Duke, N.C. State, and UNC. But when one team goes further into postseason play, and the others return home in defeat, the papers and stations double-down on their coverage of whichever is still standing with a chance to "win it all."

In the summer of 1992, George Lynch and Eric Montross—the stalwarts in UNC's upcoming season—were fishing at a pond about fifteen miles west of Chapel Hill. In the solitude of the rowboat, they shared their mutual frustration over Duke's nonstop publicity of late and pledged they would lead their teammates back to New Orleans

INTRODUCTION

for the 1993 Final Four so Smith could win a second NCAA title in the Big Easy.

Montross is still remembered for his bloody battle with Christian Laettner in UNC's 1992 upset of the top-ranked and 17–0 Blue Devils at the Smith Center. Students rushed the court afterward, which angered Smith because, he said, "We're supposed to beat Duke." Krzyzewski regretted the game for a different reason. "Bobby [Hurley] broke his foot, and if he doesn't sit out three weeks we might have been undefeated that season with what I thought was my best team," he said of his second straight NCAA champs.

Fourteen months later, Lynch, Montross, and the rest of the Tar Heels took the stage and celebrated with the packed Louisiana Superdome. They had beaten Kansas in the semifinals and Michigan's Fab Five in the final to bring home Carolina's third national championship trophy, including Frank McGuire's miracle 32–0 season of 1957. UNC was back on top and Duke's dream to three-peat was over, ended by Jason Kidd and Cal in the second round as Blue Devils All-American Grant Hill hobbled with a foot injury.

Now Mike had two and Dean had two. And then came an occurrence that was to be repeated two decades later. In 1994, Duke returned to the championship game and lost to Arkansas on a last-minute 3-pointer by Scotty Thurman. In 2016, a year after the young Blue Devils had won Duke's fifth NCAA title, UNC reached the championship game and lost on a buzzer-beating long ball by Villanova's Kris Jenkins.

The best rivalry in college basketball ebbed and flowed through the rest of the 1990s, when each school reached five Final Fours. Krzyzewski missed almost a full season with medical problems in 1995, and two years after his return Smith's long-anticipated retirement ceded the mantle to Coach K.

His teams whipped Carolina 15 of 17 games during a stretch from

1999 to 2005, and Duke enjoyed an unprecedented run of winning the ACC regular season and/or conference tournament for an astounding 10 consecutive seasons (1997–2006).

In 1998–2000, the Blue Devils went 46–2 in the ACC regular season, including a pulsating 1998 comeback win over the Tar Heels at steamy Cameron for Krzyzewski's 500th career victory. Duke also was beating Carolina in most head-to-head recruiting battles (Shane Battier, Elton Brand, Mike Dunleavy) and getting players from as far away as Alaska (Trajan Langdon and Carlos Boozer).

The twenty-first century featured long, grinding campaigns for both programs, with Duke on top during the early years while Carolina collapsed in turmoil after inexperienced Matt Doherty succeeded Bill Guthridge, the successor to Dean Smith. The veteran team Doherty inherited in 2001 did win at Cameron for UNC's first victory there since 1996 but paid the price in two subsequent meetings that season, including a humiliating 26-point beat-down for the ACC tournament title in Atlanta, where Doherty swore the game clock never moved whenever he looked at it.

After the 79–53 blowout of the Tar Heels before the biggest crowd in ACC tourney history, and marking the 600th career victory for Coach K, the Blue Devils won a third NCAA title over Arizona back in Minneapolis, where they had stripped the nets for their second national championship nine years earlier.

Doherty's second team posted a school-worst 8–20 record, snapped a plethora of streaks begun by Smith and extended by Guthridge, and was on the verge of UNC's largest losing margin at home against Duke when Krzyzewski called off the dogs with a timeout and 30-point lead. "There has been great basketball played in this building before, and there will be again," he yelled at his smirking players. "So, go out there and finish the game, shake their hands and walk off the court."

It turned out that two of Doherty's three highly recruited freshmen the next season—Raymond Felton and Rashad McCants—helped him win his *last* regular-season game against the Blue Devils, in March 2003. But not before Doherty and Duke assistant coach Chris Collins engaged in a foul-mouthed, chest-bumping incident that had the irritated Krzyzewski wishing the game and eventual three-point loss had ended right then and there. The often fiery coach was turning into more of a diplomat. "It was like an alarm clock, game over, we lost," he said.

After Carolina finished 19–16 and missed the NCAA tournament for a second straight year, a third coaching change in six seasons brought Roy Williams back to his alma mater from Kansas in April 2003, fifteen years removed from the UNC bench as an assistant next to Smith. "The family business needs you," Smith told his protégé.

By then, Duke and Krzyzewski were the most prominent names in college hoops, and Williams vowed to restore unity on and off the court among dissenting players, disenfranchised former Tar Heels, and disgusted fans. He also intended to sign five-star recruits who could rival Duke on the floor.

Williams, a virtual unknown when he landed the Kansas job in 1988 with the help of KU alumnus Smith, was now a renowned name in his own right after winning more than 80 percent of his games coaching the Jayhawks. In the summer of 2000, he had turned down the chance to return to Chapel Hill when Guthridge stepped down after three seasons; Williams cited pledges he had made to his last recruiting class at Kansas. Potential pros Nick Collison, Drew Gooden, and Kirk Hinrich had said they would go to KU only if Williams agreed to coach them as long as they were in Lawrence, and they had all just finished their freshman season.

So Williams stayed, led the Jayhawks to the third and fourth Final Fours of his tenure there, and then went home to North Carolina after losing the 2003 national championship game to Syracuse. He returned largely because Smith asked him again and Williams' father and older sister were in failing health back in his native Asheville. He had been out recruiting for Kansas when his mother died in 1992, and he wanted to be closer this time to his remaining childhood family members. Estranged father Babe Williams died of cancer in 2004, and sister Frances succumbed after a short battle with dementia in 2005.

His first season as head coach at UNC was more about restoring a winning culture and work ethic to the Carolina program, which was wrought with distrust and infighting from having lost 36 games in the last two seasons. Williams found the players in such bad physical condition less than a month after the 2003 season ended that several almost puked when he put them through a 28-minute workout just to see what he had for a new team.

He reviewed the stats and saw guys were doing things—like shooting 3-pointers—beyond their capabilities. In individual meetings, he told each of them what he expected, and if they could not obey he would help them transfer to another school. Jackie Manuel, who had been Doherty's whipping boy, was one of them and agreed to stay, and he became the defensive stopper the rest of the team eventually followed.

In Williams' first two games against Duke, the Tar Heels let Chris Duhon drive the length of the court to steal a two-point overtime victory at the Smith Center, and in the rematch at Cameron, McCants had the ball in the frontcourt in the final seconds when Carolina trailed by three, but Duke's aggressive defense forced a turnover. Williams cajoled them to a 19–11 record and back into the NCAA tournament, but so much remained to get his program where he wanted it. The Blue Devils finished first in the ACC regular season and reached their fourteenth Final Four.

INTRODUCTION

After a grueling first season getting players, alumni, and fans back on the same page, and with UNC's six-year record against Duke at 2–15, change came dramatically in the 2005 game on Senior Day at the Smith Center. The Blue Devils were on the verge of winning their fifth straight over Carolina, holding a nine-point lead with a little more than three minutes left to play. Williams called timeout, told his players to get their heads up, and said something that, at the time, he thought might be blarney.

"We're going to win this game," he yelled at them. "If you all do everything I tell you to do, I guarantee you we're going to win this game. It's got to be a total commitment. You have to do it right now better than you have ever done it before. And if you do that, if you'll give me total commitment on every possession, I promise you we're going to win this game!"

Clearly a last-ditch effort to save a game that had all but slipped away, what other choice did Williams have? He later admitted to "maybe lying" because he had nothing else to say. But his team took it to heart, kept Duke marksman J. J. Redick scoreless in the second half, and closed with an 11–0 run to win 75–73 on a three-point play by freshman Marvin Williams as the Teflon roof nearly blew off the dome. "The loudest I have ever heard any building anywhere," Williams said after winning his first ACC regular-season championship as a head coach.

A month later, his Tar Heels were in St. Louis for the Final Four when Williams ran into Redick, who was there for a college all-star game after the Blue Devils had been ousted in the Sweet 16. "You may not believe me, but I'll be pulling for you this weekend," Redick told Williams, who replied, "You're right, I don't believe you." In addition to everything else about the rivalry, Krzyzewski had just surpassed Dean Smith's record with his sixty-sixth NCAA tournament victory before losing to Michigan State.

Carolina went on to win a seminal national championship that one-upped the Blue Devils, defeating top-ranked Illinois at the Illini orange–festooned Edward Jones Dome. Williams' first NCAA title was the school's fourth, and the remarkable turnaround brought Carolina Basketball back together. Smith, Michael Jordan, and Phil Ford joined the team celebration in the locker room, during which Williams pointed to them and said to his players, "They are what made North Carolina basketball great, and now you all are part of that forever."

Upon returning to his home in an upscale Chapel Hill golf course community, several signs were in Williams' front yard, one reading, "Thanks for 'Heeling' our team."

Four players left and became NBA draft lottery picks that spring, but 6'9" Tyler Hansbrough enrolled before the next season, and among other things, he helped Carolina beat Duke more often. The Tar Heels won six of eight matchups in his four years at Chapel Hill. They also added two more Final Four trips, losing to Williams' former Kansas team in San Antonio in 2008 and completing a destruction of the tournament field with six victories by double figures in 2009. Carolina dismantled Michigan State for the championship at Ford Field in Detroit, less than a hundred miles from the Spartans' East Lansing campus, on Monday night.

It was another chance to celebrate, and a large Tuesday crowd, coincidentally on a teacher workday in Chapel Hill, assembled at the Smith Center and watched on the big video boards as news helicopters tracked the path of police escorts and two buses leaving the airport with the team and traveling party. The buses rolled into Chapel Hill and took a victory lap of sorts through campus before parking behind the arena.

Inside, the digital boards lit up with the final score: UNC 89, Michigan State 72 . . . 2009 National Champions. An estimated 12,000 people had shown up for the welcome-home party, and they cheered loudly when the weary team filed onto the stage, some holding up mini camcorders to record the moment. Final Four Most Outstanding Player Wayne Ellington wore one of the nets they stripped after the game and, at the end, Williams carried out the NCAA trophy. "These young men gave me one fantastic ride," he said to a huge roar.

There was no mention of Durham, except for the introduction of longtime Tar Heels radio broadcaster Woody Durham, who hosted the celebration. After about thirty minutes of speeches by several players, the team gathered around its coach for one last time that season and walked off to resume lives that had been changed forever. Carolina was back on top of the college basketball world after a four-year record of 124–22, including 70–7 the last two seasons. But eight miles away Duke was getting ready to counter.

The Blue Devils were in a bit of a slump, if you can call averaging 27-plus victories and capturing three ACC tournament championships over the prior five years a slump. They had come to believe that March was their month, but were under fire from critics for lacking quality play by their big men. Duke had not returned to the Final Four since a 2004 semifinals loss to Connecticut in San Antonio, falling three times in the NCAA Sweet 16, once in the second round and once in the first March Madness game they played in 2007.

However, Krzyzewski returned one of his most experienced squads for the 2009–10 season while Carolina had lost all five starters, four to the NBA. The Blue Devils were led by multiskilled and vastly underrated junior forward Kyle Singler, two sharpshooting guards—senior Jon Scheyer and junior Nolan Smith—and two senior post men who were turned into exceptional role players, bearded Brian Zoubek and Lance Thomas, an erstwhile top 10 high school recruit.

The next time a national championship celebration occurred in the Research Triangle, Duke held it after that excellent and efficient

2010 squad clobbered Carolina at Cameron by 32 points, swept both the ACC regular season and tournament, and reached the 11th Final Four of Krzyzewski's career, tying Smith for the second most of any coach to date, behind UCLA's John Wooden.

The Final Four was in Indianapolis, the site of Duke's first NCAA championship in 1991, and the Blue Devils won their fourth national title by out-slugging rugged West Virginia and outlasting Cinderella Butler, which twice had shots to win the game. Besides the thousands of Duke fans across the country, most everyone else was pulling for Brad Stevens' Bulldogs to shock the world. They almost did.

At the reception at a crazy Cameron on Tuesday, April 6, Krzyzewski said he loved his team and singled out Nolan Smith, whose deceased father, Derek, had played for Louisville and defeated Duke in the 1986 national championship game, Coach K's first Final Four. The packed arena cheered Smith and chanted "one more year!" for Singler, the Most Outstanding Player of the Final Four, who indeed did return with Smith for their senior seasons.

This 2010 team was not mega-talented like the Laettner-Hurley-Hill champs of the early '90s, but it embraced the challenge of the newest buzz phrase in sports: Everyone did his job, especially the big guys inside who came to relish the dirty work of grabbing rebounds and starting fast breaks or relocating the ball outside for open 3-pointers. Duke teams were rarely dominant on the backboards, but this one finished seventh in the country in offensive rebounding percentage and knocked down 301 three-balls for the season, many coming on second-chance possessions.

Five years later, Duke won it all again and tied Carolina for NCAA championships with five. Jahlil Okafor, Tyus Jones, and Justise Winslow were the only one-and-dones for Krzyzewski through 2018 who found the pot of gold at the end of the freshman rainbow. It was a shooting star, almost like a summer romance that was over way too soon and could not have been as satisfying for Coach K as the 2010 team that was more vintage Dewan Smith, winning with system over talent and mind over matter.

The Tar Heels pulled ahead with their sixth in 2017, defeating Oregon and Gonzaga in tense Final Four games remembered more for their poor shooting than for better rebounding, playmaking, and defense. At one point during that 2017 season, Duke and UNC had split their most recent 96 meetings and scored exactly 7,437 points against each other.

In both 2017 and 2018, each team won at home during the regular season and then met in the semifinals of the ACC tournament in Brooklyn. The favorite lost that third game (UNC in '17 and Duke in '18) but advanced further in the NCAA tournament, demonstrating that what happens between Duke and Carolina is often anomalous to the rest of college basketball. That is the unique nature of the Blue Blood rivalry.

CLASSES THAT RESTORED THE RIVALRY

Duke
Freshman Class of 2003
Sean Dockery
Lee Melchionni
Shavlik Randolph*
J. J. Redick
Michael Thompson*
Shelden Williams

Freshman Class of 2004
Patrick Davidson
Luol Deng*
Joe Pagliuca

Freshman Class of 2005
David McClure
DeMarcus Nelson

Freshman Class of 2006
Eric Boateng*
Jamal Boykin*
Jordan Davidson*
Josh McRoberts*
Greg Paulus
Martynas Pocius

UNC
Freshman Class of 2003
Raymond Felton*
Damion Grant
Sean May*
Rashad McCants*
David Noel
Byron Sanders

Freshman Class of 2004
Reyshawn Terry

Freshman Class of 2005
Wes Miller
Quentin Thomas
Marvin Williams*

Freshman Class of 2006
Mike Copeland
Bobby Frasor
Marcus Ginyard
Danny Green
Tyler Hansbrough

(*) **Did not stay four years**

1

HANSBROUGH INDOOR STADIUM

Tyler Hansbrough is not sure he had met or even heard from Roy Williams while Williams was still head coach at the University of Kansas, which is about six hours to the northwest of Poplar Bluff, Missouri, where the Hansbrough family lived. After Williams left KU for his alma mater in April of 2003 to coach the Tar Heels, the recruiting began in earnest.

Hansbrough was recruited by Bill Self, who succeeded Williams at Kansas, and admits he might have gone to KU if not for the coaching change. Painfully shy 6'9" kids from small towns who love their families—and hate to fly, which he did—prefer to drive down the interstate rather than make a plane change to North Carolina. But Hansbrough (as well as his parents) favored the UNC coach after getting to know him.

Williams first saw Hansbrough play at the Nike All-American camp in Indianapolis the summer before the big blond's junior year in high school. "I was watching everybody that day, but I kept noticing this 6-9 kid who was running the floor and banging into everyone,"

Williams recalled in his autobiography, *Hard Work*. He said although Hansbrough was "not that skilled and doesn't look pretty, he plays the way I want a big man to play." After watching Hansbrough in another tournament later that summer and going to see him three or four times as a high school junior, Williams had to have him, another big Midwestern post man like Raef Lafrentz and Nick Collison at Kansas. Whether flying a private plane or puddle jumper into the Poplar Bluff municipal airport, it became a familiar trip for Williams.

On one of those visits, during an observation-only period of the recruiting calendar, Williams watched Hansbrough and his teammates lift weights at 7 a.m. and shoot around at 7:30 before school started. He then returned at 8:00 that night to see the team play pickup games. In between, Williams went golfing with four or five coaches from the high school. Aware that Duke had already visited with Hansbrough's coach, John David Pattillo, Williams said to Pattillo, "I can only say hello to Tyler, but can you remind him that when Coach Krzyzewski came here he just watched pickup games, but I've watched him lift weights, watched him shoot, and then stayed all day and watched the pickup. That's the way I'm going to do it. I'm going to try to outwork everybody."

Williams said he thought it was something that might appeal to Hansbrough, one of the hardest-working high school players he had ever seen. Williams grew more impressed when he learned the Hansbrough family story. Tyler was in between younger brother, Ben, and older brother, Greg, who at one point was projected as the best athlete.

At seven years old, Greg was diagnosed with an inoperable brain tumor that was basically a death sentence. Father Gene Hansbrough, an orthopedic surgeon, scoured the country for other opinions about his son's condition and found one at the Mayo Clinic in Minnesota, where a neurosurgeon said he would perform the operation but gave

Greg only a 50-50 chance to recover and have any quality of life. Greg survived, and with permanent disabilities became Tyler's hero. Greg made the Poplar Bluff basketball team, playing basically one-handed, and later turned into an accomplished long-distance runner and author who penned his own story. Tyler wore Greg's No. 50 uniform and kept that number through college and his professional career.

By the summer of 2004, Hansbrough had moved Duke out of his final four schools of Kansas, Kentucky, Missouri, and UNC. The closer he got to Williams and the Carolina program, which included getting snowed in during an official visit in January of 2004 and an unofficial return on a beautiful summer day the following June, Duke fell further down the list. Hansbrough had watched the Duke-UNC rivalry on TV, like most other college basketball fans around the country, but said he did not have a particular favorite at that time. That began to change on his trips to Chapel Hill.

"Before I committed to North Carolina, I was pretty neutral," Hansbrough said years later. "I enjoyed following the rivalry as a big fan of the game. It was just kind of cool to watch and imagine playing in some day."

True to his word, Williams kept outworking every other school chasing Hansbrough. He sent on average three handwritten notes a week to Hansbrough's home, all including a thought for the day from his practice plans. When he found out from his father that Tyler only opened the envelopes with a UNC Basketball return address, Williams then sent something almost daily.

Williams left in August for the 2004 Olympic Games in Athens, where he was Larry Brown's assistant coach, and figured Hansbrough would announce his decision while he was overseas. On August 5, Williams called assistant coach Joe Holladay at 5:00 in the morning and learned Hansbrough had picked UNC. He had his next star signee, although he had no idea of the once clumsy kid's upside.

An entire season of high school and college basketball remained before Hansbrough arrived in Chapel Hill, part of a highly rated recruiting class that included 6'3" combo guard and coach's son Bobby Frasor, 6'5" athlete and defensive ace Marcus Ginyard, 6'5" explosive scorer Danny Green, and 6'7" banger Mike Copeland.

Even after his Tar Heels won the 2005 NCAA championship, Williams thought Sean May would return for his senior season and allow Hansbrough to come off the bench as a freshman in 2006. May had been the best player in the country over the last month of the season—with eight straight double-doubles from Duke game to Duke game capped by 26 points and 24 rebounds on Senior Day against the Blue Devils in the regular-season finale. After winning MVP in the NCAA East Regional and Most Outstanding Player in the Final Four, May decided his pro stock would never be higher. After all, he had 26 points and 10 rebounds in the national championship game against Illinois, surpassing his father, Scott's, performance (26 and eight) in undefeated Indiana's 1976 NCAA title victory over Michigan.

May joined freshman Marvin Williams, whose tip-in gave UNC its last lead in the national championship game, and fellow juniors Raymond Felton and Rashad McCants in the 2005 NBA draft, the first time four players from one school were lottery picks the same year. (Duke had four first-round picks in 1999, but only three were in the lottery.)

With those four and the team's three seniors gone, Carolina lost 90 percent of its scoring, 79 percent of its rebounding, and 122 blocked shots. The exodus left Roy Williams with one of his youngest teams for the 2006 season.

Suddenly, Tyler Hansbrough was the new center of attention for the Tar Heels, and Williams still had no idea how that would work out. Then Duke stars J. J. Redick and Shelden Williams announced they were forgoing the NBA draft to play their senior years, bent on getting back to a second Final Four and winning it this time. Duke had blown a big lead against UConn in the 2004 national semifinals, and the return of Redick and Williams installed the Blue Devils as the nation's top-ranked team heading into the new season.

Top recruit Shaun Livingston had gone straight to the NBA and 2004 freshman Luol Deng turned pro, but they had finished 27–6 in 2005 and won their sixth ACC tournament in the last seven years. Duke had lost only Daniel Ewing from its starting lineup and added freshmen Josh McRoberts, a versatile 6'10" forward rated Hansbrough's equal coming out of high school, and plucky point guard Greg Paulus, who was also a high school football star and eventually used his fifth year of college eligibility to play quarterback as a graduate student for Syracuse in fall of 2009.

After Carolina's national championship, the Blue Devils remained masters of the rivalry, having beaten the Tar Heels in 15 of their last 18 meetings while in the midst of an unprecedented string of ACC regular-season and tournament titles. Still, knowing UNC had cut down the last nets the previous April wasn't lost on Shelden Williams. "I want to accomplish some of the things Carolina did," the reigning National Defensive Player of the Year said upon announcing his return with Redick. Projected high first-round draft choices, Redick and Williams had made first-team All-ACC, and Redick was a unanimous All-American, the Rupp National Player of the Year, and ACC Player of the Year in 2005. Duke was loaded, a consensus No. 1 pick in the polls.

The Blue Devils ran out to a 17–0 start and multi-game lead in the 2006 ACC regular-season race before losing to Georgetown at the MCI Center in Washington, D.C. They then won four more to stand 21–1 going into the first Carolina game on February 7 in Chapel Hill. The Tar Heels—starting three freshmen, junior Reyshawn Terry, and senior David Noel—had opened the season unranked and got off to the expected uneven start. They had won three straight, were 14–5, and climbed back into the rankings at No. 23 before Hansbrough's debut against the team he had once admired from afar.

"I was pretty programmed the minute I got to North Carolina to start hating Duke," Hansbrough said. "For some reason, it kind of felt natural to me, the way it was supposed to be. They're a different school than us, kind of an uppity private school. I was a small-town country boy, so it didn't really fit with me."

After their last meeting, Carolina's stirring comeback victory at the end of the 2005 regular season, the heat was rising in the rivalry. Roy Williams had not only beaten Duke for the first time at UNC but also landed another recruit both schools wanted for the freshman class of 2007. Brandan Wright, a 6'9" forward from Tennessee, had committed to the Tar Heels the previous October after all the scuttlebutt had him wearing royal blue.

Williams had offered a contingent scholarship to 6'8" Thaddeus Young, who signed with Georgia Tech after Williams rescinded the tender. "I told [Young] that Brandan was coming in for a visit, and that if Brandan accepted the scholarship offer, it was going to be his," Williams said. Although Wright had made official visits to Carolina and Duke when each school was hosting the other during the 2005 season, he showed up on his own at UNC's first preseason practice of the fall, called Late Night with Roy, the following October. "Brandan did not surprise me, he surprised everyone else," Williams said. "J. J. Redick told me at the [2006] Final Four, 'You really surprised us.' I sort of smirked a little bit because I thought we were doing pretty well with Brandan from the start."

Wright and fellow commits Ty Lawson and Wayne Ellington, hotshot prep All-American guards, gave Williams his first top-ranked incoming freshman class at North Carolina.

Despite losing Wright, Duke still had signed its own studly list of recruits the previous November, including 6'5" shooting star Jon Scheyer and Ellington's Philadelphia high school teammate Gerald Henderson Jr., the 6'5" son of the former NBA star, and a future Hansbrough antagonist. But Wright's decision left Krzyzewski and his staff scrambling for a power forward, and they immediately went after 6'9" Lance Thomas, a highly rated New Jersey prospect who had committed to Arizona but wanted to wait until the spring to sign. He did, with Duke.

Helping turn the tide for Thomas was Krzyzewski's appointment as U.S. national team coach for the 2008 Summer Olympics in Beijing. He was the first college coach to hold the position since NBA players were allowed to compete in 1992. The job would not only keep Coach K in the news through the off-seasons to follow, it fulfilled a fantasy for the former Army captain and West Point graduate, who had closely followed international basketball long before serving as an assistant to Chuck Daly on the original 1992 Dream Team in Barcelona. And it began a vital second career for the Duke coach.

On the court, the Blue Devils seemed to be just fine, too, especially with their 17-game winning streak that opened the 2006 season. Their narrowest margin of victory was 10 points in all but three games before the loss to Georgetown, but a seductively dangerous trend was developing. Redick, who finished the season second in the nation in scoring (26.8 points per game), was ringing up higher and higher numbers—three 40-point games and, in February, five straight of at least 30. He was on his way to setting Duke and ACC all-time scoring records, and he also broke Art Heyman's school career record of 19 games with 30 or more points.

But with Shelden Williams the only other double-digit scorer on the team, Duke was becoming too dependent on Redick, whose teammates found themselves playing tentatively. Krzyzewski, who turned the team over to Redick before the season, told him, "I'm okay living and dying with the shot you take." Duke fans wondered why the athletic McRoberts wasn't used more as an inside-outside threat. Sophomore starter DeMarcus Nelson had a nagging foot injury, and Paulus suffered similar freshman adjustment problems that had plagued starting point guard Bobby Hurley sixteen years earlier. The Blue Devils temporarily dropped to No. 2 in the polls behind Connecticut, heading into the first game against UNC in Chapel Hill on February 7, 2006.

Duke began aggressively, whistled for four fouls in the first six minutes, and did not get into the bonus until the final seconds of the first half. Leading by five, the Blue Devils were hooted off the court and had a shouting match in their locker room, criticizing the calls and yelling at one another about lackadaisical play against an opponent they were supposed to rout. Krzyzewski calmed them down, and Duke scored the first 12 points of the second half, forcing six straight turnovers, which prompted a livid Roy Williams to pull all five starters.

"At that point, we could have lost by a thousand points," Williams said, angered that his team did not meet the challenge and especially by the nonchalant play by some of the greener Tar Heels not named Hansbrough. "I hate 'cool' and have always hated anything about being 'cool.'"

That tantrum might have been the turning point of the season for his young team, which rallied and actually took a five-point lead with less than five minutes left. But Redick scored 11 points in the last 4:22, including three 3-pointers, and finished with 35 points, the most ever by a Duke player on UNC's home court. The Blue Devils survived 87–83. The Tar Heels shot only 40 percent compared to Duke's 49 but were buoyed by dominating the offensive boards, 22–7. Hansbrough, Noel, and Danny Green each pulled down nine rebounds, matched only on the Duke side by Shelden Williams, who led the ACC in rebounding that season with 10.7 a game. The Blue Devils hung on in part because McRoberts had his best college game to date, scoring nine points in the second half and finishing with 17.

Hansbrough scored 14 points as one of five teammates in double figures and remembered being exhausted all night, attributing it to the intense energy on campus before the game. He discovered that the vibe from other students, the constant well-wishing, and his phone blowing up with ticket requests from people he hadn't heard from in months, unnerved him.

"I had worn myself out before the game," Hansbrough said. "I was so nervous, hadn't slept very well the night before. I didn't know what to expect because it was my first big-time rivalry game. I remember when the game started it was a big sigh of relief, finally we're going to get this thing going. We can quit studying the scouting report and having tough practices, we can just go out and play.

"Shelden was pretty strong; I hadn't faced too many guys with his strength. He was a big load for me to handle. J. J. came out and hit us right from the beginning and never took his foot off the gas pedal. When we lost, we knew we had to do a lot of things to prepare for the next one, like guard J. J. a little better, limit his touches that led to some easy baskets."

With a 9 p.m. tip-off, the day had lasted forever, and though Hansbrough did not conserve his own strength, he learned from it. The Chapel Hill police and fire departments had prepared more than forty-eight hours for a celebration, which never materialized, but the Tar Heels went on a winning streak after that. They caught veteran Boston College as the second-best team in the conference heading into the regular-season rematch at Duke and Senior Night for Redick and Williams on Saturday, March 4.

Anticipation had built, since Carolina won six straight games and the Blue Devils regained the No. 1 ranking the week before after winning 10 of their last 11. The Heels' own hot spell had moved them up to No. 13 in the national rankings.

UNC had lost four in a row at Cameron, with Hansbrough and fellow freshmen Frasor, Ginyard, and Green facing their first game in the famous cauldron. They all got it from the Crazies the moment they appeared for informal warm-ups. The students had been camping at Krzyzewskiville since early January. Two months in a tent made them even crazier than usual, and they were incensed when learning a group of UNC student impostors had infiltrated their ranks to get into the game.

"I remember getting chills because this is what I watched on TV," Hansbrough said. "To see the students surrounding the whole gym, and they were on me from the minute I stepped on that court; it's an atmosphere like none other, and I had never been in that building before, unlike anything I'd ever experienced."

Hansbrough said he fed off the heavy razzing and extra time on Coach K Court before tip-off and felt even more amped in the barren visitors locker room. While Redick, Williams, Lee Melchionni, and Sean Dockery received their senior send-offs, Roy Williams told his players to expect a punch in their collective face, but they could survive it. He said they were the only group in the country that could ruin Duke's Senior Night, calling such an upset "stealing their brownies." His current team had won five straight ACC games on the road, better than the 2005 NCAA champs had done, and he reminded his new players of that distinction.

The haymaker Williams referred to was Redick hitting four of his first five shots as Duke blew out to a 13–3 lead before the first TV timeout, beginning as if he were chasing more history. He had already passed Johnny Dawkins, a former All-American and now Krzyzewski's assistant coach, as Duke's career-scoring leader two weeks earlier against Miami. The next week he eclipsed Wake Forest legend Dickie Hemric to set an ACC record, ironically, with a season-low 11 points against a tough Temple defense and nasty Philly crowd. And the most prolific 3-point shooter in the twenty years the long ball had been part of the college game looked ready to do a number on the Tar Heels in his home finale.

After all, prior Duke All-Americans had done something similar. Dick Groat set a Duke record with 48 points against Carolina in 1952 in his last home game, leaving the court in tears. Art Heyman said so long to Duke fans and the Tar Heels with 40 points and 24 rebounds in 1963, exiting to a three-minute standing ovation. Christian Laettner scored 26 against UNC, including five 3-pointers, in his swan song of 1992 and after the game promised that he and his mates would come back to Durham with Duke's second consecutive national title. They fulfilled that vow a month later.

When Redick gunned in those four early shots, one while falling over, Carolina fans grumbled with apprehension, "He might get 50 tonight." And when his second 3-pointer went in, Cameron vibrated from its sixty-six-year-old foundation, and indeed it looked like Groat, Heyman, and Laettner would have to slide down a seat.

But, truth was, Redick had been in a shooting slump for a few weeks, and some Dukies feared he might lose his touch again. Even his coach acknowledged that the pressure of chasing the scoring records had an effect on his shooting star. "When he doesn't have his look, it has a negative impact on our team," Krzyzewski said.

After Williams said to his youngsters, "I told you so," they settled down and climbed back in the game. By halftime, Carolina had actually taken three leads and trailed by a point. Indeed, Redick seemed to be pressing in his last Cameron appearance of a spectacular scoring career and, guarded mostly by freshman Ginyard, made only one more field goal and finished shooting 5-for-21, 2-for-10 from 3-point range. Shelden Williams was keeping Duke in the game, on his way to 18 points and 15 rebounds and averaging a double-double for the second straight season. Krzyzewski complained that his senior center and soon to be school's all-time best rebounder was unappreciated due to all the attention on Redick.

As in the previous game at the Smith Center, however, UNC controlled the backboards, led by Noel, a former two-sport high school star in Durham who grabbed 12 rebounds in his last chance to win at Duke. Frasor's 3-pointer with about 12 minutes left in the game gave the Tar Heels a lead they extended to 11 before Duke made a last push, cutting the deficit to eight with a little less than four minutes remaining. Green grabbed a defensive rebound that led to a delay-game possession and Hansbrough having the ball at the top of the key with the shot clock running down; he let it fly with five seconds left.

"They made a run, and hitting that three kind of put a dagger in them," Hansbrough said. "David came over and gave me a big chest bump, and we hugged right there. This was his last chance at Duke, and it was kind of cool to know we were going to win the game."

The Blue Devils rallied one last time and had a chance at a 3-pointer to tie, but Redick could not get a shot off, and Green stripped the ball away from Dockery. Hansbrough iced it in the final seconds with a pair of free throws, as Carolina's four freshmen outscored Duke's four seniors, 55–51, in the 83–76 upset

"We ran off the court and were all excited about getting back to Chapel Hill," he said. His father was still leading the wild cheering behind the Carolina bench that erupted when the game ended.

Hansbrough now had the full measure of the rivalry. A quiet downtown Chapel Hill exploded with revelers emerging from bars and restaurants and students sprinting from all corners of campus for a celebration that, frankly, few expected with Duke being so heavily favored. "It's amazing to see and terrifying all at the same time, how quickly a sea of humanity can descend on Franklin Street," Chapel Hill police chief Chris Blue said.

"Friends were texting us on the bus ride back, and we all went down there," Hansbrough said. "It was like we won the national championship, bonfires, people celebrating. I was shocked, never had experienced anything like that. I think it hit me right there what beating Duke meant."

Hansbrough's 27 points and 10 rebounds on national television earned a 10th ACC Rookie of the Week honor and catapulted him to become the first unanimous freshman All-ACC selection. He tied Redick and Shelden Williams with 324 first-place votes. Hansbrough also got three votes for ACC Player of the Year, the other 105 going to Redick, who made unanimous first-team All-America and won the Wooden and Rupp awards as National Player of the Year. Roy Williams swamped the field for ACC Coach of the Year after taking a team picked to finish sixth to second place with a 23–8 overall record and another bid to the NCAA tournament.

And, too, the Tar Heels had duplicated their feat of 1994, when they upset second-ranked Duke 87–77 in the home finale for Grant Hill, another four-year player and consensus All-American.

"Sorry we couldn't get it done tonight; Carolina played great," Redick said in his farewell speech to the Cameron fans who stayed around for his final words after a game that had been seen in more than 3 million homes, the highest rating ever for college basketball on ESPN. "The good thing is the season is far from over."

In the throes of the slump, Redick had missed 15 of his last 16 shots against UNC and went into the postseason having made only 23 of his last 80 attempts. He recovered by averaging almost 24 points in the ACC tournament and earned his second straight MVP as the Blue Devils edged Boston College in a hotly contested championship battle. Duke won a second consecutive tournament, its seventh in the last eight years and tenth overall for Krzyzewski, who was coaching his 1,000th college game. The victory also meant Duke had won both the outright regular-season and tournament titles for the fifth time in the past twenty-one years. No other ACC school had done that in the same span.

Carolina, which had climbed to No. 10 in the polls after the victory at Duke, lost to 11th-ranked BC for a second time that season in the ACC tournament semifinals. By winning eight straight games before that defeat, the Tar Heels had improved steadily in the amalgamated data used by the NCAA tournament selection committee. Most bracketologists had them as a No. 2 or No. 3 seed in the Greensboro pod for the first two rounds along with top-seeded Duke.

Duke was a lock to receive its 10th No. 1 NCAA seed, which tied UNC for the most since the seeding system began in 1979. But would Duke and Carolina play in the same venue for the first two rounds for the second straight year? In 2005, both had opened the tournament in Charlotte, where the top-seeded Tar Heels had an overwhelming partisan crowd that had bought up most of the tickets anticipating correctly that its team would be there.

The ACC had exercised the right to reserve 1,000 tickets for the 2006 games in Greensboro so its competing teams could have more access to them, and even Greensboro Coliseum managing director Matt Brown said he expected both Tobacco Road rivals to be there.

In recent years, the NCAA had encouraged feedback from the schools in the Big Dance and heard about the crowd reaction in Charlotte. In 2006, since Duke had swept both the ACC regular season and tournament, allowing the more populated Carolina fan base to create the same hostile atmosphere seemed unfair. Blue Devils fans had purchased all available tickets, thirsting for a chance to return the favor from the year before. Duke officials denied rumors they had lobbied the NCAA to send their archrivals to another pod in another city. And when UNC was shipped to Dayton as the No. 3 seed in the Washington, D.C., (East) Region, Carolina conspiracy theorists had a field day.

By being placed in the Friday–Sunday pod in Dayton, Carolina and sixth-seeded Michigan State could meet in a second-round rematch of last year's Final Four game, if not the same teams, since the programs had lost a dozen players combined from their 2005 rosters. CBS tentatively scheduled its late game Sunday afternoon to be from Dayton at 4:30 p.m., which would have attracted a huge audience watching the "name" schools.

If there was any such plan, the Spartans foiled it by losing in the first round to mid-major George Mason, one of the teams that CBS analyst Billy Packer had ridiculed for being invited to the sixty-eight-team field. After Carolina edged Murray State in the first round, CBS bumped the UNC–George Mason game to regional status at an earlier time and missed an even bigger story when the Tar Heels squandered a 14-point, first-half lead and found themselves in a dogfight by settling for too many 3-point shots against the underdog Patriots' zone, missing 20 of 30 attempts.

The resulting 65–60 loss to an 11th seed at first looked like UNC's most embarrassing defeat since its first-round ouster by 14-seed Weber State in 1999, even though the Tar Heels' 23–8 record far exceeded all predictions. The 2006 season was supposedly a bridge year to 2007, when Williams could reload with a star-studded freshman class. Still, Williams called it "the most fun year I ever had coaching in my life. Very seldom have we been the underdog, very seldom have I had a leader any better than David Noel, and very seldom have we had freshmen tough enough to say we were going to be freaking good."

Duke moved through its Greensboro games with victories over Southern University and George Washington, but still had to face the sting from season-long criticism of favorable officiating, which had become something of a national story in recent years.

In a first-round win, Redick and Shelden Williams combined for more points (59) than the entire Southern team. The Blue Devils were booed steadily by George Washington fans throughout a dominating second-round victory over the eighth-seeded Colonials, during which Williams surpassed Mike Gminski as Duke's all-time leading rebounder. The Blue Devils moved on to Atlanta wearing the same villain's hat from their appearance there in 2004, when a *Washington Post* story first publicized the "great level of hatred" they felt from opposing fans across the country.

Support was no more bountiful this time at the Georgia Dome, where Duke faced an aggressive LSU team embodying the old adage that the SEC has athletes while the ACC has basketball players. The Tigers' 6'6" freshman Garrett Temple swarmed Redick, bumping and jostling him into another bad shooting game. Redick's misfires led to a halftime exchange between Krzyzewski and chief assistant Dawkins, who wanted to get the ball more to post men Shelden Williams and Josh McRoberts inside against LSU sophomore Glen "Big Baby" Davis. Williams wound up with 23 points and 13 rebounds and as many shots (18) as Redick. Temple played 40 minutes of dogged defense on Redick, who got no help from the officials, one of whom, Jim Burr, had worked four Duke games that season including the win in Chapel Hill.

Even when Redick wasn't forcing shots or moves to the basket, his wide-open teammates often looked too scared to go get the ball and shoot it if they did. After one high-flying stretch when freshman McRoberts twice dunked and gave Duke a tie or lead, LSU took the game higher above the rim and left the Blue Devils, including

Williams and McRoberts, flatfooted under the basket. The Tigers' freshman Tyrus Thomas blocked five shots, including a soft, left-handed layup attempt by Paulus that best depicted the difference in athleticism on the court that night.

Williams concluded his college career with his 21st double-double of the season. It ended with three mostly dominating NCAA tournament games, in which he averaged 23 points, 15 rebounds, and five blocks. But even he was helpless in the last five minutes against this jacked-up opponent. At one point with none of his LSU teammates in the lane, Big Baby Davis missed a free throw and stepped in to claim the rebound while four dazed Dukies simply stood there.

Duke shot a dismal 28 percent for the game and 19 percent from the 3-point arc. Besides Redick, who missed 15 of his 18 shots including all nine of his 2-point attempts and six of nine long balls, the rest of the team combined to make only two of 17 from 3-point range. And LSU hardly played a flawless game, missing 11 free throws and making careless turnovers in the second half that Duke couldn't convert into points. The 62–54 loss by the top-ranked team stunned college basketball but hardly Krzyzewski, who had recognized his team's limitations all season while compiling a phenomenal 32–4 record playing basically three guards and seven guys.

"We are who we are," he had said several times. Over the years since then, Krzyzewski talked about Redick, a Duke fan since he was eight, not fulfilling his dream of winning a national championship with the Blue Devils.

Redick left the court in tears, failing for the fourth time to reach his ultimate goal. He remained perhaps Duke's greatest player, a two-time National Player of the Year whose No. 4 jersey hangs in the rafters of Cameron, where he had explosive scoring binges that had the Crazies chanting, "J. J. Redick, Dy-No-Mite!"

But his legacy also included his flops in the NCAA tournament in which he reached only one Final Four and never won that national championship. His superlative college career had seasons that ended with a combined 13 field goals in 60 attempts (22 percent) in four NCAA tournament elimination games. "I've moved on with my life, but it would have been nice to win a championship at Duke," said Redick, who has gone on to play twelve seasons for five NBA teams and has averaged making 41.5 percent of is 3-pointers.

Though living in Redick's shadow, Shelden Williams also finished as Duke's best career shot-blocker and long ago earned the nickname "Landlord" for how he patrolled the lane. He became the third Blue Devil ever to register a triple-double when he had 19 points, 11 rebounds, and 10 blocks against Maryland as a senior and was the first player in NCAA history to surpass 1,750 points, 1,250 rebounds, 400 blocks, and 150 steals. Like Redick, he could have set those records only by staying all four years. Recognized as a slightly better pro prospect than Redick, at least in the NBA draft, Williams was picked No. 5 by the Atlanta Hawks compared to Redick's No. 11 selection by Orlando. In 2008, Williams married Tennessee All-American Candace Parker, the national player of the year who went on to an all-pro career in the Women's NBA and also won two Olympic gold medals.

For both Duke and Carolina, the shock of losing to such decided underdogs in 2006 was somewhat lessened in their respective regional championships. For the eighth time in nine years, Duke's vanquisher went on to the Final Four or national championship. LSU beat second-seeded Texas to take Duke's place in Indianapolis. (From 1975 to 1990, something similar happened to UNC when Dean Smith coached.) The Tar Heels were spared a measure of embarrassment this time when Cinderella George Mason stunned top-seeded UConn to join LSU, UCLA, and Florida in the Final Four, and the Gators went on to win their first of two consecutive NCAA titles.

HANSBROUGH INDOOR STADIUM

The Final Four went off without Duke or Carolina for only the fifth time in 21 years; one of the schools (or both, as was the case in 1991) had been to 18 of the last 25 and 20 of the last 29. Since the ACC was formed in May 1953, the two teams together had played in more than 50 percent of the Final Fours, better than all other ACC schools combined and every other conference except the Big Ten. That ratio remained for the following twelve years, when the rivalry grew closer in head-to-head meetings.

The 2007 season marked the first time in ten years that Carolina's basketball program was viewed as superior to Duke's, but with it came the same pressure to produce the Blue Devils carried over that period.

Even though Redick and Williams had completed their eligibility, typical expectations remained for Duke, which opened as the 12th-ranked team in the country and climbed to No. 5 after a nine-game winning streak from November to early January. But ACC play began with consecutive losses to Virginia Tech at home and at Georgia Tech. Duke won five in a row, then lost four straight and fell out of the polls for the first time since 1996, the year after Mike Krzyzewski missed most of the season due to back surgery and exhaustion.

These Blue Devils had become offensively challenged. Four players averaged in double figures, led by junior DeMarcus Nelson with 14 points a game. However, the team shot almost 200 fewer 3-pointers than the year before and made a lower percentage of them amidst mounting controversy over the Blue Devils' ineffective inside game. Sophomore Josh McRoberts was the roster's best big man, averaging nearly eight rebounds, with no one else getting more than 5.4 a game. Freshman bigs Brian Zoubek and Lance Thomas were still learning, averaging a combined 7.1 points and 4.7 rebounds. The enormous

Zoubek frustrated some Duke fans by playing barely seven minutes a game due to injuries, and Thomas caught the brunt of jokes that there must be a Delilah on campus who, like with Samson, sheared the dreadlocks he had as prep star.

The Tar Heels also had a head problem. They had opened as the No. 2 team in the country but lost to Gonzaga in the preseason NIT at Madison Square Garden in their fourth game of the season. A few of the players came out wearing white headbands, and after the 82–74 defeat an annoyed Roy Williams ordered them off for good.

"It irritated me because they just decided to do that on their own," he recalled. "Gonzaga beat us, and then I told our players, 'By God, this is my team and this is the University of North Carolina and we don't wear that crap.' To me, the headbands made them look like individuals, and we got beat that night by a better team."

Carolina promptly ran off 12 straight wins, rose to No. 1 in the polls, and Williams reached his 500th career victory faster than any other coach in history. The three freshman McDonald's All-Americans had joined sophomore Hansbrough and senior Reyshawn Terry as starters. Lawson, the mercurial-but-moody point guard, sharpshooter Ellington, and Wright—with the seven-foot wing span—gave Carolina potentially one of the best lineups in the country. But Williams spent the season periodically pissed off at a team that eventually lost five ACC games to unranked opponents. He threw Lawson out of one practice for not hustling and threatened to leave him home for the game at Virginia Tech. Lawson played well in a foul-plagued 24 minutes in Blacksburg, and Hansbrough had 19 points and 15 rebounds. Still, the Tar Heels could not contain the Hokies' guards in their first of two losses of the season to the unranked football school.

As usual, Duke brought out the best in the better players. In the teams' first meeting at Cameron, Carolina rallied from a five-point deficit at halftime and 10 points with 17 minutes left to outscore the

Blue Devils 39–23 down the stretch. Wright had 11 of his 19 total points in the second half, when Hansbrough pounded in 12 of his 16 and Lawson 11 of his 15 as the Tar Heels flexed their superior size and skill to win again in Durham. The Blue Devils fell to 5–5 in the ACC, and four days later lost at Maryland, leaving them below .500 for the first time since 1996. The game against Carolina, however, was a breakout performance for freshman Scheyer, who foretold his shooting prowess with 26 points, including four 3-pointers that had some fans thinking he might be the next Redick.

By the rematch in Chapel Hill on March 4, 2007, Duke was back up to No. 14 in the polls against the fourth-ranked and heavily favored Tar Heels. It was never close after five UNC players scored in a 12–0 spurt less than five minutes in. The lead grew as high as 16 in the second half and was 12 when Williams sent a sub to the scorer's table with 18 seconds left in the game. Hansbrough stepped to the foul line after having already totaled 26 points, and 16 rebounds—his best overall performance in the rivalry to date. He missed the first free throw and the second rolled off the rim.

Hansbrough followed his shot, came down with his ninth offensive rebound, and pump-faked his way up to the basket. Meanwhile, Duke freshman Gerald Henderson had soared for the ball from the right side of the lane and crashed, elbow first, on top of Hansbrough. The direct blow split open Hansbrough's nose and blood gushed out as the aggressive player nicknamed Psycho T scrambled to his feet ready to fight before teammates and officials restrained him. Hansbrough went to the locker room with the trainer and a photographer in tow.

"Blood was everywhere; it was like I was choking on my own blood," Hansbrough recalled of his red-stained face and uniform. "I said to the photographer, go ahead and get some good pics; I figured he'd never show anybody else, but I still see them everywhere now."

BLUE BLOOD II

Williams, whose 100th head coaching victory at Carolina would be clearly overshadowed, and Krzyzewski stood side by side as the officials looked at the TV monitor, called a flagrant foul, and ejected Henderson, who was escorted through the visitors tunnel to a shower of boos. To many UNC fans, it was an intentional foul aimed at hurting their newest hero, although on the CBS broadcast Billy Packer insisted it was merely a high-speed collision by two big bodies and Henderson should not have been banished.

"I've played basketball for a long time and it was a dirty play, fouling someone like that," Hansbrough said. "Everybody wants to break it down, but if you want to hurt somebody that's how you foul somebody. I've never seen anyone come down, elbow right to my face. But that's not to say Gerald Henderson isn't a good person."

On the bus ride back to Durham after the 86–72 loss, Henderson texted high school teammate Ellington, apologizing to Hansbrough and saying he meant no harm. Henderson was clearly frustrated by not only losing again to Carolina but from a season unlike he expected when he signed at Duke. The 6'5" guard was an aggressive player by nature, having grown up around pro basketball watching his father, Gerald Henderson Sr., play for seven NBA teams in 13 seasons.

The celebration on Franklin Street was more subdued this time for Carolina's third straight win over Duke. Not all of the players went, most of them still worried about Hansbrough's condition. Those who did noticed a white bedsheet already hanging outside the ATO fraternity house with black letters painted, "Fuck Henderson."

"I didn't like it in the press conference when it was suggested . . . that I should have taken Tyler out," Williams said of his decision to leave Hansbrough on the court when his team had a comfortable lead in the final minute. "Duke's starters were still in the game. The crazy thing is that I had a substitute for Tyler at the scorer's table. If we hadn't missed that stupid free throw, none of that would have happened."

Two victories over Duke marked the first time Williams had swept the Blue Devils since his return to UNC. The Tar Heels' 11–5 league record earned a tie for first place with Virginia, which they had defeated by 10 points in their one scheduled meeting.

Wright easily won ACC Rookie of the Year and later became Carolina's second one-and-done in three years, after Marvin Williams in 2005. Hansbrough earned unanimous All-ACC for the second straight season but finished a distant third in the Player of the Year voting behind winner Jared Dudley of Boston College and Al Thornton of Florida State. His 18.4 scoring average and 7.9 rebounds per game seemed to be taken for granted after his splashy freshman debut.

The ACC suspended Henderson for the first game of the ACC tournament in Tampa, which Duke lost to N.C. State. The week of bad publicity and boos when Henderson came out with the team in street clothes led Krzyzewski to say his player had become a victim. That aggravated UNC's Williams, who said, "Tyler was the guy who had the nose broken. That really bothered me, even though I knew Mike was trying to take care of his player."

Hansbrough and Henderson admit not talking to each other for ten years until, in late 2017, they surprisingly launched a *Tobacco Road* podcast. The premiere episode was titled "The Incident" and over the first fourteen minutes both had their say about the foul. "As you go up, the ball gets knocked back, and the only thing that remained there in that space happened to be your nose, your face," Henderson told Hansbrough. "My eyes were closed as it was happening, and I just wildly took a swipe down . . . with my elbow . . . I was hitting anything that came in that direction."

"I'm over it," Hansbrough countered sarcastically. "I don't need a petting zoo now."

With the broken nose, Hansbrough played with a plastic mask, which his surgeon father found for him after his son rejected several heavier models the UNC medical staff tried. While sympathetic fans at the St. Pete Times Forum wore replica masks, Hansbrough was bothered by the apparatus and played ineffectively in the tournament. But three freshmen—Wright (MVP), Lawson, and Ellington—led the all-tourney team for the first time in ACC history as the Tar Heels defeated Florida State and Boston College, both by 15 points, and outlasted N.C. State 89–80 to win their first ACC championship in nine years.

As the top seed in the NCAA East Regional, Carolina defeated 16-seed Eastern Kentucky in Winston-Salem and moved on to a tough second-round game against ninth-seed Michigan State. Hansbrough, who played with a different mask and had 21 points and 10 rebounds in the first game, kept the mask on at first against the rugged Spartans, but after being banged around during the opening minutes he ripped it off during a timeout and, as Williams recalled, "threw on his cape instead and played like Superman the rest of the game." He scored 33 points as the Tar Heels won 81–67 and Williams stayed unbeaten against Sparty coach Tom Izzo. (Williams was 7–0 against Izzo until Michigan State drubbed UNC in 2017 at the PK80 tournament in Portland, Oregon, honoring Nike co-founder Phil Knight's eightieth birthday.)

Meanwhile, Duke lost the last four games of an up-and-down season that finished 22–11 and 8–8 in the ACC, tied for sixth place. It ended the Blue Devils' amazing run of ten years having captured the regular-season and/or tournament championships, a streak that might never be matched in any conference.

What had suddenly become an ordinary sixth-seeded 2007 Duke

team missed 12 free throws and committed 17 turnovers in a 79–77 upset loss to unranked and 11-seed Virginia Commonwealth, marking the third time Krzyzewski had gone out of the NCAA tournament in the opening game. In his first trip to the Big Dance, in 1984, Duke went down to the Washington Huskies and future NBA star Detlef Schrempf in Pullman, Washington. Then came those seven Final Fours in nine years and two consecutive NCAA championships before Coach K began his second rebuilding job at Duke in 1996, a season that ended with a first-round loss to ninth-seeded Eastern Michigan. Two more one-and-done NCAA tournaments came for Krzyzewski in the next century, and Tar Heels fans still gloated that Roy Williams had never lost a first-round game in twenty-nine postseason appearances.

In the 2007 Sweet 16 at the Meadowlands in New Jersey, Carolina fell behind quicker No. 5–seeded Southern Cal by 16 points early in the second half. At about the time CBS broadcaster Jim Nantz read a statement on national TV that UNC cheerleading mascot Jason Ray had been struck by a moving vehicle while walking outside his hotel that morning and was in critical condition, the Tar Heels came to life.

Sparked by the offensive rebounding of Marcus Ginyard, they ran off 18 straight points over eight minutes and somehow pulled out the 74–64 win. Ginyard had three put-backs, including one for a three-point play, and finished with 10 points and nine rebounds in his best college game to date. Hansbrough had his worst game at UNC, finishing with four points and five rebounds, stymied by USC freshman Taj Gibson, who finally fouled out during Carolina's comeback. Wright picked up the big-man slack with 21 points and nine rebounds, as Carolina moved on to the East Regional final against Georgetown. It came 25 years after their classic matchup in the 1982 national championship game, won by Michael Jordan's jumper for Dean Smith's first NCAA title.

Williams did not sleep well on Saturday night, having learned that Jason Ray's condition had worsened. (Ray died early Monday, March 26, 2007.) Once, the clock read 4:44 a.m., and Williams thought it might have been an omen that his team was going back to the Final Four. Carolina led Georgetown by 10 points with seven minutes remaining before an epic collapse began when Danny Green missed a long jumper from right in front of the UNC bench about 10 seconds into the shot clock. A string of poor possessions followed; the Hoyas tied the game and then outscored Carolina 15–3 in overtime. The Tar Heels' season came to a shocking end, finishing 31–7.

"We all thought we had that game in the bag and were going to the Final Four," Hansbrough said. "We were really upset and, as a team, it drove us to work harder over the summer."

Three days later, Williams received word he had been elected to the Naismith Basketball Hall of Fame, joining Smith and Krzyzewski for basketball's highest honor. The induction ceremony followed in September, and twenty-two of Williams' former players from Kansas and UNC showed up in Springfield, Massachusetts. He was accompanied on the stage by Smith, who beamed with pride as his decorated protégé read the speech he had written himself in longhand. Over the next five years, cognitive dementia would rob Smith of most of his cherished memories.

In that fall of 2007, Carolina seemed positioned to continue its dominance over Duke in both the rivalry and their program accomplishments. The Tar Heels and Tyler Hansbrough had two more visits to Cameron ahead, attempting to be the first team to beat the Blue Devils there four straight years with Krzyzewski on the bench. UNC fans hoped they could continue calling Duke's hallowed home court "Hansbrough Indoor Stadium."

RECRUITING THE BIGS (6'8" OR MORE)

Duke	UNC
Lance Thomas	Brandan Wright*
Brian Zoubek	Alex Stepheson*
Jamal Boykin*	Deon Thompson
Kyle Singler	Ed Davis*
Taylor King*	Tyler Zeller
Miles Plumlee	John Henson*
Mason Plumlee	David Wear*
Ryan Kelly	Travis Wear*
Amile Jefferson	Harrison Barnes*
Alex Murphy*	James Michael McAdoo*
Marshall Plumlee	Desmond Hubert
Jabari Parker*	Brice Johnson
Rodney Hood*	Joel James
Semi Ojeleye*	Kennedy Meeks
Jahlil Okafor*	Isaiah Hicks
Brandon Ingram*	Justin Jackson*
Chase Jeter*	Tony Bradley*
Jayson Tatum*	Garrison Brooks
Harry Giles*	Brandon Huffman
Marques Bolden	Sterling Manley
Javin DeLaurier	Walker Miller
Marvin Bagley III*	
Wendell Carter Jr.*	

(*) **Did not stay four years**

2

"HIS WILL EXCEEDS HIS SKILL"

Only twice in their storied history had both rivals been ranked higher when they played. In 1994, Duke with Grant Hill was No. 1 and defending national champion Carolina No. 2 for their February 3 game in Chapel Hill, won by the Tar Heels 89–78. Four years later, on February 5, they held the same positions in the polls, and the Antawn Jamison–led Tar Heels won again at the Dean Smith Center by a surprising 97–73 score.

Mike Krzyzewski, who had been through so many of these, called the "atmosphere for a Duke–North Carolina game, whether here or there, the best of any place because, for whatever reasons, people in the stands feel privileged to be there, like they are going to be part of an amazing event. It's almost like the arena has a soul, a life that day that cannot be duplicated."

For the first meeting of the 2008 season at UNC, Duke was ranked second and Carolina third when Carolina's starting point guard, Ty Lawson, had to sit out with a sprained ankle. Brandan Wright, who had 29 points and 14 rebounds in two games against the Blue Devils as a freshman, also was gone after becoming the Tar Heels' second one-and-done in three years and the eighth pick in the 2007 NBA draft.

Even though their best rebounder, Josh McRoberts, also had turned pro in the off-season after a relatively disappointing two-year college career, the Blue Devils had won 19 of their first 20 games in 2008 when they bused over February 6 to play the 21-1 Tar Heels. They shot lights out, especially from 3-point range, and six players finished in double figures. They were led by junior point guard Greg Paulus, who drained six of his eight 3-pointers, and emerging stars Kyle Singler and Jon Scheyer, who kept the anxious Carolina crowd groaning.

Singler and Scheyer would be the heart and soul of a national championship team two years later and also the target of opposing players and fans. Both were sweet shooters, with Singler also a notorious trash-talker, especially after making a tough shot, telling the man trying to guard him he had no chance. Singler's nose was broken several times in his career from a purposely placed elbow. Scheyer was also a fierce competitor whose face often contorted during heated moments. Photos of his weird expressions trolled the internet as a contender with the high-strung Paulus for the latest in a long line of Duke's most disliked players.

But then, Tyler Hansbrough had developed the same reputation with Dukies, who were relieved that not even his monster game of 28 points and 18 rebounds and UNC's decided advantage on the offensive boards (20–11) could offset the team's poor shooting. In the second half, the Tar Heels missed 24 of their 36 field goal attempts and 10 of 12 from behind the arc. For the game, Duke made 44.8 percent of its 3-pointers (13 for 29).

"If you have good shots and you are going to be a good shooter, you've got to shoot the frickin' ball on game day," Roy Williams fumed after losing 89–78, the exact score, if not the outcome, as in 1994. "It doesn't do any damn good to shoot the ball during the week. You've got to shoot the ball well on game day or you're not as good a shooter as everybody says you are."

That was fatal for a team playing porous defense, ranked 246th in the country in points allowed and 110th in opponents' field goal percentage. "We just watched guys drive by us without stepping into the lane, and finally our last line of defense had to help," Marcus Ginyard, supposedly the team's defensive stopper, said afterward, "and that was what gave them so many open shots."

Duke led all the way after taking control in the first half and ended the game with its largest margin of the night. Leaving town still with one loss and undefeated in the ACC with a two-game lead over Carolina, Krzyzewski looked like he had another Final Four contender or at least a conference champion.

"This is a pretty special team to me right now," he said after ending his first three-game losing streak to UNC in 12 years. "I mean, we are 20–1 and 8–0. We know who we are, a very unconventional team. We are not a very strong physical team; you just have to hope that you don't get killed by somebody's strength."

But Duke did slip up, losing at unranked Wake Forest and Miami and dropping to No. 6 in the rankings before the regular-season finale against Carolina, which had climbed atop the polls with a 28–2 record and 13–2 in the ACC. The Tar Heels were riding a seven-game winning streak in which they had defeated every opponent but one by at least 10 points. Hansbrough led the ACC in scoring and rebounding on his way to a unanimous Player of the Year vote, sustaining perhaps the best season of his life. After successive victories at Cameron, they *knew* they could make it three in a row in 2008.

An emotional ceremony preceded the tip-off. For the second straight March, UNC had lost a highly recognized student. A year after mascot Jason Ray was struck and killed by a passing SUV during the NCAA tournament in New Jersey, two gang members from Durham invaded the off-campus house of widely admired student-body president and Morehead Scholar Eve Carson. They robbed, kidnapped, and shot her to death in the early morning three days before the game. Carson, a senior set to graduate with honors the following May, was beloved on the Carolina campus and a wild basketball fan, who was quoted in *The Daily Tar Heel* newspaper, "I love Roy all the time."

Several of Williams' players who knew Carson personally went to the vigil at the Dean Dome, attended by thousands of students and hundreds of alumni.

Williams was torn up, also having to relive the death of Ray, a registered organ donor who had been in the news over the last year for having extended the lives of several terminally ill recipients. "We're supposed to die before our children," Williams said. "I cannot imagine what the parents of Eve and Jason have gone through. For us, it's just an awakening, to be more aware each day that what we do is entertainment. It's a game."

Krzyzewski reached out to Williams about the idea that his staff put on the same blue and white ribbons as the Carolina coaches would wear. UNC also sewed an "EVE" patch on every uniform jersey, and dozens of students, alumni, and fans put on "EVE" stickers. The college communities came together as the two teams knelt arm in arm at center court before the game and led a moment of silence for Carson, a touching tribute and reminder of the mutual respect between the rabid rivals.

Duke led only twice, in the first minute and then with 5:47 to play after making a stunning comeback from 11 points down in the second half behind Scheyer's scoring. The Tar Heels' 42–31 halftime lead was punctuated by Danny Green's flying dunk over Paulus, which became an iconic photo in Duke-Carolina annals. After the Blue Devils fought back to go ahead 68–66, UNC scored the last 10 points of the game, two each by Wayne Ellington, Hansbrough, and Lawson and four by Green, including another dunk with 30 seconds left. The 76–68 win clinched a second straight ACC regular-season title and again spoiled Duke's Senior Night, this time for leading scorer DeMarcus Nelson.

Hansbrough, one of four Carolina players in double figures, finished with 16 points and 15 rebounds but, ironically, did not go to the foul line. It was the second of three times that happened in his 142-game college career as the NCAA all-time leader in free throws made (982).

The Blue Devils' fast start to the 2008 season skidded to three losses in their last seven regular-season games, but Krzyzewski had earned his 800th career victory with a one-point comeback win at N.C. State, when a furious Coach K turned the huddle over to his team in a last-ditch effort to erase an eight-point deficit. "For a couple of late timeouts, I let anyone who would actually want to talk—and say something that somebody would listen to—run the huddle," Krzyzewski said. "Teams become really good when they talk to each other. What happens is, they take ownership. We never took ownership until late in the second half."

Carolina went to the ACC tournament in Charlotte a heavy favorite to repeat as champion. In between the two semifinal games on Saturday, Dean Smith limped onto the court as UNC's honoree in the ACC Legends ceremony. His gimpy knee had been replaced the previous December, and cardiological and neurological complications from the surgery led to progressive cognitive impairment. Smith was still able to kid with fellow inductees, including former Duke All-American Mike Gminski, who once wanted to play for Smith.

The Tar Heels had rallied to defeat Virginia Tech in the first semifinal on Hansbrough's dramatic put-back baseline jumper, and they had to do it again on Sunday against a Clemson team that had already lost two overtime games to them during the regular season. Hansbrough, who finished with 66 points and 26 rebounds in the tournament, earned the MVP award, and was joined by Ellington and Ginyard on the all-tourney team. They secured a second straight No. 1 NCAA seed, back in the East Regional, and played their first two weekends in North Carolina.

Duke, which lost to Clemson in the ACC semifinals, again did not make it out of the first weekend of the NCAA tournament, beating Belmont in the Round of 64 in Washington, D.C., before bowing to unrelenting West Virginia two days later. The Blue Devils, second-seeded in the West Regional, led by five points at the half and then were bludgeoned on the boards by the No. 7–seed Mountaineers, whose 45–19 rebounding advantage in the game rekindled criticism of Duke's soft inside play.

After showing so much promise throughout most of the season, the 2008 Blue Devils lost three of their last five games and finished 28–6, having fallen out of the top 10 in the national rankings. But there certainly were good omens for the future. Singler was named ACC Rookie of the Year after averaging 13.3 points and 5.8 rebounds, and Paulus shot 42.3 percent from 3-point range on a team-high 196 attempts.

Again, the comparison to Carolina was pronounced. The Tar Heels blew out unranked Mount St. Mary's and Arkansas, going over 100 points twice in Raleigh. They returned to the (NBA) Bobcats Arena in Charlotte, the site of their ACC championship just two weeks before, and pulled away from 21st-ranked Washington State (coached by Tony Bennett, who would eventually move on to Virginia) in the Sweet 16.

Next up for a trip to the Final Four was No. 13 Louisville and its tournament-tested coach Rick Pitino and fifth-year center David Padgett, who ten years later would be thrust into the role as interim coach when the school fired Pitino after an FBI investigation into alleged cheating. Carolina held off the high-speed Cardinals down the stretch, beginning with Lawson's 3-pointer from the corner to protect the lead and then atypically when Hansbrough went out to the left elbow to hit clutch face-up jumpers and ice the 83–73 win. The East Regional title exorcised the ghosts of the collapse against Georgetown the year before as the Tar Heels–heavy crowd rocked the building.

Jay Bilas, the former undersized center at Duke, was on loan from ESPN to call the game for CBS. He effused over the guts of his fellow big man. "There is no one with a bigger heart in college basketball," he said of Hansbrough, who finished with 28 points and 13 rebounds and the regional MVP award. "His will far exceeds his skill."

The dramatic victory also pushed UNC past Duke in the eyes of the media. "North Carolina has clearly been the better team the last couple of years," Bilas said.

"All of a sudden, Carolina's won two ACC titles in a row, Carolina's the one going to the Final Four," added noted sports author Barry Jacobs. "The real question is: Has the balance shifted? Or is this just a good team pulling astride?

"To some extent, the UNC family rallied around Roy Williams. He was perceived as the savior . . . it infused everyone with more of a sense that we don't want to play second fiddle to Duke anymore—we don't have to."

The 2008 Final Four in San Antonio featured the inevitable

matchup once Williams left Kansas for Carolina, since most years both programs were contenders for the national championship. Even though Bill Self was welcomed warmly as Williams' successor at Kansas, some Jayhawks fans still held a grudge from 2000 when Williams turned down the Carolina job the first time it was offered and said he was staying at KU until he died or retired. After that, UNC fans were sore at him for three years.

The speculation and story lines went mad the week of the Final Four, where Memphis and UCLA were playing what seemed like a preliminary to the Kansas-Carolina main event on semifinal Saturday at the Alamodome. Everyone wanted to know how Williams felt about going against his "old school." The Carolina coach answered every question patiently and appeared relaxed going into what the media had turned into World War III.

But San Antonio had not been good to the Tar Heels in the 1998 Final Four, where they were clearly the best team but lost to Utah in the semifinals in Bill Guthridge's debut season as the successor to Dean Smith. Williams had his own bad memory of the Alamo City, a 16-point drubbing of his Jayhawks by top-seeded Illinois in the 2001 regional semifinals. But this time his team was *playing* Kansas in a game he would never schedule.

Perhaps unwisely, Williams reached out to Self to discuss "handling the situation the right way." But Self, who was having his own problems escaping his predecessor's long shadow, cut the phone call short by saying, "I've always handled this the right way."

Williams tried to treat it like his previous five Final Fours, enjoying the open practices on Friday when he knew envious coaching colleagues were watching from the stands. But the side show following him—from North Carolina to Texas—might have literally made him sick. He caught a flu bug somewhere and woke up Saturday morning feeling terrible. Although he insisted his team was ready to play great, the Tar Heels were awful from the opening tip and fell behind at one point 40–12. Although hardly household names like Carolina's weekly national TV stars, all five KU starters were good enough to play in the NBA and did. They were UNC's equal in every respect on paper and were dominant on the way to an 84–66 win that wasn't even that close.

"Coming to Carolina from Kansas, a lot of people back there had beaten up Coach Williams about it," Hansbrough recalled. "The players were trying to win for him. We got in a hole and didn't have enough energy to get out of it."

As Kansas took on Memphis Monday night, an even bigger story erupted. Williams and his wife, Wanda, stayed in San Antonio to cheer on his former team—as they had done in 1993, when his Jayhawks lost to the Tar Heels and they remained in New Orleans to watch Dean Smith win his second national championship, waving blue-and-white pompoms the entire game. On the way to their seats, Williams bumped into one of his former players who handed him a KU sticker and Williams slapped it on his sweater. The CBS cameras soon found him in the crowd and zoomed in on the sticker. It spawned dozens of different reactions, most of them negative. Asked about it during a halftime interview, Williams candidly said that with his season over, his heart was with Kansas.

"I have 19 former players at the game," he said a few months later. "I'm supposed to look down there and see Jacque Vaughn cheering for Kansas, and I'm not supposed to cheer for them? I'm about people, not buildings. I was doing what I was taught to do by Coach Smith, supporting my former players."

Williams spent part of the spring and summer stewing about the criticism, most of which came from hurt UNC fans and triumphant Jayhawks, whose team had beaten Memphis in overtime for Self's first NCAA title. While diligently preparing practice plans for what he hoped would be another national championship contender, Williams never could let it all go, saying, "Now that I've had a chance to think about it, I'd wear 12 of those suckers next time."

Down the road at Duke that spring, Johnny Dawkins left the basketball staff to become head coach at Stanford, a move some saw as the end of his chances to someday succeed Krzyzewski. That prospect always seemed unlikely; as the first of Krzyzewski's players to have his jersey hung in the rafters of Cameron Indoor Stadium, Dawkins' legacy was already secured. Why risk it for the no-win proposition of following a coaching legend?

For Carolina basketball, it was a longer off-season than a Final Four team with a 36–3 record warranted. But the loss to Kansas, Williams' failure to call timeouts in that game, and the sticker incident stuck. He groused over one poll in North Carolina that gave him a 76 percent approval rating, wondering what that other 24 percent could have wanted.

When Wayne Ellington, Ty Lawson, and Danny Green put their names into the 2008 NBA draft to test the waters, the Tar Heels immediately went into a state of flux. Without those three, their chances of repeating as ACC champions as well as returning to the Final Four would be severely compromised. Williams stayed in touch with NBA general managers he knew, gauging the interest in his three pro prospects, mainly if any would commit to selecting them in the lottery or among the fourteen top picks. Tyler Hansbrough, the reigning ACC and national Player of the Year, was a different story.

If Hansbrough hadn't turned pro after his first two seasons, he certainly wasn't passing up his senior year. The day of the deadline to enter the NBA draft, Psycho T spent the afternoon in the weight room pumping iron and seeing that Kansas loss with every lift. He refused to meet with the media and, when Williams said he had to at least issue a statement that he was staying in school, Hansbrough huffed, "Just write something you think I would say." That was it, less drama when Ellington, Lawson, and Green decided to return for the 2009 season and vaulted the team from uncertain status back to the top of the preseason polls.

Despite a fast start, the Tar Heels looked like a team already worn down by injuries to Hansbrough, freshman forward Tyler Zeller, and Ginyard. Carolina had made the covers of *Sports Illustrated* and *Sporting News* as the consensus pick to win the national championship and had blown through its first 13 games by at least 15 points. The Tar Heels were dominant even though Hansbrough missed the first two (including a home rout of unranked Kentucky) and four of the first seven games with a potential shin fracture that troubled Roy Williams, who feared the injury would threaten his superstar's professional career. Should he practice Hansbrough less, play him fewer minutes?

With a half-dozen UNC and ACC career records squarely in his sights, Hansbrough returned for good in the last two games of the Maui Classic and began his onslaught on the record book by scoring 34 points in the 102–87 annihilation of eighth-ranked Notre Dame in the final. "That was one of my best college games," he said. "People were doubting me and I took a lot of criticism. I couldn't turn on ESPN without people saying, 'He's not the same Tyler Hansbrough.' I wanted to prove I was back."

A week later, UNC was in Detroit to play Michigan State in the ACC–Big Ten Challenge at Ford Field in what turned out to be a preview of the Final Four there the following April. The NCAA had decided to experiment with the location of the raised basketball court, putting it on the 50-yard line of the football field—instead of tucking it in one end zone and closing in the playing floor with temporary bleachers like it had at past Final Fours in domed stadiums. The configuration resulted in more than 70,000 seats, most of them far away from the court, but barely 25,000 fans showed up for Carolina's 98–63 rout of the sixth-ranked Spartans, who had little home crowd advantage.

"See you at the Final Four," someone said to Williams after the press conference.

"I'll be back, and I hope my team is with me," he responded.

Over the next two weeks, Williams orchestrated the breaking of Phil Ford's all-time scoring record. Going into a home game with Oral Roberts, Hansbrough needed 34 points to surpass Ford's 2,290 mark. After he scored 26 against Oral Roberts, Williams pulled Hansbrough so he could set the record in the first half of the next game against Evansville. Ford, an assistant coach with the NBA's Charlotte Bobcats, had an off night and could be there, and as soon as Hansbrough scored his ninth point, the officials halted the game, Ford came out to congratulate his successor, and then stayed around for the press conference to discuss relinquishing a record that had remained for thirty years.

Next up was Duke's J. J. Redick, the ACC's all-time scoring leader, whom Hansbrough eventually passed on March 19 in the first round of the NCAA tourney. He had already surpassed former Duke All-American Christian Laettner for the most career free throws during the 2008 postseason.

The top-ranked Tar Heels remained unbeaten through the end of the calendar year.

Then, when the schedule stiffened, Williams' players started showing defensive lapses that reminded him of the 2008 season, when they didn't care much about anything but scoring. At Christmastime, they were second in the nation in average points (95.6) but 196th in points allowed (68.5). Most of them had it in their heads that they didn't have to play defense because, with Hansbrough, Ellington, Lawson, and Green, they were storming down the other end to score, every time. Or so they thought.

When ACC play began, unranked Boston College lit them up in the Smith Center for their first loss and a week later No. 4 Wake Forest outscored them by three points in Winston-Salem. It was the first time UNC had begun the ACC season 0–2 since 1997, Dean Smith's last season. That team recovered to win the ACC championship and reach Smith's 11th Final Four. Williams mentioned that and also recollected his third season at Kansas, when the Jayhawks dropped their first two Big Eight games at Oklahoma and Oklahoma State but wound up playing Duke for the NCAA title the following April.

His disheartened team seemed to brighten up as if to say, "We're still okay." But Williams also reminded them they were going back to work the next day, and the emphasis would not be on scoring.

Without their defensive ace Ginyard, who had started all 39 games as a junior but suffered a summertime foot injury that forced him to redshirt for the 2009 season, UNC did not have a leader on that end of the floor. The Tar Heels' defense improved during a seven-game stretch, when they held all but one opponent under 80 points. They were 7–2 in the ACC, tied with Duke for first place heading into their February 11 visit to Cameron Indoor Stadium with a bit of history on the line, trying to become the first team to win four straight at Duke over Mike Krzyzewski–coached teams.

"Kids can't identify with history," Krzyzewski said the day before the game, "they're too young. They're not 30-, 40-, 50-year-old people. They're kids and they need to be put into the now. And now is that this is a hell of a game. 'Now' is both tied for first place."

With the media already speculating that no team could pull a four-peat on Coach K at Cameron, Williams tried some old Smith philosophy, relishing the rare underdog role.

"You know, guys, we probably can't beat Duke again over there, all those experts they must be right," he recounted in his autobiography *Hard Work*. "It would be really hard to do that, but you know what? Nobody else in America can go in there and win this game, but we can. So let's think about how this is going to feel when we beat Duke for the fourth straight time in their own gym."

The pep talk seemed to work for the first nine minutes, but Duke rallied from an 11-point deficit to outscore the Tar Heels 34–15 and take an eight-point lead at halftime as Cameron roared like a freight train out of control. The Blue Devils did it with torrid shooting, 21 of 34 from the floor and six of nine from 3-point range, as Singler, Scheyer, Paulus, and Gerald Henderson combined for 44 of their 52 points. Carolina shot 50 percent, kept in the game by Bobby Frasor's three 3-pointers, but took a rare tongue-lashing from Hansbrough in the locker room at halftime. Williams got on them for playing "sorry" defense and on offense for letting Duke help on Lawson, who was near unstoppable one-on-one.

Then Williams diagrammed some sets to spread the floor and let Lawson drive by his defender to the basket, and over the second half the once petulant point guard solidified his campaign for ACC Player of the Year, which had started two weeks earlier when he hit a long buzzer-beater at Florida State on national television. Lawson, who had four points at the break, scored 21 in the second half as the Tar Heels shot 60 percent compared to Duke's 36 and thundered back to blow out the sixth-ranked Blue Devils 101–87. All five UNC starters finished in double figures by getting good shots and making most of them.

Carolina ran away from Duke in the closing minutes, the ending so anticlimactic that it fostered the unusual occurrence in the rivalry. After Hansbrough hit another 3-pointer (like he had as a freshman) and Lawson's old-fashioned three-point play gave the Tar Heels a 17-point lead, the home crowd began filing out in disgust before the final buzzer, leaving the few visiting fans to whoop it up in an otherwise quiet arena.

"Crickets," Danny Green said. "We heard crickets. When you leave a game on the road and you hear crickets, you know you did your job."

Even with the national championships and so many victories, that fourth straight win at Duke might just be the pinnacle of Williams' coaching career because it was such a rare accomplishment. The locker room atmosphere felt more like satisfaction than excitement. Now Franklin Street was a different story; fans gathered there to celebrate and prep for the national championship the Tar Heels were again favored to win.

By the March rematch in Chapel Hill, UNC had climbed back to No. 2 in the polls while Duke had fallen to seventh. Carolina was 12–3 in the ACC, Duke 11–4, so the regular-season finale was still for first place, although the Tar Heels had clinched at least a tie. The Blue Devils had won five straight, including winning at Maryland, where Carolina did not, and believed they could ruin Hansbrough's Senior Night like he had doused Redick's three years earlier.

Duke might have thought Hansbrough's career lasted forever, but he remembers it as a blur, and his Senior Night was so distracting that he had to ignore most of the family and friends who had come into town. "My dad would also always call me and say, 'Can you get me some tickets?' Yeah, you're my dad," Hansbrough said. "'How many do you need?' He would never tell me, he'd say, 'How many can you get?' I was also real nervous about writing and giving my senior speech for after the game."

Now the overtime loss at Maryland two weeks earlier loomed large.

Carolina had flubbed away a 16-point lead by shooting too quickly, and the outcome allowed Duke to pull within one game back in the ACC race. A loss to the Blue Devils would leave the teams tied for first place and a No. 1 NCAA tournament seed up for grabs.

At the end of the Thursday's practice before Sunday, Lawson slammed his big right toe against the basket stanchion on a fast break and limped off the court and then out of the arena on crutches. The internet message boards blew up, and "Ty's toe" became the story line heading into the game, making national news and eventually becoming a factor in President Obama's NCAA bracket pick of the Tar Heels.

Williams thought Lawson, whose dedication had been questioned in his first two seasons, wouldn't play after not coming out with the team to warm up. Turns out, Lawson was getting a cortisone shot to numb the pain in his toe. Williams had been on the underclassmen before the game to make sure the seniors went out the right way, or "I'm going to be mad at you," he said. And now he had real doubts about the outcome if Lawson could not go or was ineffective in what would also be his last game at the Smith Center.

Lawson started, wearing an oversized shoe with a steel plate to protect the toe, and struggled through the first half. Duke led 39–38 at the break. Williams grabbed Lawson on the way back to the court and said, "Put that half behind you and play your tail off this half." Lawson somehow finished with 13 points, eight rebounds, and nine assists and made a clutch three-point play with 1:03 left as the Tar Heels held on for a tense, eight-point victory. They not only won a third straight regular-season championship but in all likelihood secured a top seed in the NCAA tournament.

At that point, all questions about Lawson's toughness had been answered, but not his toe. Lawson's father thought that soaking his son's foot in Epsom salt would speed the healing process, but it did the opposite. The next day, Williams saw how swollen Lawson's toe was and thought his star point guard was done for the postseason. He held him out of the ACC tournament in Atlanta, which was a big favor to Duke. The Blue Devils were in a three-year stretch of not having won anything significant amidst continued criticism of their big men, coached by assistant Steve Wojciechowski. They had never been an inside scoring team under Krzyzewski and had not consistently outrebounded opponents since their Final Four team of 1999.

However, with senior Frasor running the point and scoring only two points compared to Lawson's 16-plus average, Carolina lost to fleet Florida State in the ACC semifinals. The Seminoles played the Blue Devils in the championship game, and with Henderson, Scheyer, and Singler scoring 70 of its 79 points, Duke won by 10. Coach K beamed over the achievement. "Really neat," he called it. "I'm good with where my team is at."

Krzyzewski, a Republican, wasn't as good with Obama picking Carolina to win the national championship, based somewhat on Obama's scrimmage with the UNC team the previous April while the Democratic candidate was on the campaign trail (after which Hansbrough said, "Fifty years from now, I will still remember playing basketball with the next president of the United States").

"Somebody said we're not in President Obama's Final Four, and as much as I respect what he's doing, really, the economy is something he should focus on, probably more than the brackets," Coach K told the Associated Press. (When the NCAA champion Tar Heels later visited the White House, Obama told the team, "Thanks for salvaging my bracket and vindicating me before the entire nation.")

Duke, second-seeded in the East Regional, joined UNC in Greensboro for the first weekend of the 2009 NCAA tournament and dispatched unranked Binghamton and Texas. Still without Lawson, the Tar Heels, seeded No. 1 in the South, crushed Radford as Hansbrough passed Redick as the ACC's all-time scoring leader. Carolina then had its scariest postseason moment when falling behind LSU by five points with 12:25 left in a second-round game. Lawson had returned but wasn't doing much to that point. Williams called a rare timeout and barked at his team, which included three seniors and two juniors he figured were going pro. "Is this the way you want your careers to end?" he asked angrily. "Then keep playing like this!"

Behind a suddenly engaged Lawson, Carolina scored 11 straight points and held the Tigers to one basket for nearly seven minutes while going on to win 84–70. Lawson, who had two points at the half, finished with 23, matching Wayne Ellington as high scorer. It reaffirmed Lawson's resilience and his prior selection as ACC Player of the Year, the second UNC point guard to win the award, after Phil Ford. Lawson would also finish the season as the only point guard to ever lead the Tar Heels in field goal percentage (.532).

Duke moved on to the Sweet 16 in Boston but lost to 11th-ranked Villanova at the TD Garden, where future Blue Devils Kyrie Irving and Jayson Tatum would rejuvenate the Celtics nine years later. The Wildcats crushed Duke on the boards, mainly because Singler, Scheyer, Henderson, and Nolan Smith missed 40 of 51 shots—20 of 24 3-pointers—in the 77–54 final. Duke finished 30–7 but out of the news as UNC kept rolling toward a second straight Final Four.

Stories continued to appear in the local and national press on how the rivalry had now evened up and, in some, giving the nod back to UNC as the best program. With Lawson gracing the cover of the *Sports Illustrated* Sweet 16 issue, the Tar Heels advanced to Memphis, where Williams engaged in an old tradition of spitting in the Mississippi River for good luck and a new tradition of walking the ducks to the lobby at the famed Peabody Hotel, where his team stayed.

Carolina easily beat Gonzaga after Williams altered how his team defended ball screens, holding the Zags to seven of 23 from 3-point range while Carolina canned 11 of 19. It was something he probably should have done against Kansas the year before at the Final Four in San Antonio, where KU had 17 assists on 34 made baskets and shot 53.1 percent. Williams was notoriously stubborn to change anything that had helped him win almost 80 percent of his games. He often joked that he has had only one wife (Wanda) and used the same golf putter for decades.

In the South Regional final, the Tar Heels took on Oklahoma and All-American Blake Griffin, the 2009 National Player of the Year, who was averaging better than 22 points and 14 rebounds per game. By denying Griffin the ball with a double-team early in each of the Sooners' possessions, Carolina raced out to a 13–2 lead on its way to a 72–60 victory. Lawson won the regional MVP with a combined 40 points and 14 assists in the two games at the FedEx Forum.

Oklahoma was coached by former Dukie Jeff Capel, who would lose that job two years later and wind up on Krzyzewski's bench and eventually become the architect of the Blue Devils' recruiting emphasis on one-and-done high school stars.

UNC had now won four NCAA tournament games by double digits and returned to Ford Field, the site of the ACC–Big Ten Challenge game in which Williams' team had crushed Michigan State. The Spartans also were back for their seventh Final Four. This time, more than 70,000 fans attended, the first national semifinals to eclipse that mark. But the rows of seats sloping dramatically away from the raised playing floor made the crowd seem relatively quiet for the Saturday Final Four. The Tar Heels eliminated Villanova in an ugly defensive struggle, and Michigan State defeated UConn to set up a rematch for the national championship.

Spartans coach Tom Izzo, who had not beaten Carolina with Williams as the coach, said a victory for his team would boost a city and state ravaged by the economic meltdown of the time. Williams, who had labeled this Final Four as a "business trip" for his team, tried to make a joke and said he "had a cause, too, to win the national championship, period, the end." But it didn't exactly end there. "If you told me that if Michigan State wins, it's going to satisfy the nation's economy, then I'd say, hell, let's stay poor for a little while longer." Not funny to many people who heard it on cable TV and read it on websites and in newspapers.

The game, however, was a laugher, which made the predictions of *both* CBS analysts Greg Anthony and Seth Davis that Michigan State would win seem foolish, considering the Tar Heels were blowing through the tournament to that point and had already beaten the Spartans badly on the same floor in December.

Carolina, the best running team in college basketball, had compiled the largest total point differential in NCAA tournament history in their five previous wins, and Izzo suggested his team would also play up-tempo. "Detroit, defense, and destiny" were the three reasons for an upset offered by Davis, a Duke graduate. He should have known that while most of Motown favored Michigan State, a hostile atmosphere was really more helpful to UNC. The fans were still too far away from the floor to be a factor, but Williams pulled out the old Frank McGuire "us against the world" mantra to keep his team focused on getting off to a great start. "Remember what happened last year," he harped all weekend, a reference to the Kansas disaster.

"I *love* playing on the road," he said at Sunday's press conference; his team had played 22 games away from Chapel Hill and won 19 of them.

Because their offensive numbers were so impressive, with four future pros in the starting lineup, most fans and media hadn't noticed that after two years of constant criticism from Williams his team had become a defensive force as well.

Lawson and Ellington made Michigan State's guards Kalin Lucas (the Big Ten Player of the Year) and Travis Walton (the league's Defensive Player of the Year) look like they couldn't cut it against the ACC. Lawson's seven steals in the first half tied a Final Four record (his eighth in the second half broke it), and Ellington's 17 points against Walton catapulted Carolina to an NCAA title game high of 55 in the first half and a 55–34 lead, a record for the biggest margin at intermission. That's when enough fans switched over to *Dancing with the Stars* that the ratings plummeted. Anyone who turned back to check the score saw that the lead remained 20 points midway through the second half, chasing away the viewing audience for good. The 89–72 triumph gave the Tar Heels an average victory of 20 points in the tournament, and they were the first team since Duke in 2001 to win all six by double digits. Surely Williams would have bettered 76 percent in a new appreciation poll.

But all of that made his second national championship feel different for Williams, who had won this time with players he had recruited, not inherited, as he had in 2005 when he rescued the program from the disastrous Doherty days. And the reaction was also not the same back home, less overt appreciation, no signs in his yard; the feeling of entitlement had seemingly returned to Carolina Basketball. He did receive a congratulatory letter from Bob Knight, who said winning the NCAA tournament when everyone expected you to was the greatest accomplishment under the most pressure.

The players who had withdrawn from the NBA draft returned, this time victoriously, to the biggest stage and boosted their pro stock. Lawson proved he was talented *and* unselfish, and Ellington, the Most

Outstanding Player in the Final Four, moved up on first-round draft boards closer to Hansbrough, who went No. 13 to the Indiana Pacers. Lawson (No. 18) and Ellington (No. 28) were both drafted by Minnesota.

Danny Green went from an undrafted projection to a second-round pick. He signed with the San Antonio Spurs and became the best pro of all his teammates. The Hansbrough–Green–Frasor–Mike Copeland class had gone 124–22 over four years, akin to what Duke teams led by Christian Laettner (123–26), Shane Battier (133–15), and Jason Williams (95–13) had done at the turn of the last two decades.

In just six seasons, Roy Williams had tied his mentor with two national championships at Carolina, which Smith had reached in his thirtieth year. Williams' Tar Heels had now won two NCAA titles since the Blue Devils' last in 2001.

But only one starter from the championship team and another from 2008 would be returning—Deon Thompson, the 2009 team's fifth option on offense, and defensive ace Ginyard, who missed all but three games of the season with a foot injury. Carolina faced a certain rebuilding job until Williams could sign another stellar recruiting class.

Ownership of the rivalry seemed secure in the short term, but Duke had different plans, borrowing a philosophy from Carolina that would prove equally successful.

TWENTY-FIRST-CENTURY RIVALRY STATS
Overall record: Duke 558–125, UNC 499–188

- Average record: Duke 29.4–6.6 (ACC); UNC 26.3–9.9 (ACC)
- 30-win seasons: Duke 9, UNC 7
- Top 10 finishes: Duke 17, UNC 10
- Top 25 finishes: Duke 18, UNC 14
- No. 1 finishes: Duke 4, UNC 1
- Head-to-head: Duke 27, UNC 16
- Duke wins in Smith Center: 11
- UNC wins in Cameron: 7
- ACC regular-season championships: UNC 9 (2 shared), Duke 5 (2 shared)
- ACC tournament championships: Duke 10, UNC 3
- National titles: Duke 3, UNC 3
- Final Fours: UNC 6, Duke 4
- Sweet 16s: Duke 14, UNC 10
- NCAA wins: UNC 48, Duke 46
- First-round losses: Duke 3, UNC 0
- NCAA tournaments: Duke 19, UNC 16

Note: The twenty-first-century list includes one season under Bill Guthridge and three under Matt Doherty for UNC.

3

THE WORMS TURN

Recruiting is the lifeblood of any college athletics team. The best coaches can't consistently win championships without also having the best players. Duke and North Carolina had combined to match UCLA in number of national championships with 11 through the 2018 season and won more conference titles than any other basketball programs because they had Hall of Fame coaches who turned high school stars into All-American players and, many of them, future pros.

The Blue Devils and Tar Heels had been going after many of the same recruits for more than fifty years in all sports, but primarily men's basketball because both of their programs had sustained national success under the growing spotlight. Until the explosion of the internet and social media, most of that recruiting was hidden from the public, but it was just as fervent (maybe more so) for Art Heyman in 1959 as it was for Harrison Barnes in 2009. The schools got on recruiting rolls that reflected their on-court success at the time.

In the early 1960s, after Duke stole Heyman away from Carolina two months before enrollment, coach Vic Bubas was the master recruiter. He followed up by landing prep stars Jeff Mullins and Jack Marin, while young, struggling UNC coach Dean Smith could only watch and learn. Bubas, who built four ACC championship and three Final Four teams from 1961 to 1966, did lose a celebrated target, 6'5" forward Bill Bradley from Crystal City, Missouri. Bradley had committed to play for the Blue Devils until he was laid up with a broken leg the summer before school opened. While recuperating, Bradley read about the U.S. government and Foreign Service programs offered at Princeton, which had also recruited him. Deciding that was the field he would enter after his basketball career ended, future U.S. senator Bradley made the last-minute switch to the Ivy League school. (Bubas gained a measure of revenge by beating Bradley and the Tigers 85–74 at what was then called Duke Indoor Stadium his sophomore year.)

Smith broke through in recruiting by pulling off a surprising upset with Larry Miller, a Pennsylvanian who liked the idea of being a foundation more than just one of the bricks. With Miller and two recruits from North Carolina high schools—Rusty Clark and Bill Bunting—that Smith wrangled away from Duke, the Tar Heels won three consecutive ACC titles and reached three Final Fours at the end of the decade. Then Smith had a Bradley-like loss when 6'11" Tom McMillen of Mansfield, Pennsylvania, knuckled under to family pressure to play closer to home and jilted Carolina for Maryland on enrollment day. McMillen was the second schoolboy to have his picture on the cover of *Sports Illustrated*.

Nevertheless, UNC dominated recruiting in the early 1970s and beat Duke on the court, losing only Dick DeVenzio to Bubas while signing Dennis Wuycik, Steve Previs, and George Karl to take over the Pennsylvania landscape. After Bubas retired, Carolina reached the 1972 Final Four with those three players and returned in 1977 with stars named Phil Ford and Mike O'Koren, who only briefly considered the Blue Devils.

Duke responded by capitalizing on perhaps the greatest recruiting mistake Smith ever made, turning down an interested 7-footer named Mike Gminski, who wanted to play for the Tar Heels but was incorrectly deemed too slow by Smith and his assistants. Gminski went on to win ACC Rookie of the Year in 1977 and Player of the Year in 1979, as Carolina failed to sign a star center during the "G-Man's" career. With Gminski, the Blue Devils won two ACC championships and reached the 1978 NCAA title game, losing to Kentucky. Forty years later, Gminski confirmed that if UNC had offered him a scholarship, he would have accepted.

Duke had also won the recruiting battle for Gene Banks, the school's first African American basketball star, largely because Banks played in high school for Joey Goldenberg, a close friend of Duke coach Bill Foster. After Foster left for South Carolina in 1980, Mike Krzyzewski arrived and worked to catch and surpass Smith and UNC in recruiting.

Coach K's first major signing victory over the Tar Heels came with Danny Ferry, who had grown up a Carolina fan but fell for Krzyzewski's hard sell. He became a rising Duke star in 1985. "He is the first big-name player we beat them for," Coach K said of Ferry, who was a National Player of the Year and two-time All-American. Ferry played in three Final Fours, still owns the Duke single-game scoring record (58 points), and was the first player in ACC history to score 2,000 points, pull down 1,000 rebounds, and dish for 500 assists. The Tar Heels won two ACC regular-season titles and one tournament championship but did not make a Final Four during Ferry's career; however, they played his teams dead even in head-to-head matchups, splitting 10 games, most of them brutally rough affairs.

Duke controlled the early 1990s while capping off a run of seven Final Fours in nine years after beating Carolina in recruiting unstoppable star forward Christian Laettner, gutsy point guard Bobby

Hurley, and the great Grant Hill, another onetime Tar Heels fan. Smith won the recruiting battle for 7-footer Eric Montross, who led UNC to the 1993 NCAA championship after Duke had won back-to-back titles the previous two years.

UNC signed Jerry Stackhouse and Vince Carter, who both visited Duke, but after Krzyzewski returned from an illness in 1995 and rebuilt his program a second time, he made a clean sweep over Carolina, beginning with Shane Battier in 1997, Duke's only star recruit of the era to stay all four years. The recruiting dominance continued with Elton Brand, Corey Maggette, Will Avery, Jason Williams, and Mike Dunleavy—first-round NBA picks who along with second-rounder Carlos Boozer gave up ten total seasons of college eligibility.

When Roy Williams returned to UNC in 2003, he planned to resurrect Smith's program and duplicate the one he had for fifteen years at Kansas, seeking a solid base of four-year players with occasional early departures to the NBA. Meanwhile, Krzyzewski went in the other direction and ramped up his pursuit of players he knew would not stay four years, all the way to taking full freshman classes of potential one-and-dones. His wholesaling of high school stars who had to spend at least one year in college due to the new NBA minimum age limit of nineteen started even *before* Duke hung its fourth NCAA championship banner with a veteran group of role players who looked more like one of Smith's Tar Heel teams.

The season after Carolina roared through the field to win the 2009 national championship, Krzyzewski thought he had a good team that could be great the following year. On October 22, 2009, Kyrie Irving announced on ESPNU that he would sign with Duke. The 6'2" senior from St. Patrick's High School in New Jersey was the best player in his state and one of the most coveted prep guards in the country, a sure-shot college All-American and future NBA first-rounder. He pretty much declared himself a one-and-done after donning the Duke cap on national TV.

That was okay with Coach K. Looking ahead to 2010–11, he was assembling a roster that was packed with scorers like Kyle Singler and Nolan Smith, shooting stars Seth Curry (Steph's kid brother, who had transferred from Liberty), and Andre Dawkins. And Krzyzewski had more size than perhaps he ever had on one team in 6'10" brothers Miles and Mason Plumlee and 6'11" Ryan Kelly. Kelly, from Raleigh, followed Shavlik Randolph as the first in-state five-star recruits not to pick Carolina since David Thompson way back in 1972. Irving would be Duke's new point guard, and Krzyzewski was missing only a swing man to replace 6'6" Jon Scheyer, who was graduating after the 2010 season. He had targeted the top player in the 2010 high school class, 6'8" Harrison Barnes of Ames, Iowa, who was being recruited by every major school in the country, including Carolina.

Barnes had all the makings to be another Grant Hill: smooth, swift, athletic with the DNA of a family that had been around education for a generation. Barnes teamed with future Creighton All-American Doug McDermott to lead Ames High School to back-to-back undefeated seasons (53–0) and state championships, averaging 27.1 points, While a senior Barnes collected 10.4 rebounds, 4.0 assists, and 4.0 steals, finishing as Ames' all-time scoring ace. He was a five-star recruit in every rating and the consensus No. 1 target of 2010, earning co-MVP at the McDonald's All-American game and named Mr. Basketball USA.

And, clearly, Duke was the early leader for Barnes, who took his official visit to Durham during his junior year, when UNC held the No. 1 ranking for the first seven weeks of the 2009 season with Duke not ranked higher than fourth. The worm apparently turned away from the Blue Devils on that visit.

As is custom, Barnes and his mother, Shirley, sat directly behind the Duke bench, where they could stand during timeouts and look into the huddle and right at Krzyzewski crouched in front of his team. It was not a particularly good game for the Blue Devils, who faced their coach's fuck-filled criticism for much of the afternoon. Afterward, Shirley Barnes told her son, "It's your choice, but I would never want my son playing for a coach who talked to his players like that."

Bobby Frasor, who heard Krzyzewski's worst during Carolina's four straight victories at Cameron Indoor Stadium, told the website *Deadspin* in 2012, "You don't realize how much he curses and how much he's on the refs all the time. I remember someone telling me about [former Duke player and transfer] Taylor King during his freshman year and how he thought his name was 'motherfucker,' because that's how Coach K got his attention. I don't know how true it is. I mean, he's a great coach and I'm not going to deny that at all, but the way he handles his players or acts with the refs and media, sometimes it kind of rubs people the wrong way."

That was coaching business as usual for Krzyzewski, who despite his polished corporate image over the years could still lace into his players with a string of profanities that had caused several families sitting too close for comfort at cramped Cameron to request seats farther away from the bench. With Coach K, most of his players came to accept it as necessary motivation, given Duke's long-term success.

The other X factor in Barnes' recruitment was UNC's Williams, who always prided himself on outworking rival coaches. With three private planes at his disposal, Williams counted eleven trips he made to Ames, compared to three by Krzyzewski. In the sophisticated software days when computers could track the destinations of aircraft based on their registration numbers, Duke knew Williams was repeatedly flying to Iowa. During one of his last trips, a Krzyzewski assistant called the Barnes home to confirm that Carolina had gone in after Duke's final visit. When told they didn't know Williams was following them in, Shirley Barnes said, "You never asked me."

Barnes informed the six finalists, which also included Iowa State, Kansas, Oklahoma, and UCLA, that he would deliver his college decision by Skype, the first known recruit to use the computerized video communication tool, on November 13, 2009, at 2 p.m. Eastern time. That was the day of Duke's first game of the 2009–10 season, and the Blue Devils were ranked No. 9 in the country. Carolina was 2–0 at that point and ranked No. 6, astonishing considering how the rest of the Tar Heels' season went. All six schools had to rearrange their schedules and scramble to set up computers with Skype capabilities to watch Barnes' proclamation. "That's another one I probably felt better about than the general public did," Williams said after hearing Barnes mention his name, reaffirming that hard work can get the job done.

Williams has always liked the early signing period, so high school seniors can get their decisions out of the way and have fun playing their last year and then graduate without the pressure hanging over their heads. And he really liked it for Barnes and his fellow signees Reggie Bullock and Kendall Marshall, because the Tar Heels would eventually lose 12 of their last 16 ACC games—including the tournament—fall out of the polls, and miss an NCAA bid for the only time in Williams' first fifteen years at UNC. Duke all the while was ascending toward the Final Four, including a 32-point revenge beatdown of Carolina at Cameron. Would Barnes have made a different choice if he waited until after the season?

It was reminiscent of Raymond Felton, Sean May, and Rashad McCants signing with Matt Doherty in the fall of 2001, after which Carolina finished the 2002 season at 8–20 amidst massive turmoil in the program, eventually costing Doherty his job. Would they have gone elsewhere had they waited, and not been Tar Heels when Williams returned in 2003? Or would Williams have come back at all with the cupboard so bare?

Two years later, Carolina won the NCAA championship with those three players at the core of his team.

Duke's failure to land Barnes was compounded in the 2011 season when Irving missed all but 11 games with a torn ligament in his big toe, and the Blue Devils did not fulfill Krzyzewski's prophecy of winning the national championship. But he had done it a year earlier.

Entering the new decade, Duke still considered itself to have the best program in the country over the last ten years, if not the prior twenty. The Blue Devils had dominated the ACC since Krzyzewski's return from missing most of the 1995 season, and they reached three Final Fours and won the 2001 national championship. Carolina's sample size was smaller, but even more impressive: three Final Fours and two NCAA titles in Roy Williams' first six seasons. Duke regarded Carolina's run during the Hansbrough era as a natural ebb and flow of America's best college basketball rivalry.

Krzyzewski's long-range goal for his program mirrored Dean Smith's of sustained success, rather than winning an occasional championship and then disappearing for a few years. Like Smith, Krzyzewski recognized that staying high in the polls each year perpetuated national publicity that enhanced recruiting. And Duke had the data to support its coach's method. Since the 1997–98 season, the Blue Devils were ranked No. 1 during nine seasons for a total of fifty-six weeks. UNC was second with five seasons for thirty-four weeks. Duke had also surpassed Carolina in final No. 1 rankings, five times compared to two. Both were at or near the top of most of these metrics.

"There are swings that happen in each program; you might have one team for a four-year period that is really difficult to beat,"

Krzyzewski said in 2012. "They had that with Hansbrough, and we had it with a few of our teams in the 1990s and early 2000s."

And without Hansbrough and three other starters gone to the NBA, the drop for Carolina was expected to be steeper than usual in 2010. After all, the Tar Heels had lost 7,309 career points from the departed players and, off the 2009 NCAA champions, 70 percent of their scoring, almost half their rebounding, and more than two-thirds of their assists. Although in some corners expectations were still high.

They returned two veterans (Deon Thompson and Marcus Ginyard) who had started 131 games and two rising sophomore big men (Ed Davis and Tyler Zeller) who had pro potential but wound up missing a combined 24 games with injuries.

Into January 2010, the teams were actually running pretty close. Through January 10, UNC was 12–4 and ranked No. 9 in the country. That had included a win over Nevada in November for Williams' 600th career victory, still the fastest coach to reach that milestone.

Duke finished January with a 17–4 record and No. 8 in the polls. But the rivals soon started in opposite directions. Crippled by injuries and Williams' worst-shooting team, the Tar Heels collapsed into a 2–10 stretch that left them unranked with a .500 record and already on the outside looking in at an NCAA tournament bid. Meanwhile, the Blue Devils were finding their stride after adjusting to Krzyzewski's tallest team—a bevy of big men all close to seven feet with specific roles, and four returning starters from 2009 (sans Gerald Henderson, who turned pro after his junior season).

The Duke streak kicked into overdrive in Chapel Hill for the first meeting of 2010, with Carolina trying to pull itself from a six-out-of-seven-loss tailspin. Holding a 28–27 lead after one half of dreadful shooting by both teams, the Blue Devils blew the game open in the last seven minutes behind Scheyer's 11 points, and they beat the Tar Heels on the backboards for the first time in years. Scheyer and

Singler combined for 43 points and made all nine of Duke's 3-pointers, sending UNC to a fourth straight loss and snapping a second three-game losing streak to the archrival in four years.

"It just sucks losing to these guys," Nolan Smith said after the 64–54 victory. "To do it the amount of games we did in a row, and now to finally get this win, it feels great. We played a good game and hopefully we can start this stretch of us winning games against them."

By the rematch at Duke more than three weeks later on Scheyer's Senior Night, Carolina had split its last six games and had some reason to believe it could win a fifth straight time at Cameron. But coming off their only loss in the last nine games (at Maryland), the Blue Devils were not letting this one get away after hearing about "Hansbrough Indoor Stadium" for the last four years. They jumped on top from the opening tip and led 53–26 at the half, sparked by Singler's 19 points and his trash-talking to the Tar Heels. Scheyer finished with 20 points in his last game on Coach K Court; he had been perhaps Duke's most selfless player in his career, starting off at small forward and ending up sharing point guard duties with Smith.

"I was trying to remember that moment, keep the picture in my head," Scheyer said of his postgame adulation from students and fans. He was to end his career as Duke's ninth all-time scorer and third in both total free throws made and percentage.

"You never go into a game thinking you're going to blow somebody out by 30," Scheyer said of the 82–50 thrashing. "But once we get a lead like that, we really want to have a killer instinct and put them away. I thought we never let off the gas."

The emergence of senior post men Brian Zoubek, who had 13 rebounds to go along with eight points, and Lance Thomas continued to redefine the new Blue Devils, who finally found big guys to control the glass on both ends of the floor. They gave Duke a six-plus advantage on the backboards for the season. The Blue Devils reclaimed first place in the ACC and went into the postseason as a projected top seed in the NCAA tournament.

After UNC's worst loss to Duke since 1964, the Tar Heels finished 5–11 in the ACC and a three-way tie for ninth place, their lowest in fifty-seven years of conference play.

"It was like they were trying to make up for losing the last four years in one game," Roy Williams said of Duke. "And it felt to us like they did."

Indeed, it was Duke's most lopsided home win over Carolina, which had its lowest point total of what had long since become a lost season. It almost assured the Tar Heels the dubious distinction of following up their national championship by not even making it back to the Big Dance.

"In my 22 years as a head coach, I've never had the combination of problems and mistakes and injuries we had to overcome," Williams bemoaned. "Starting out we knew we might have trouble shooting the ball from the 3-point line; that came to fruition (32.8 percent). We were also concerned with the backcourt play because nobody had actually done it, so turnovers became a big problem for us. It's what the season was; so many things that could go wrong did go wrong."

Duke, on the other hand, had developed an unusual juggernaut. Sure, the Blue Devils were still launching almost 20 3-pointers per game, but their inside play was not geared to scoring, only creating open looks for those outside shooters. Among Zoubek, Thomas, the Plumlee brothers, and Ryan Kelly, none made 100 shots in the 40-game season. Amazing for just under 35 feet of big men who played 39 percent of the minutes and scored only one-fourth of the team's total points. Not exactly your recipe for a national championship.

The evolution of Duke's 2010 team began after a shocking loss to VCU in the first round of the 2007 NCAA tournament, when some in the Blue Devils' own fan base thought the program might be slipping and Coach K was losing his magic touch. Their last NCAA championship had been in 2001, for Duke six long years ago, and their last Final Four was in 2004.

Duke finished the 2007 season 22–11 and tied for sixth in the ACC, the lowest league finish since Krzyzewski's lost season twelve years before. Carolina had swept the home-and-home series, dethroned Duke as ACC regular-season and tournament champion, and built a power of its own behind a team of five-star recruits.

"You come to Duke and you expect to win. You learn that you have to earn everything you get. It's eye-opening," said Zoubek, who was part of a highly touted class that included Scheyer, Thomas, and Henderson, all McDonald's All-Americans. "We had to figure out a way to win; we needed each other."

While Duke was going through a five-year stretch without a Final Four appearance, Carolina went to three Final Fours and won two national championships and three straight ACC regular-season titles.

But the shock from that loss to VCU didn't last long for the Blue Devils. Playing in the shadow of Tyler Hansbrough's Tar Heels, Duke came back to win 28 games in 2008 and 30 in 2009 with the addition of Singler and Nolan Smith. The Blue Devils placed second in the ACC both years and won the 2009 conference tournament when Carolina's Ty Lawson sat out with an injured toe. (Ironically, it was Duke's 17th ACC tourney championship, tying UNC for the most.) They also returned to winning NCAA games, but still lacked the post play they had not had since Shelden Williams departed in 2006.

Duke had bolted to fast starts in 2008 (22–1) and 2009 (18–1), so winning the preseason 2010 NIT over Arizona State and UConn didn't seem like a big deal except it began to define the team as different from its predecessors of the last decade. Under aggressive coach Jim Calhoun, 13th-ranked UConn had won two national championships and returned the core of its 2009 Final Four team. The Huskies were built to beat up most Duke teams physically, but not this one. The Blue Devils won what was more like a backyard brawl, 68–59, shooting only 28.4 percent but out-banging UConn on the boards by 13 rebounds. While taking 52 of Duke's 74 shots and making only 13, Scheyer, Singler, and Smith saw the signs of the toughest team they had played on.

They lapsed by losing in the ACC–Big Ten Challenge at Wisconsin, a team they had beaten by 24 points two years earlier. "We won the UConn game playing the way we knew we had to play, with rebounding and defense," Thomas said. "And then we got arrogant against Wisconsin because we beat them really bad before. We thought it would be really easy."

Scheyer said the loss helped "define our team. We found out we couldn't just outscore people anymore." Singler, who had a career-high 28 points in Madison, agreed.

So did Krzyzewski, who knew for these Blue Devils to be successful they would have to be unlike all his others. "Just because you have four starters back and four of your five leading scorers doesn't mean you can play the same way offensively," he said of his constant tinkering with lineups, offensive sets, and even a zone defense he was learning from Jim Boeheim, his Olympic assistant and Syracuse coach.

The Blue Devils were already connecting with one another, but their own tragedy strengthened that bond. After defeating St. John's at home, the players and coaches found out the sister of freshman guard Andre Dawkins had been killed in a car wreck on the way to the game from the family's home in Virginia. "We were there for Andre, wanted to be there," Krzyzewski said. "We came together as a group for him."

Dawkins went home for the funeral during a ten-day break and returned to play in every game as the Blue Devils won seven straight, including a 35-point blowout of 15th-ranked Gonzaga in New York, after which the team scattered for Christmas break. Thomas, from New Jersey, made his partial jewelry purchase that would be investigated and dropped two years later. The winning streak lasted through a solid victory over Iowa State at the United Center in Chicago, where Scheyer scored 31 points in his homecoming game in front of hundreds of his family, friends, and fans.

Duke, now fifth-ranked, faced four road trips in the next seven games and lost three of them, including a 12-point thumping against No. 7 Georgetown at the Verizon Center in Washington, where President Obama and VP Joe Biden sat courtside. The loss dropped Duke to 17–4 and to No. 11 when the next poll came out. A horrible performance, Krzyzewski called it. On the bus ride to the airport, he told his staff to "flush this game" and that more changes were coming. He began by insisting that at practices, in huddles, and every chance they got, the Blue Devils locked arms in a circle and broke by chanting "Together!"

"Like a chain, knowing that they aren't in this alone, no weak links," said Krzyzewski, who had imposed other gimmicks throughout his career, such as having his players kissing the Duke logo at center court at Cameron before games.

He also decided that Zoubek, the 7-footer with a menacing beard, deserved more playing time after shaking the injuries that had plagued most of his college career. Coach K began platooning his post men, using Zoubek and Thomas together and the Plumlee brothers playing side by side most of the time. He also held individual meetings with all of his bigs, no longer including Singler, who had moved out to the wing and was playing all over the court in Duke's motion offense.

In different iterations, Krzyzewski heard the same thing. Zoubek said he wasn't sure what to do with offensive rebounds he grabbed.

Thomas had improving numbers, but still felt like he was half the high school star who averaged a double-double. And the Plumlees were worried about taking each other's minutes. The veteran, Hall of Fame coach further shook up his team.

Beginning with the home game against unranked Maryland on February 13, 2010, seniors Zoubek and Thomas were his starters and he gave each of them a specific assignment. Krzyzewski told Zoubek what to do with those offensive rebounds, and it wasn't to go back up with the ball unless he had an uncontested dunk. The term "relocation" became part of the Duke lexicon, and Zoubek's job was to find Scheyer, Singler, or Smith on the perimeter and fire the ball back out to the open man. Coach K convinced Thomas that he could be as valuable as a rebounder and defender as he could by averaging 20 points a game. Zoubek and Thomas bought in, and Duke's immediate future changed.

The Blue Devils lost only one more ACC game, a close defeat at Maryland, which got a key late basket by ACC Player of the Year Greivis Vasquez before a wild crowd at the Comcast Center. Duke was upset because it meant tying the Terrapins for first place in the ACC rather than winning it outright. But the loss also proved they had become the kind of battle-tested team Krzyzewski wanted and added fuel for the postseason.

Now fourth-ranked, Duke won three close games in the ACC tournament in Greensboro and rallied from nine points behind against Georgia Tech in the Sunday final for its second consecutive tourney title and an amazing ninth of the last twelve years. Singler won the MVP award, and the big three—Scheyer, Singler, and Smith—were at the top of the all-tournament team voting. The title secured a No. 1 NCAA seed for the first time in four years.

Their new roles transformed Zoubek and Thomas. Both "relocators" more than doubled their assists from the year before and helped

Duke post more assists (555) than any other Blue Devils team since 2002. The duo also averaged more rebounds than points. Thomas led the nation in offensive rebounding the last six weeks of the season, resulting in a pro career he thought he had lost.

All four Blue Devils big men were single-minded in their relentless pursuit of the ball to start fast breaks from the defensive end or find shooters for second-chance points. These shooters would step into their releases rather than, as guards usually do, get the ball from one side or another and have to square up for a good look. Scheyer remained the same consistent 3-point shooter (38.5 percent) but Singler and Smith increased their accuracy along with the team, which shot its highest percentage since Redick's senior year in 2006, with 73 more attempts from behind the arc.

Still, with little margin for error, Duke needed the specialists to excel at their specialties. While the three scorers had all but 13 of the team's 70 points against 10th-ranked Purdue in the NCAA Sweet 16 on the raised court at Reliant Stadium in Houston, Zoubek's 14 boards helped the Blue Devils outrebound the rugged Boilermakers. Facing their most athletic opponent in No. 19 Baylor in what was tantamount to a road game in the Elite Eight, Singler uncharacteristically missed all 10 of his field goal attempts but Smith and Scheyer picked him up with 29 and 20 points, respectively. Thomas and Zoubek combined for 18 rebounds; Zoubek had drawn a crucial charge call when Baylor was leading by two. The Blue Devils then went on a 15–3 run and won by seven. Smith won the South Regional MVP.

Duke was going back to the Final Four with a chance to win its first national championship in nine years and counter Carolina's 2009 NCAA title. In Indianapolis, where Krzyzewski and the Blue Devils had won their first title in 1991, they would face the two toughest foes for a team their coach would not yet call great.

Second-seeded West Virginia, with its aggressive changing

defenses, was Duke's most difficult challenge of the season. The Blue Devils absolutely had to shoot the ball well at cavernous Lucas Oil Stadium, home of the NFL Colts, and they knew it. But playing in their second NFL stadium in two weeks seemed to help them further adjust to the different depth perception behind the baskets.

"We had five days to prepare for them," Krzyzewski said of Bob Huggins' intimidating Mountaineers, "their 1-3-1 zone and tough man-to-man. We moved the ball, got a lot of touches and made thirteen 3-pointers." Singler regained his shooting touch and combined with Scheyer for 63 points. Zoubek had 10 more rebounds and drew another big charge as the Blue Devils pulled away to a satisfying 78–57 victory.

Their opponent on Monday night was 11th-ranked Butler, which had won 25 straight games and become the Cinderella of college basketball. In comparison, Duke's towering team could not take the smallish Bulldogs lightly and, more important, forget that only history made the Blue Devils favorites. "We did not want the pressure of the past, because that can affect your present," Krzyzewski said, telling his players: "This is not about Duke, our name, winning a fourth national championship, or me. This is about you."

Singler said they had steely focus, their best of the season. "Once this one is over, it's over!" he shouted to his teammates before they took the court.

The game was an NCAA tournament classic, as neither team led by more than six points. Every time the Blue Devils pushed out to a small lead, the Bulldogs countered until they had the ball under the Duke basket with 13.6 seconds to play and trailing 60–59. Krzyzewski had his biggest player guarding Butler All-American Gordon Hayward on the throw-in, and Zoubek's presence forced Butler coach Brad Stevens to call timeout. Stevens switched up his in-bounder and the pass went to Hayward beyond the 3-point line.

Hayward had a poor shooting game and wanted to drive the lane and get to the foul line, where he had made eight of eight. But Singler stayed with him before Zoubek slid over and forced Hayward to the baseline, where his fall-away jumper hit the back rim. The rebound came off to Zoubek, who was fouled with 3.6 remaining. With both schools having the same color, the building had hours ago blended into a dark blue sea of true March Madness.

A 55 percent free throw shooter, Zoubek said he imagined looking at the goal in his childhood driveway before swishing the first foul shot to give Duke a two-point lead. But with his two big men in foul trouble, Krzyzewski needed to avoid overtime. He thought missing the second shot would force Butler to scramble instead of having time to set up for a 3-pointer and tie the game. He and his assistants yelled at Zoubek to miss the second, which he flicked hard at the basket. Hayward grabbed the long rebound, wheeled down court, and let fly from 45 feet. The ball was on line but bounded off the backboard and rim, and Duke began celebrating its fourth national championship. As with its first three, it came with veteran players.

The team's top three scorers—senior Scheyer and juniors Singler and Smith—all reached double figures in four of the six NCAA tournament games. And, when one of them had an off day, the other two scored enough to make up for him. The Blue Devils outshot five of their opponents and outrebounded all of them. Zoubek, who had become something of a cult figure over the last half of the season, had 60 rebounds in six games.

"We don't win without Zoubek; he was as much the story of our team as anyone," Krzyzewski said. "Butler was a great story, but our story was better. Our team was better, which is why I did not think the last shot was going in."

Stevens, who later coached Hayward and former Duke stars Kyrie Irving and Jayson Tatum with the Boston Celtics, called Zoubek "a good example for a lot of kids who aren't playing, about embracing your role, getting better, doing whatever your team needs you to do. Now you see what a powerful figure he is on that team."

The five starters scored all of Duke's points in the final game. Singler, with 40 points and 18 rebounds in the Final Four, was the Most Outstanding Player to go with his first-team All-ACC selection, ACC tourney MVP, and several All-America mentions. He was joined on the all-tournament team by Scheyer and Smith. Somehow, Zoubek, with 20 rebounds and great defense against Hayward and the Butler bigs, was left off. The Blue Devils, however, went home with what they wanted.

"For our guys to learn along the way like that is unbelievably gratifying to me," Krzyzewski said. "I don't like to say this one's better than another, but this one is really good. I've never had a group exactly like this one. I've said throughout the year that they were good . . . then really good . . . then they were really good with great character. But I told them in the locker room after the game, 'You are a great team.'

"They played as one with a collective ego. They followed their hearts, they shared their hearts. Tough as one. With no weak links."

Duke finished 35–5 and this would be its last championship team for a while without one-and-done players. The Blue Devils went unbeaten at home for the first time in seven years, won the ACC regular season and tournament and an unforgettable NCAA title. With Singler, Smith, and the Plumlees returning, Irving coming, and Seth Curry becoming eligible, Duke was positioned for another run in 2011. In fact, the Blue Devils looked set to go deep into the NCAA tournament for the next few years, especially with Krzyzewski's recruiting philosophy evolving toward more one-year players who might become NBA stars.

Duke's archrival was feeling about as low as Duke was high at this time. Carolina had completed a deflating 2010 season by posting four straight NIT wins before losing to Dayton in the championship game at Madison Square Garden and ending with a 20–17 record. In a season when quality wins were hard to find, the school did earn its 2,000th all-time victory. But it was the first time in ACC history that no UNC player received a single vote for any of the three all-conference teams, although Ed Davis (who was among the top rebounders in the league when he went down with an injury) and the still hobbling Marcus Ginyard would have received consideration had they been healthy.

With his team having lost seven of its last eight games, the weekend of February 12–13 was clearly the highlight of the season for Roy Williams. Not only did Carolina snap a four-game losing streak by beating N.C. State on Saturday afternoon, but members of Tar Heels teams from as far back as 1942 were on hand for the 100th anniversary of UNC Basketball, as Duke has done early in the 2004–05 season. Of all the former players and managers who attended, almost sixty of them had suited up in practice uniforms Friday night for an old-timers game that split the scrimmages by eras—from eighty-five-year-old Julian Smith and eighty-nine-year-old Bob Gersten to a couple of walk-ons from Carolina's fifth NCAA title team in 2009 and many more from the years in between. Current pros not at the NBA All-Star Weekend came in but did not participate in the scrimmages.

There was nary a dry eye at the sold-out Smith Center when former assistant coaches Eddie Fogler and Bill Guthridge escorted Dean Smith to midcourt to greet many of his former players. Smith, who was sixteen days from turning seventy-nine, acted like he knew everyone who approached him for a handshake or hug, but by then stories about his cognitive impairment stemming from knee replacement surgery in 2007 had been made public.

Including a moving video of Smith's career highlights, it was the ultimate tribute that everyone but Smith wanted. Gracious as ever, he acknowledged the crowd and disappeared back into the privacy he sought since his retirement. Smith made a brief appearance at halftime of the State game the next afternoon, receiving a thunderous ovation from 22,000 fans in the building that bears his name. During the procession of more than 250 basketball alumni, Smith stood next to Michael Jordan, who hugged and kissed him on the top of his head—a photo that became a piece of Tar Heels history.

Williams was in the locker room with the team at halftime but took his current players to the banquet Saturday night and instructed them to listen carefully to the speakers from each era, including the keynote address by Jordan, because he said they would all be in the same places in their lives one day. It served as an emotional juxtaposition of a rare bad season and remembrance of so many great years.

Usually finding a reason why each season is hard, Williams did not have to look very far in 2010. Long before the first game came omens. The tailspin actually began the previous June when his good friend and former Kansas athletics director Bob Frederick, the man who gave him his first head coaching job, died in a freak cycling accident in Lawrence. It left Williams with a profound sadness that carried through the summer and into the new season.

Whether or not it would be his hardest season in coaching, it was certainly his longest.

Following the 2009 national championship, Williams agreed to write his autobiography with noted author Tim Crothers, spending more than sixty hours taping interviews about his rags-to-riches life. His left shoulder, injured when he slipped on a golf course, required surgery in the fall, and he not only signed hundreds of books at scheduled events with his left arm in a sling, but ran practices and coached wearing the harness. He took enough pain and sleep medication to make him look puffy, and the candid, engaging coach acted grumpier than usual. One example: Early in the 2010 season, a rowdy visiting fan sat behind the Carolina bench at the Smith Center, and Williams had him ejected.

Williams fought the comparisons to 2006 all season, even though both teams faced similar circumstances—they followed a national championship season and had lost most of their best players. But his latest squad showed it lacked any true resemblance to the team with freshman phenom Hansbrough and the leadership that could help the struggling Tar Heels pull out of it. "In 2006, David Noel had one stretch of two or three games when he really got down on himself," Williams recalled. "But he bounced back and everyone was really impressed. That made his leadership qualities even stronger."

Williams thought, at last, the long months of injuries, insults, and frustration had ended with the loss to Dayton in New York. Then, after Duke won the national championship, he saw a full-page Nike ad in *Sports Illustrated* with a drawing of a devil's pitchfork and the caption "Order Has Been Restored." That angered the coach of Nike's flagship school, which was outselling Duke in licensed Nike apparel three to one and the alma mater of the owner of Nike's top brand (Jordan Jumpman). Exactly what order had been restored?

"I was dumbfounded, and they've heard about it," Williams said. "I was not pleased, did not like it, will never like it, will never understand it, and will never forget it. They said it was somebody in their marketing department, and their response was the order that had been restored meant that after all the upsets, at the end a No. 1 seed won the tournament, and it had nothing to do with the state of college basketball."

He didn't buy that explanation and said, eventually, Nike higherups apologized to him and admitted the ad never should have run.

Williams was also miffed when nationally syndicated talk show host Colin Cowherd kept insisting that "Duke is the only college basketball team that moves the dial." A mediocre team notwithstanding, Carolina had played in the highest-rated regular-season TV games. Duke's two-point victory over Butler, a real-life *Hoosiers* story, had drawn the highest rating for a national championship game since, well, UNC's 2005 NCAA title victory over Illinois in St. Louis.

"The highest-rated game in the ACC last season was North Carolina–Texas, the second highest was North Carolina–Michigan State," Williams said. "Three years ago, the highest-rated TV game in ESPN history was North Carolina vs. Ohio State. The highest-rated game in the ACC seven years in a row has been North Carolina–Duke. Anyone who makes those statements doesn't know what the crap he's talking about."

Williams was buoyed by having freshmen Harrison Barnes, Reggie Bullock, and Kendall Marshall joining the program for the 2011 season, filling the shooting and ball handling holes that plagued the perimeter and doomed the Tar Heels in 2010. Plus, 6'11" Tyler Zeller and stretch forward John Henson were developing into future high NBA draft choices. So, as is always the case with the Blue Blood rivalry, it was Carolina's turn to reload and try to catch Duke in 2011 and perhaps go back on top the following year.

Krzyzewski and his fourth national champions weren't quite done celebrating, however, accepting an invitation to the White House for May 27, 2010, for a marginally comfortable ceremony with President Obama. The president began his remarks in the Rose Garden by acknowledging with a smirk that he had picked North Carolina in his 2009 bracket to "win it all . . . it was nothing personal, just trying to win some money . . . I was right. [And Obama got to host the Tar Heels a year ago, as well].

"Coach K wasn't too happy; he basically told me to stick it . . . or stick to my day job. And this year he went out with these guys and he won, so he said [we'll] come to the White House and crow about it."

Needling himself, which was also applicable to the Blue Devils, the POTUS said, "Payback is sweet, isn't it, Coach?"

He mentioned the several Duke connections to the White House, gave a shout-out to co-captain Jon Scheyer, "my homeboy from the Chicago area," and recalled how he had campaigned in Medford, Oregon, "in the gym where Kyle Singler grew up, so I was the second-most famous person to ever show up in Medford." He recognized Greg Zoubek as "the only player that Coach K had allowed to grow a beard . . . somebody who's overcome a lot in college to set a Duke record for most offensive rebounds in a single season."

Obama finished by praising the Blue Devils as "a bunch of throwback guys who hustled and worked and had fun together and played by one of Coach K's philosophies. Think of the hand, if you attack with your five fingers open, you're more likely to break a finger, but if you bring them together to make a fist, you can really pound somebody. Very subtle, Coach K."

That was the very analogy Roy Williams used when he took over a fractured UNC program in 2003 and won two national championships between Duke's third and fourth. Williams rekindled admiration from a future president, whom his inner circle knew as a Tar Heels fan all the way back to Michael Jordan's championship days with the Chicago Bulls.

More gracious was Obama's praise of a Duke basketball program, with all upperclassman starters, for working off the court to support elementary education from Read with the Blue Devils in the schools to the Emily K Center, named for the coach's late mother and devoted to helping at-risk youngsters. There would be another visit before Obama left office, far more nonpartisan for both parties.

BRANDING CAMPAIGN
Mike Krzyzewski
Record 1981–95: 358–127
Winning percentage: .645
ACC regular-season titles: 4
ACC championships: 3
Final Fours: 7
NCAA championships: 2

* * *

Record 1996–2018: 669–152
Winning Percentage: .773
ACC regular-season titles: 8
ACC championships: 11
Final Fours: 5
NCAA Championships: 3

COMING HOME
Roy Williams
Record at Kansas: 418–101
Winning percentage: .805
Big 8/12 regular-season titles: 9
Big 8/12 championships: 4
Final Fours: 4
NCAA championships: 0

* * *

Record at UNC: 424–126
Winning Percentage: .772
ACC regular-season titles: 8
ACC championships: 3
Final Fours: 5
NCAA Championships: 3

4

THE BRANDING OF COACH K

While he sat out most of the 1995 season with back surgery and related exhaustion, Mike Krzyzewski had already built the Duke brand into one of the most influential in the history of college basketball. From 1986 through 1994, the Blue Devils had reached seven Final Fours in nine years, played in five national championship games, and won back-to-back NCAA titles, a stretch of consistency surpassed only by UCLA's 10 NCAA titles with John Wooden as coach from 1964 through 1975.

Similar to how Dean Smith had turned North Carolina into a national brand through 20 years of assorted championships, nationally televised games, and All-American players from Phil Ford to James Worthy to Sam Perkins and Michael Jordan, Duke took over in the 1980s and made Danny Ferry, Christian Laettner, Bobby Hurley, and Grant Hill into modern-day rock stars often welcomed by screeching girls in hotel lobbies. Krzyzewski was their coach then, but the players were the real stars of that time.

When he returned in the summer of 1995 and began a second

rebuilding of the Duke program, Coach K assembled a group of handlers led by former sports information director Mike Cragg and included Krzyzewski's wife, Mickie, to ramp up his personal brand.

A first move was to create the Legacy Fund, which was solely dedicated to men's basketball and eventually raised $50 million to endow the program with coaching salaries and new facilities. The fund eased tension with the Iron Dukes over the practice of splitting up athletic money among the varsity programs at Duke after paying for all scholarships.

The minimum contribution for the Legacy Fund was set at $1 million, and Grant Hill kicked it off with the first gift. Krzyzewski made all of the requests for gifts personally, and it helped that most of the million-dollar donors lived across the country and didn't need scarce season tickets, just VIP treatment for certain games, with Duke rolling out the red carpet for them. First-class airfare and five-star accommodations were among their perks, besides sitting behind or near the Duke bench for the games they did attend.

His new marketing team embarked upon prioritizing his schedule while furthering the Coach K brand, which would maintain Duke's as well. He quit all outside activities that weren't worth the time spent and money they paid and concentrated only on opportunities that increased his wealth, highlighted his relationship with Duke, aligned him with certain charities, and made his name as big, or bigger, than the school he worked for.

His income and power at the private university had already reached unprecedented heights for a coach and would, eventually, exceed the highest-paid doctors at the Duke medical center. "No one ever expected the [1991–92] back-to-back thing to happen, and when it did he moved into the position of getting anything he wanted," a former Duke athletic employee said. And when Krzyzewski returned from his medical leave, after Duke's 13–18 record in 1995, he quickly reclaimed his power by replacing almost his entire coaching and support staffs and made sure everyone knew he was back for good. Like a West Point–trained military leader, Coach K took command.

After his team won the 1997 ACC regular-season title, buoyed by Krzyzewski's first transfer, Roshown McLeod, he hired superagent David Falk, who became famous and filthy rich representing Michael Jordan. Falk had convinced Nike to introduce the first athletic shoe not only endorsed by a pro athlete but *named* for him—the Air Jordan. Based in Washington, D.C., Falk Associates Management Enterprises (FAME) already represented Georgetown's bigger-than-life coach John Thompson. The agency was expanding its client base into sports and entertainment, and Krzyzewski was becoming a superstar who could benefit from association with both genres.

Falk and Coach K's teaming up was recognized for more than mere involvement with Jordan, UNC's most famous sports alum. Falk was known to be at odds with Dean Smith, who referred to him as "a gofer" when he worked for former Davis Cup captain Donald Dell at the ProServ agency, and Smith resented the millions in commissions Falk made on Jordan's business deals, which included Coke, Gatorade, McDonald's, and the 1996 hit movie *Space Jam*. Smith always controlled which agents his players considered, and Falk never signed another from UNC after Smith apparently thought he hadn't told the truth while pursuing Tar Heels All-American center Brad Daugherty, the No. 1 pick in the 1986 NBA draft.

The association with Falk and FAME also gave Krzyzewski something Smith never had, an agent to manage and expand his personal investment interests (Smith had a financial advisor, accountant, and good friend Bill Miller from Charlotte). And it further accentuated the political differences between the Tobacco Road icons.

Smith was a longtime liberal who backed Democratic causes. He stayed away from personal endorsements and never allowed commercial signage at Carmichael Auditorium or the Smith Center. Miller pushed UNC to pay Smith on the high end of the market for college coaches, Smith received one of the country's largest stipends from UNC's contract with Nike, and the Carolina Basketball School summer camp made untold thousands that went mostly to his staff members who ran the sold-out sessions. Growing up in a thrifty middle-class Kansas family with a father who coached and a mother who played the organ in church, Smith never craved a lavish lifestyle as an adult but did like to travel first-class, wear expensive clothes, and eat at the best restaurants.

Besides being a registered Republican who hosted political fundraisers, Krzyzewski was also known as a capitalist. The man whose first salary at Duke in 1980 was $48,000 had a modest way of life raising three daughters in a northern Durham neighborhood; the son of high school dropouts in Chicago was now making more money than he had ever seen in a bank account and wanted to ensure the financial future of his children, whom he tried to incorporate into his business dealings, and grandchildren. One daughter directed external affairs for the Legacy Fund, another served as team psychologist, and the third coauthored several of his books.

His flirtations with the Boston Celtics in 1990, Portland Trail Blazers in 1994, and eventually the Los Angeles Lakers in 2004 put pressure on new Duke presidents and/or coaxed more money for himself, his coaches, and the Duke physical plant. After the Blue Devils reached the 1999 NCAA championship game, Duke named the Cameron floor Coach K Court with painted logos in front of home and visiting benches. And after they won their third NCAA title in 2001, Krzyzewski signed a multimillion-dollar "lifetime" contract extension and took on the title of special assistant to President Nan Keohane.

"We were able to do a few things for Mike in his contract," athletics director Joe Alleva acknowledged when Krzyzewski turned down the Lakers, even though critics scoffed that Falk had orchestrated the ploy to make sure new Duke president Richard Brodhead got the full measure of Coach K's importance. (It was similar to how Dean Smith maneuvered Dick Baddour into the AD's job at UNC in 1997 over the objections of Chancellor Michael Hooker, who favored fund-raiser and former Tar Heels quarterback Matt Kupec.)

It also put Falk into motion finding the business deals that would satisfy all of Coach K's requirements. Under Falk, Krzyzewski's endorsement opportunities multiplied. He earlier had done a series of Final Four "Yes, I am" promos for CBS, playing off the difficulty of pronouncing his name (Coach "Krushelooffski"); now he sought serious commercial messages, and having signed on with the Washington Speakers Bureau commanded high-paying, sometimes six-figure, gigs with corporations and executive clubs.

Later in 2004, American Express hired Krzyzewski to do a series of TV ads on the Duke campus in which he said, *"I don't consider myself a basketball coach. . . . I look at myself as a leader who happens to coach basketball,"* and in a not-so-subtle recruiting pitch that said of his players, current and future, *"When they get into the workplace, they're armed not just with a jump shot or a dribble. I want you armed for life."* The AMEX ads ran in nonrecruiting periods and incensed many of his peers when Coach K's not-so-subtle pitch reached millions of viewers during the 2005 NCAA tournament telecasts.

Also in 2005, Krzyzewski signed on with XM Satellite Radio to do a weekly show called *Basketball and Beyond,* during which he began to interview some of the biggest names in athletics and entertainment. His guest list ran the gamut of the alphabet from Bill Belichick of the New England Patriots to rival Roy Williams early in the 2017 season, when UNC went on to win the national championship. In the digital age, almost all of Krzyzewski's shows and interviews became available on his personal website, CoachK.com, which covers both the man and his basketball program exclusively. Several of the six books he has coauthored have been best-sellers, including *Five-Point Play* on the 2001 NCAA title season, a joint effort with acclaimed historian of American leadership Donald T. Phillips, who has written extensively on Abraham Lincoln.

Krzyzewski also launched corporate academies and adult fantasy camps where business executives spent $10,000 a pop for three days of (re)living glory days scrimmaging on the Cameron court. Camp participants were coached by former Blue Devils, ate dinner with Krzyzewski, and listened to talks about team-building and motivation. The Fuqua School of Business at Duke held an annual Coach K Leadership Conference, which, if not increasing his wealth, certainly added to his brand recognition.

Smith did very little of that, and Williams had quieter, almost private, corporate involvements. Through Learfield Communications and Tar Heel Sports Marketing, Williams was paid upward of $10,000 to speak to groups that included Blue Cross Blue Shield of North Carolina—a UNC sports sponsor—and he usually split the money between gifts to the Lineberger Cancer Center at UNC, his primary charity, and his children, Scott and Kimberly. Williams also has done soft endorsements by wearing TAG Heuer watches and (Alexander) Julian's menswear from the Chapel Hill native who has designed Tar Heels uniforms since 1992.

After growing up in the mountains of North Carolina even poorer than Krzyzewski, Williams drew total annual compensation of more than $4 million, but wasn't among the top 20 highest-paid college basketball coaches in the country. He also made less than half of his competitor eight miles down the road.

Williams began his college coaching career as a part-time assistant to Dean Smith for $2,700 a year, and after getting the head job at Kansas said he was making more money than he thought they printed. He became comfortable beyond his wildest expectations and usually matched what he raised to fight cancer, the disease that took two family members and, for twenty-four days in 2011, Williams thought he might have in his own kidneys.

Krzyzewski was known to give money back to Duke in various ways, including the Duke Children's Hospital; he has also generously supported the Emily K Center named for his late mother, and the Jimmy V Foundation, among other nonprofits.

Since Duke and UNC teams continued to wear Nike shoes and apparel, both basketball coaches received the largest chunk of annual payments Nike made to its marquee schools. In 2017, Nike named its new 47,000-square-foot workout facility in Oregon for Coach K.

One of the most effective yet understated parts of Krzyzewski's branding campaign was remaining the head coach of USA Basketball for almost eleven years and winning three Olympic gold medals, restoring American pride.

That pride had been shattered in 2004, when UNC alum Larry Brown coached the Olympic team in Athens and, coming off winning the NBA championship with the Detroit Pistons, looked like the perfect choice to continue U.S. dominance in basketball.

But as the Pistons were defeating the Lakers in five games of the 2004 NBA Finals, Brown learned he had lost most of the Olympic squad from the previous summer that had qualified for pool play. That team went 10–0 and won by an average of 31 points per game at the 2003 FIBA Americas Olympic qualifying tournament in Puerto Rico, twice beating the Argentina team that would upset the Americans at the Athens Olympics the following summer.

Nine players dropped off the original roster, citing personal reasons that included fear of terrorism three years after 9/11, family concerns, marriages and pregnant wives or fiancées, and injuries. NBA All-Stars Ray Allen, Mike Bibby, Vince Carter, Jason Kidd, and Tracy McGrady were among those who helped defeat Argentina by 33 points for the FIBA championship and then opted not to go to Greece. With several other NBA veterans too exhausted from the playoffs and Kobe Bryant in the middle of rape allegations in Colorado, the Olympic selection committee had to scramble for replacements to join the three players who stayed on the team—Allen Iverson, Tim Duncan, and Richard Jefferson.

USA Basketball was not the one-man operation it became, and several ladles were in the Olympic soup. NBA commissioner David Stern pushed for adding LeBron James and Carmelo Anthony, who had just finished their rookie seasons, to promote their burgeoning careers. Neither played as much as he wanted and both late teens were immature pains in the ass to Brown and his coaching staff, which included Roy Williams.

There was also a significant drop-off in experience and talent, and it turned out to be America's youngest Olympic team with NBA players, averaging a little less than 24 years old. They also had precious little time to practice together. The U.S. lost to Argentina 89–81 in the semifinals and defeated Lithuania to win the bronze medal. Brown caught the brunt of the criticism, coaching what one writer called "at best the nation's D-Team that was sent to Athens."

For Williams, the Olympic experience was so forgettable that its only mention in his autobiography was about being in Greece when he learned Tyler Hansbrough had committed to the Tar Heels just before his senior season in high school. Williams said in an interview three years later that he never was so happy to set foot back on American soil and begin coaching his second season at UNC, the team that went on to win his first national championship the following April.

"In Puerto Rico, we had the best talent and best character guys, and we won easily," Williams said. "In 2004, the NBA put a couple of kids on the team who weren't ready. LeBron was a year out of high school and Carmelo didn't want to be a role player. We traded Jason Kidd for Stephon Marbury. The negative things being said about Larry just weren't fair."

Marbury, who had the reputation as a lightning rod, called it the "worst 38 days of my life" and was nearly sent home by Brown for complaining about the same style of play the head coach had used with the Pistons to win an NBA title in Detroit.

Williams had more bad memories from Athens than failing to come home with the gold medal. While he was breaking up a rowdy party that included James and Anthony, a few players insulted him and left Williams visibly shaken by the incident.

The trip soured Williams on ever coaching in the NBA despite regular offers, especially when former Tar Heel Mitch Kupchak ran the Lakers. As an assistant to Brown, he saw how some of the pro egos destroyed that team and decided to remain a college coach until retirement. Then the Olympic job went to his prime recruiting rival.

In the summer of 2005, USA Basketball named Jerry Colangelo managing director of the men's national team. Colangelo, chairman and CEO of the NBA Phoenix Suns, apparently ruled out elevating Brown's top assistant Gregg Popovich, head coach of the San Antonio Spurs, to succeed Brown. Popovich won a third NBA title that year as the Spurs coach, but Colangelo perhaps needed to make a clean break from Brown's Olympic staff. Instead, he called a meeting of experienced coaches, among them Hall of Famer Dean Smith, who led the 1976 U.S. team of college stars to the gold medal in Montreal and knew how the job had changed since then, especially with the reclassification of NBA players as "Olympic amateurs."

"A bunch of names were up on the white board, all with stellar won-loss records," Colangelo said. "Dean Smith voiced loud support for Mike Krzyzewski. Now Duke and Carolina aren't like any other rivalry. They play for blood, so when Coach Smith told us that no one will connect with and motivate the players like Coach K, the whole crowd went silent. That was a big moment for us."

The following October, with support that mushroomed from Smith's recommendation, Krzyzewski was offered and agreed to take over as the Olympic coach for the 2008 Summer Games in Beijing.

By the time Coach K convened tryouts in Las Vegas during the summer of 2006, James and Anthony were proven pros and NBA All-Stars, and they made America's newest Dream Team. But winning wasn't automatic; Krzyzewski's first international team as head coach lost to Greece in the 2006 World Cup semifinals. It turned out to be his only defeat in 89 qualifying tournaments, and Olympic games.

In time, Krzyzewski repaired what was broken with USA Basketball and made competing for their country important again to the pros who comprised the entire team. One Olympiad wouldn't be a huge recruiting advantage for Duke, but eleven years as the national men's team coach and overseeing all America-sponsored youth programs gave him a unique dynamic and higher profile over all other college coaches.

For example, during the summertime dead period for college recruiting, Krzyzewski was free from NCAA restrictions to attend and observe practices for all of the USA age groups, talk to the players, and meet with them as a group. According to several coaches who handled those teams, room assignments were decided by USA Basketball (aka Coach K). So a player on the 18-and-under team who was already committed to Duke could wind up staying with a kid whom Krzyzewski was still recruiting, or two younger top priorities for Duke might be roommates. His colleagues coaching those youth teams had their own advantages, but none carried the clout of Coach K.

Perhaps the biggest benefit of coaching NBA players and directing them to gold medals was that Krzyzewski could claim (justifiably so) that he knew more about what made a successful pro and could prepare Duke players for the NBA better than any other college coach. That was undoubtedly the hottest button for so-called five-star recruits who thought they were going to "the league" after leaving school. And Krzyzewski's record of getting his Blue Devils drafted in the first round was surpassed by only Kentucky in the ten years leading up to the 2018 draft.

Whether or not Kobe Bryant, James, and other members of the Olympic teams shared with prep stars their experiences playing for Coach K, they were free to do so. Other coaches have their own former players in the NBA but can barely use them in recruiting because, as alumni, they are considered "representatives of the school's athletic interests" and prohibited by NCAA rules from fully participating.

USA Basketball had only amateur players until 1992, and for years it struggled to raise money and fund the Olympic team. Now the organization was flush with cash. Besides corporate sponsorships, a big part of that underwriting came from the NBA, which contributed millions to the Olympic effort so players and coaches could be paid nicely and travel first-class with their families to the Summer Games.

Krzyzewski was a beneficiary of this. He took his wife, children, grandchildren, and his personal entourage to Beijing, London in 2012, and Rio in 2016, presumably all at USA Basketball expense.

For some coaches, Krzyzewski's Olympic gambit was unpopular if not loathed. Beyond what he was making, Coach K had become so influential and an institution all to himself that criticism from his competitors mattered little. Besides, he had checkmated his profession by putting Olympic basketball back together and winning three golds, so any public criticism could be seen as unpatriotic. Some college coaches considered his position a definite recruiting advantage that would resonate as long as he remained at Duke and had helped him become dominant in signing one-and-done players. And there were resentments in the NBA that Popovich, who had five NBA championships with the Spurs equal to Krzyzewski's five NCAA titles through 2018, would have to wait until he turned seventy-one to coach the 2020 Olympic team in Tokyo.

And "Pop" only got the position after Stern retired in 2014. Stern had fined Popovich and the Spurs $250,000 in 2012 for not taking stars Tim Duncan, Tony Parker, Manu Ginobili, and Danny Green to Miami for the fifth game of a six-day road trip toward the end of the regular season and did not inform the NBA or the Heat that he was sending them home. Stern was succeeded by Duke graduate Adam Silver, who has served on his alma mater's Board of Trustees. Perhaps Popovich was to take over when Krzyzewski first said he would not coach the Olympic team a third time, but Stern and Silver blocked the appointment and Coach K agreed to stay on for more brand-building.

Having established his own personal brand, Krzyzewski began talking to top recruits about doing the same, from 2010 with silky smooth Harrison Barnes (whom he lost to Carolina) through 2018 with Spartanburg, South Carolina, slammer Zion Williamson (whom he stole from favored Clemson). Before he pulled out the Duke cap, Williamson tipped it off by saying he wanted to build his own brand. Where else did an obvious one-and-done player get that if not from a coach who probably showed him a PowerPoint presentation on brand-building on their official recruiting visit? Even in recruiting, Duke had become more hi-tech than most schools.

When Barnes left UNC in 2012 after two All-ACC seasons, he used those exact words as one of his goals—"building my own brand"—upon declaring for the NBA draft. Roy Williams won Barnes over with other recruiting tactics, but brand-building was not part of his shtick.

Duke had two players who stayed one season before 2006, when the NBA implemented its minimum draft-age requirement of nineteen.

Corey Maggette, a sculpted 6'6", played for only the 1999 Blue Devils, who were among the deepest and most talented of Krzyzewski teams, with ACC Player of the Year Elton Brand and All-ACC guards Will Avery and Trajan Langdon and forwards Shane Battier and Chris Carrawell. Nicknamed the Alaskan Assassin, Langdon took a redshirt season due to a knee injury and turned into the most prolific 3-point shooter in Duke history until J. J. Redick made more.

Maggette looked like a potential star for the only ACC team to run the table (16–0) in a nine-school league, and the Blue Devils went on to win 37 times before succumbing to a late UConn rally in the 1999 NCAA championship game in St. Petersburg, Florida. But he turned pro after that season, upset with his role coming off the bench, and a year later he admitted he took cash from former AAU coach Myron Piggie during summers in Missouri.

After applying to enter the 1999 NBA draft before the underclassman deadline, Maggette went No. 13 in the first round to the old Seattle SuperSonics before being traded to Orlando. He played 14 seasons for six NBA teams, eight with the L.A. Clippers, for whom he set franchise records in free throws attempted and made. After Maggette admitted to accepting money from Piggie, the NCAA cleared Duke for having no knowledge of it when Maggette signed. Piggie eventually went to prison for committing mail fraud and failing to file a federal income tax return. Among the original charges was fraud against four universities, including Duke—akin to the 2017 federal probe claiming certain coaches funneled money to players from shoe companies.

Luol Deng also played at Duke before the one-and-done rule. He was attending a New Jersey prep school when Krzyzewski took his 2002–03 team to London for two October exhibition games—in the city where Deng's Sudanese family had immigrated. The family got to meet the coaches and watch the Blue Devils play. After some coaches complained about Duke's junket with the fall semester in progress, the NCAA prohibited overseas trips once classes had started. In Deng's one season with the Blue Devils (2003–04), he appeared in all 37 games and started 32. He averaged just over 15 points in 30 minutes, as Duke went back to the Final Four for the first time in five years and blew another lead to UConn, this time in the Saturday semifinals.

A high NBA draft prospect from the start, the 6'8", 220-pound Deng became the 10th freshman in ACC history to lead all rookies in scoring, rebounding, and field goal percentage. After the season, the native of Wau, Sudan, declared for the NBA draft and went No. 7 in the first round to the Phoenix Suns, who immediately traded him to the Chicago Bulls. In the middle of his 10th season with the Bulls, Deng was traded to Cleveland. The two-time NBA All-Star also played for the Miami Heat and finished his 14th professional season in 2018 with the Los Angeles Lakers.

From 1999 to 2009, Duke also lost Brand, Avery, Jason Williams, Mike Dunleavy, Carlos Boozer, Josh McRoberts, and Gerald Henderson with years of eligibility remaining, but Krzyzewski's run of one-

and-done players did not start until the 2010–11 season with New Jersey point guard Kyrie Irving.

A McDonald's All-American and one of the most highly coveted guards in the country, Irving was part of the 2010 FIBA Americas Under-18 championship team and later shared co-MVP at the Jordan Brand Classic with Harrison Barnes, one of Krzyzewski's top targets to play with Irving. Instead they became college rivals.

Irving, a 6'3" combo guard, set the world afire during his first eight college games, averaging 17.4 points, 5.1 assists, 3.8 rebounds, and 1.5 steals, including an abbreviated college high of 31 points (plus six rebounds, four assists, two steals, and two blocks) against Draymond Green and No. 6 Michigan State in the ACC-Big Ten Challenge at Cameron.

Shooting 53.2 percent from the floor, Irving was the true point guard the 2010 Duke national champions did not have. With ACC Player of the Year to be Nolan Smith and Seth Curry on the wings, Kyle Singler and three big men at least 6'10", the Blue Devils opened the 2010–11 season ranked No. 1 and stayed there through 15 straight wins. Among them was a blowout of UNC-Greensboro for Krzyzewski's 880th career win, which moved him past Dean Smith for No. 2 (behind Bobby Knight) among all-time Division I coaches.

Unfortunately, Irving's college career had all but ended in the eighth game, a rematch of the 2010 NCAA championship against Butler at the Izod Center in the Meadowlands, not far from Irving's home in West Orange, New Jersey. Playing with a sprained right big toe in the second half, Irving scored 21 points in the 82–70 victory. After the game, he was diagnosed with a severe ligament strain, which sidelined him all the way through the ACC tournament (missing 26 games) before being cleared to return. By then, Duke had lost four times and relinquished the ACC regular-season title to a resurgent

UNC, which went from ninth place in the ACC to first behind freshmen Barnes and Kendall Marshall, sophomore John Henson, and junior forward Tyler Zeller. Also, Nolan Smith had taken over as lead guard for the Blue Devils, complicating Irving's return for the NCAA tournament.

Accustomed to having the ball, Irving had it for his first eight games at Duke and now had to take it back from Smith or, essentially, play out of position. After defeating Carolina in the ACC tourney championship game in Greensboro, No. 1–seeded Duke reactivated Irving for the NCAA opener against Hampton, an 87–45 blowout. He played a little more in the narrow second-round win over eighth-seeded Michigan, which was Krzyzewski's 900th career victory.

At the Sweet 16 in Anaheim, Irving regained his old game, scoring 28 points. But the rest of the Blue Devils were not in sync. Smith shot 3-for-14 and missed his three 3-pointer attempts, and regular-season starter Curry was relegated to nine minutes and two points. Miles and Mason Plumlee combined for 10 points and 10 rebounds, but neither could handle Wildcats big man Derrick Williams, who scored a career-high 32 points, including five 3-pointers and pulled down 13 rebounds. As a close game at halftime slipped away in front of essentially an Arizona home crowd, the TV caught Coach K mouthing to one of his assistants, "It's not our night."

"The tournament is cruel," Krzyzewski said after losing a chance to repeat as national champions, which the Blue Devils had done in 1991 and '92. "It's an abrupt end for everybody when you don't win."

Third-ranked Duke finished the season at 32–5, giving Krzyzewski his NCAA-high 12th season of winning at least 30 games. Irving entered the NBA draft and Cleveland made him the No. 1 overall pick, Duke's first since Elton Brand in 1999. Irving was guaranteed $23 million for four years, compared to Brand's $9.95 million for three, as first-round contracts had almost doubled over the twelve-year span.

After playing only 11 college games, Irving won the 2012 NBA Rookie of the Year award, receiving 117 of a possible 120 first-place votes. He was also the only unanimous selection to the All-Rookie team after averaging 18.5 points, 5.4 assists, and shooting 46.9 percent from the field, including 39.9 percent on 3-pointers, for the Cavaliers before LeBron James' return to the franchise.

Surprisingly, second-seeded Carolina made it further than Duke in the 2011 NCAA tournament, winning three games that included Zeller, Henson, and Barnes showing their potential by combining for 84 points in a first-round romp over Long Island University. The Tar Heels missed a return to the Final Four by losing the East Regional championship game to fourth-seeded Kentucky in Newark, New Jersey. They never did play against Irving but, ironically, had won a second-round game over the Washington Huskies, who were led by guard Isaiah Thomas. Six years later, Thomas was a key player in the big trade that sent Irving from Cleveland to Boston to play for Brad Stevens, the Butler coach when Irving was injured.

Carolina finished 29–8 and ranked seventh nationally. The following season, Krzyzewski's next one-and-done would have his greatest moment at Duke while breaking the Blue Blood rival's heart on its home court.

Roy Williams spent a lot of time with then Celtics coach Doc Rivers, recruiting his son, Austin, the top high school guard in the country the year after Irving was.

That was before Rivers committed to the University of Florida and two-time national champion coach Billy Donovan while leading

Winter Park High to its first Florida state title, in 2010. Continuing to be pursued by the other Power Five programs, Austin rescinded his pledge to Donovan and, as Irving had done, made Team USA for the FIBA Under-18 Americas Cup that June. The Under-18 coach was Jeff Capel, a former Duke player and then the Oklahoma coach. In the gold medal game against Canada, Rivers set a Team USA record with 35 points and followed that up by earning co-MVP recognition in the Elite 24 all-star game with 25 points, four rebounds, and four assists.

To no one's surprise, including UNC's Williams, Rivers committed to Duke in September before his senior season in high school. With Irving having turned pro and Nolan Smith graduated, starting point guard for the Blue Devils was open again. Rivers won the role in preseason and wound up playing more minutes than anyone else on the roster, although he never became a favorite of the fans.

He is best remembered for one shot and one loss during his one season at Duke.

The shot came on February 8, 2012, against the fifth-ranked and favored Tar Heels in Chapel Hill. UNC led by 10 points with less than three minutes remaining, but turnovers and missed free throws narrowed that margin to two points, and Rivers found himself with the ball on the right wing being guarded by the long-armed Zeller. He pump-faked a drive and rose up for a 3-pointer. Veteran Duke radio broadcaster Bob Harris, who called more than 100 Duke-Carolina basketball games for forty-one years before retiring in 2017, described it this way:

"Nine seconds left and Rivers comes front court . . . Rivers works to the right side, he'll try to step back with one second left . . . lets fly . . . got it! The Blue Devils win it over North Carolina! 85-84! Oh my gosh! I do not believe this!"

Doc Rivers, on hand behind the Duke bench and dressed in royal blue, led the celebration onto the court as the Blue Devils mobbed his son while a stunned capacity crowd filed out of the Smith Center.

The Tar Heels, who earned their record 14th top seed, opened the 2012 NCAA tournament in the same pod as Duke at the Greensboro Coliseum and dispatched Vermont in the afternoon session. Many UNC fans returned for the evening doubleheader to razz their archrivals and got what they never expected in the second-seeded Blue Devils game against No. 15 seed and unranked Lehigh. Playing without junior forward Ryan Kelly and against the then-unknown C. J. McCollum, Duke trailed the underdog Mountain Hawks for most of the game. Lehigh played in the Patriot League, which awarded only need-based scholarships.

McCollum took nearly half of his team's shots and scored 30 points as Lehigh pulled off a 75–70 upset of the eighth-ranked Devils, who were basically playing a road game in a coliseum filled with thousands of Tar Heels faithfuls.

"I've never seen anything like it," Lehigh forward Justin Maneri said. "We came to the [open] practice the other day and as soon as we walked in they were going crazy for us and we're like, 'What's going on?' They were screaming, 'Go, Lehigh, beat Duke!' I've never seen two schools that hate each other so much."

A two-time Patriot League Player of the Year, McCollum proved his performance was no fluke with a 17-point career average through six NBA seasons with Portland, including a 50-point game in 2018. Rivers scored 19 points against Lehigh but was part of a team effort that missed 20 of 26 3-pointers. Mason Plumlee also had 19 points, making all nine of his field goal attempts, and 12 rebounds, one of the best games of his junior season. Duke dropped its last two tournament games (ACC and NCAA) and its season ended abruptly at 27–7.

Rivers, who averaged 15.5 points, made first-team All-ACC and was Rookie of the Year, but his 71–79 assist-to-turnover ratio painted him as a ball hog in the minds of some ACC fans. He ended his jaded relationship with college basketball quickly, turning pro after the season and was picked 10th in the 2012 draft by the New Orleans Pelicans. Rivers eventually played for daddy Doc with the Los Angeles Clippers, the first such father-and-son duo on the same team in NBA history.

The Blue Devils lost in the NCAA Round of 64 for the second time in six years (2007 versus VCU), but it would not take long for that to happen again. They had no one-and-done players the next season and, tellingly, went deepest in March Madness since winning it all with a veteran team in 2010. The revised branding campaign for Coach K and Duke basketball continued with mixed results, while Krzyzewski stayed on as the USA coach for two more Olympics.

DROUGHT NUMBERS (2011–14)

Duke

Record: 115–27
Winning Percentage: .765
ACC regular-season titles: 0
ACC tournament finals: 2
ACC tournament titles: 1
NCAA tournament record: 5–4
Sweet 16s: 2
Final Fours: 0
One-and-dones: 4
First-round draft picks: 7

UNC

Record: 110–35
Winning Percentage: .681
ACC regular-season titles: 2
ACC tournament finals: 3
ACC tournament titles: 0
NCAA tournament record: 7–4
Sweet 16s: 2
Final Fours: 0
One-and-dones: 0
First-round draft picks: 6

5

THE DROUGHTS

The last time four years had passed without Duke or Carolina in the Final Four was 1973 through 1976. Honest.

Four frustrating seasons separated the Blue Devils' fourth national championship in 2010 and their fifth in 2015, and it was an even longer six seasons between the Tar Heels' fifth NCAA title in 2009 and their next Final Four in 2016.

During that four-year drought, Duke won 115 games and one ACC tournament championship but did not reach a Final Four. And the Blue Devils continued a famine with no outright first-place finishes in the ACC regular season, which reached twelve years in 2018.

The Tar Heels missed the Big Dance in 2010 but came back to win regular-season conference titles outright the next two years before heartbreaking and heart-stopping trips to the Final Four—a runner-up finish in 2016 and the championship in '17, when they cut down the nets for a sixth time.

Duke regained control of the rivalry's head-to-head score, winning 12 of the last 19 games through the 2018 season, sweeping the home-and-home series twice, and winning two of three ACC tourney matchups. But Carolina had a better NCAA tournament run, going 22–7 compared to the Blue Devils' 17–7 over the same eight-year span that included Duke's 2015 national championship.

So which school, argued rival alumni and fans, played the better basketball?

"They are two magnificent programs, and Roy and I are lucky to be caretakers of this rivalry," Mike Krzyzewski said before the first game of the 2018 season. "There are other great rivalries, but they all have a way to go before equaling Duke–North Carolina."

How did those Blue Blood battles go between the national championship years for each school? What were the best games, the biggest upsets, the closest calls, the stars of the night in prime time on national television? And how could such a drought occur with both programs producing thirteen first-round NBA draft choices over the four years?

Preseason polls picked Duke to repeat as 2011 NCAA champion with an experienced team that welcomed newcomers Kyrie Irving and Seth Curry. Carolina slowly shook off the turmoil from a disastrous 2010 in which the Tar Heels nosedived from a 12–4 start to a 16–16 record before a trip to the NIT, Williams' first-ever appearance in that tournament.

While Irving's injury hampered the Blue Devils' chances to go back-to-back as they did in 1991 and 1992, they still had a veteran core of Nolan Smith, Kyle Singler, Mason and Miles Plumlee, and Ryan Kelly, plus sophomore guards Seth Curry and Andre Dawkins, all of whom played in all 37 games. Irving's untimely return to the lineup late in the season was not unlike that of injured rookie sensation Kenny Smith when he rejoined Carolina's 1984 juggernaut with a fractured wrist. The Tar Heels, top-ranked for almost the entire season, got bounced out of the ACC tournament (by Duke) and the NCAA Sweet 16 (by Indiana) despite having future first-round NBA draft picks Michael Jordan, Sam Perkins, and Brad Daugherty as other starters.

Coming off 17 losses—the most in Roy Williams' coaching career—and a ragged start to the new season, just getting into contention to win the 2011 ACC regular season was a miracle in itself. The Tar Heels opened ranked No. 8 but fell out of the polls after going 4–2 in their first six games as junior point guard Larry Drew II continued his spotty play. They remained unranked for nine weeks.

However, the terrible 2010 season produced a couple of pluses besides the emotional 100th anniversary celebration of UNC basketball, when an ailing Dean Smith got to visit with most of his former players a last time. One was the signing of recruits Harrison Barnes, Reggie Bullock, and Kendall Marshall, who became an important freshman trio for the Tar Heels in 2011. Another was the continued blossoming of John Henson, who moved to power forward after Ed Davis had suffered a season-ending injury, and Tyler Zeller, who after missing 14 games established himself as the Tar Heels' five-man of the future.

Starting spots in 2011 were cleared for Zeller and Henson after Deon Thompson completed his eligibility and Davis turned pro. Marshall replaced Drew as a starter after 17 games in the 2011 season, and Drew cleaned out his locker and bolted home to L.A. The Tar Heels had won four straight with Marshall in the lineup, and Drew saw the writing on the wall even after making nine assists in what would be his last game.

Carolina won 17 of its last 19 games, falling at Georgia Tech by 20 points and at fifth-ranked Duke 79–73 after leading by 16 late in the first half. Nolan Smith and Curry combined for 56 points and eight assists in the dramatic comeback win while new nucleus Henson, Zeller, and Barnes totaled 47 points and 31 rebounds in a defeat that still served notice to a national television audience.

Thus, the only surprise about the mild upset of the Blue Devils in Chapel Hill three weeks later was that it secured first place in the ACC for the soon-to-be sixth-ranked Tar Heels. Fans rushed the court after the 81–67 victory, hoisting up Marshall, who had 15 points and 11 assists. The ESPN.com headline read: "North Carolina Steals ACC Title from No. 4 Duke."

"The last 10 months haven't been very easy a lot of times, but that crowd in that locker room has been fantastic," Roy Williams said. "As a coach, where you get your strength is your relationship with the players . . . how they allow you to coach them. This group has just been phenomenal to work with."

The Blue Devils shot only 35.5 percent, missing 21 3-pointer attempts, compared to 52.4 percent for UNC, which got 18 points from Barnes and two double-doubles—the 15 points and 11 assists from Marshall, 10 points and 12 rebounds from Henson. A week later, seniors Smith and Singler, who were first-team All-ACC selections, helped Duke return the favor in the ACC tournament, winning the championship game even more decisively 75–58. Smith, who was unanimous all-conference and Player of the Year, captured the Everett Case MVP award after averaging 18 points and 6 assists in the Devils' third straight tourney title and ninth of the new century. Smith and Singler were joined on the all-tournament team by Barnes and Zeller. Barnes set an ACC tournament record for a freshman by scoring 40 points in the semifinals against Clemson.

After Duke lost in the 2011 Sweet 16 to Arizona, ending Irving's one-and-done college career, and the Tar Heels fell to Kentucky in the Elite Eight, Carolina seemed to have more time on its side. Returnees Zeller, Henson, and Barnes made second-team All-ACC notice, Marshall third team, all with room for improvement.

On April 20, Woody Durham announced he was stepping down after forty years as the Voice of the Tar Heels on the school's radio network. Durham had called more than 1,800 Carolina football and basketball broadcasts, including twenty-three bowl games, thirteen Final Fours, and six national championship games. He was succeeded by thirty-two-year-old sidekick Jones Angell, like Durham a UNC graduate.

The following June, Dean Smith and Coach K shared a stage one last time, when both received the Naismith Good Sportsmanship Award (along with the late N.C. State women's basketball coach Kay Yow). For Smith, who was escorted by Roy Williams, this was his final public appearance. Williams spoke for Smith, who sat between Krzyzewski and Charlie Scott, UNC's first black scholarship athlete and the ACC's first African American star.

"I feel inadequate up here; how do you represent Coach Smith?" Williams said.

"Lou Gehrig might have been the luckiest person in the world," Scott said of the famed New York Yankees slugger who died at age thirty-seven of amyotrophic lateral sclerosis (ALS), which became known as Lou Gehrig's disease. "But all of us who played for Coach Smith, we were the luckiest people in the world."

Krzyzewski interacted playfully with Smith, who acknowledged the standing ovation from the crowd with a nod and hand wave. "It was like two generals now in peace, being able to sit there," said Coach K, the former Army captain. "I felt his respect for me, and I hope he felt my respect for him. That was a really important moment for me; observing him, studying him, and competing against him for so many years. That had a big impact on me becoming better, because he is as good as there has been."

Smith continued to visit with former players and friends during the limited time he spent at his office in his namesake arena. In November 2015, he was awarded the Presidential Medal of Freedom from Barack Obama at the White House. Dr. Linnea Smith received the award on her husband's behalf, and Williams was among the small group of family and colleagues who attended the ceremony. Poignantly, Scott, the figure most personified by Smith's support of the civil rights movement, was inducted into the College Basketball Hall of Fame in the same month.

Duke, ranked No. 6, won its first seven games of the 2012 season, including a 74–69 victory over Michigan State at Madison Square Garden when Krzyzewski passed Bob Knight for the most career wins (903) in Division I history. Knight, who coached Krzyzewski at Army, was doing commentary for ESPN, and the friends of forty-five years embraced during an emotional ceremony after the game.

Duke was 19–4 and Carolina 20–4 when the teams met in February 2012, and Austin Rivers' dramatic Dean Dome buzzer-beater gave the Blue Devils a one-point victory. The Tar Heels built a 13-point lead early in the second half behind Barnes, who scored 19 of his team-high 25 points in the final twenty minutes. Duke rallied and Zeller missing two free throws with 13.9 seconds remaining left UNC with a precarious two-point lead. Rivers' winner was his sixth 3-pointer and gave him a season-high 29 points, which went a long way toward his winning ACC Rookie of the Year.

"It was a great basketball game," Krzyzewski said. "North Carolina, I still think, is the best team in our league. They are so big and have guys who can take the game over. Austin was magnificent. We had a play called that he could either take it to the basket or shoot it; he shot it and it was all net."

Carolina fed off the startling loss in the March rematch at Cameron, where Duke replayed the famous game-winner on the video screen before the opening tip and the Crazies chided Zeller for missing crucial free throws in the first game.

"I told my teammates I thought that was disrespectful, and we need to go out here and prove a point," Marshall said. "It left a bad taste in our mouths, and we wanted to come out and play well tonight."

As he did almost every year, Williams told his players before the game they were the only team that could upset their fourth-ranked hosts, and the Tar Heels proceeded to double up Duke at the half, 48–24. The Blue Devils had made an astonishing comeback from 20 points behind midway through the second half to win at N.C. State back on February 16, but such a rally wasn't happening on this night.

The five UNC starters, who would all be in the NBA within two years, scored in double figures, and the Tar Heels outrebounded Duke 45–28 to win at Cameron for the first time since the Tyler Hansbrough era. Following the 88–70 trouncing, Williams promised them, "If you play like you did tonight, we'll be playing on Monday night in April."

After Duke finished one game behind regular-season champion UNC in the ACC race for the second straight year, Krzyzewski said that after 31 games he still didn't know what to expect from his fourth-ranked, 26–5 team, and he came out with one of his classic analogies.

"We were just kind of overwhelmed, by them and the situation," he said. "It's like a surprise gift, you know? You open it up, and for the most part, it's been a nice surprise. I never have any idea of what's inside the present. And today there was nothing. It was an empty box."

His Blue Devils never did surprise him, losing to Florida State in the ACC tournament semifinals and to Lehigh in the NCAA tourney shocker that sent them home for good.

Carolina's plans for the postseason received two bad breaks. In its ACC tournament opener in Atlanta, a win over Maryland, Henson fell on his left wrist and sat out the semifinal victory over N.C. State and the championship game loss to Florida State. The wrist healed by the second-round NCAA tournament game, against Creighton, when Henson tallied 13 points, 10 rebounds, and four blocked shots.

But late in the second half, Kendall Marshall went sprawling when fouled under the basket, and the left-handed point guard suffered a fractured right wrist. The top-seeded Tar Heels clever playmaker, who already had set the ACC single-season record for assists with 351, was in tears in the locker room over the prospect that the rest of his season might be over.

"When you go to the Sweet 16, it's supposed to be a lot more fun than this," a distraught Williams said in the postgame press conference.

"I just want to be here for my team," said Marshall, his eyes red. "It is what it is. We're not saying that I'm not going to play. We're not saying that I'm going to play. Bottom line, it's a fracture and now I have to deal with it."

He remained in street clothes on the bench when Carolina played at the Edward Jones Dome in St. Louis, site of Williams' first national championship in 2005, with reserve Stilman White filling in at point guard. White recorded 13 assists and no turnovers in the two games. The Tar Heels escaped Ohio University in overtime, then fell to second-seed Kansas in the regional final 80–67. The game had 15 ties and 13 lead changes, but the Jayhawks ended White's Cinderella story with a 12–0 run in the closing minutes, which sealed another win over KU's old coach. Although Williams had left the school nine years earlier, he was still booed by opposing fans and taunted with signs.

"Too emotional for me. That's the bottom line," he said, calling Kansas his second-favorite school. "I don't think it'll ever feel good for me, regardless of the outcome. I don't think I'll ever feel comfortable with it."

A second straight advance to the Elite Eight would be impressive for most college programs, but not with Carolina's pedigree in a season that the Tar Heels expected more. If not for the injuries, they might have made a 19th Final Four appearance and perhaps won their sixth NCAA championship earlier than in 2017. Duke, of course, also had a number of teams over the years that fell short of expectations.

No. 1–ranked Kentucky reached the 2012 title game in New Orleans on the Monday night Williams had referred to a month earlier after the win at Duke. Many Tar Heels fans thought the return of the Final Four to the Big Easy, where Dean Smith had won his two national championships, would work for Williams' team as well, but the injury to Marshall killed that karma.

John Calipari's Wildcats defeated in-state rival Louisville in the Saturday semifinals, and he won his first national championship (Kentucky's eighth) by beating Kansas after taking two previous schools, Massachusetts and Memphis, to the Final Four. Within weeks he received a contract as the highest-paid coach in college basketball, surpassing Krzyzewski, who would reclaim the top spot in 2015 with annual salary and bonuses estimated at more than $10.7 million.

In May 2012, Williams asked ESPN commentator and former Tar Heels sharpshooter Hubert Davis to drop by the basketball office. Davis, forty-one at the time and still holder of the best career 3-point percentage (.435) in Carolina history, had settled with his family in Chapel Hill after playing twelve years in the NBA. He had moved his way up as a college basketball analyst with ESPN and held a summer camp on the UNC campus. His life was good with a six-figure income and working full-time a few months a year.

"I thought Coach Williams wanted me to move around some camp dates so they wouldn't conflict with the Carolina camp," Davis recalled.

Williams wanted something else. After seven years as a player and assistant coach at Kansas, and nine more as an assistant to Williams at UNC, Jerod Haase had accepted the head coaching position at Alabama-Birmingham. Williams asked Davis to join his staff without any coaching experience.

Dean Smith had done something similar, hiring Phil Ford from a bank job in 1988 after Williams was named head coach at Kansas. All aspects of the position could be taught, except true love of school. A year after Davis was hired, veteran assistant Joe Holladay retired, and then in 2017 assistant C. B. McGrath became head coach at UNC-Wilmington, leaving Davis as the third in command, behind longtime aide Steve Robinson.

Davis, who made second-team All-ACC as a senior in 1992 and scored a career-high 35 points at Duke in his last regular-season game, represented the first former Tar Heels player on Williams' Carolina coaching staff. He wouldn't be the last. Former 1990s walk-on Brad Frederick, now an assistant, was hired in 2013, and Sean May, the 2005 Final Four Most Outstanding Player, came on in 2015 and later moved up to director of basketball operations.

Carolina lost four starters to the first round of the NBA draft (lottery picks Barnes, Marshall, and Henson, plus Zeller) off the team that finished ranked No. 4 in the country. That purge matched what happened following the 2009 championship season but wasn't quite as severe as losing the top seven players from the 2005 NCAA champs. The future did not look so bright for the 2013 season. The Tar Heels, younger and smaller, opened ranked No. 11, but fell out of the rankings with three losses before conference play began. One to Butler in Maui, Williams' favorite place on the planet, had him spitting out pieces of a filling he dislodged by grinding his teeth so hard during the 82–71 loss to the unranked Bulldogs. Even after scrapping its way back for a 12–6 record and third place in the ACC, his team never returned to the polls.

Duke fielded a team that looked more like Carolina than its recent rosters. With no freshman starters and decent depth, the superstar-less and preseason No. 8 Blue Devils raced up the rankings after beating their first 15 opponents, including No. 2 Louisville and No. 4 Ohio State. They seemed to be playing on borrowed time, with Jabari Parker, the Gatorade and McDonald's High School Player of the Year, coming the next season and Mississippi State transfer Rodney Hood, perhaps the most talented player on campus, practicing every day as he sat out his required redshirt year.

Balanced scoring, with five starters averaging in double figures, gave Krzyzewski a team he could more easily work with and better hone in fundamentals than the Rivers-dominated 2012 club. Duke had already played 23 games, winning 21 of them, and had risen to No. 2 in the polls, before hosting unranked Carolina on February 13. The Blue Devils had to rally from a second-half deficit behind two key 3-pointers by reserve guard Tyler Thornton. Mason Plumlee's foul trouble forced Krzyzewski to go small and match UNC's new four-guard lineup of 6'6" sophomore shooter P. J. Hairston joining Reggie Bullock, Marcus Paige, and Dexter Strickland. They combined for 56 points, but Carolina missed seven critical free throws down the stretch and wound up going 13-for-23 from the foul line in Duke's 73–68 win.

"If I knew how to fix the blessed thing, I would have fixed it," Williams said. "The bottom line is we didn't make free throws and we're not a good free-throw-shooting team in games."

Coach K saw it as the glass half-full, saying, "Thornton was the hero tonight. He wasn't going to let us lose."

In the game before the rematch in Chapel Hill, the Blue Devils capped off their third undefeated home season in four years by also giving their coach his 953rd career victory with an 85–57 romp over Virginia Tech; significantly, it marked his 880th victory at Duke, surpassing Dean Smith's 879 for the most all time at one school. Since the first 73 of Krzyzewski's career wins came at Army, passing Smith in any manner gave some Blue Blood fanatics reason to crow and wave placards at Cameron, especially with the third-ranked Blue Devils visiting still unranked UNC for the regular-season finale four nights later.

Pregame was your typical madness, amplified by the Tar Heels' six-game winning streak and chance to catch Duke for second place in the ACC. Plus, one-and-done prospect Andrew Wiggins was watching from a baseline seat right in front of the student section. Then a scorching Seth Curry hit his first seven shots, Duke jumped out to a 14–0 lead, and led by 18 points at halftime, spoiling Senior Night for UNC's Strickland almost before it began.

"I wanted to come in and set the tone for my team that we could win in this environment," Curry said, finishing with 20 points on his way to second-team All-ACC.

Senior center Mason Plumlee had a career night with 23 points and 13 rebounds. The second of three brothers to play for Duke led the All-ACC voting when it came out the following week. The Blue Devils completed the 69–53 blowout and finished second in the conference, one game behind Miami, dropping Carolina to third.

"Seth's performance in the first half, he's just the best player on the court," Krzyzewski said. "In the second half, we had the best player on the court in Mason."

Even though an obvious starting spot was wide open at UNC, and video promotion of the Carolina heritage was ramped up, Wiggins chose Kansas the following May. His decision was seen as Roy Williams' first big recruiting loss that seemed linked, at least in part, to the emerging academic scandal on campus. The loss to Duke with

Wiggins watching was also Williams' first losing Senior Night as a head coach in fifteen years at Kansas and ten at UNC.

The second-ranked Blue Devils stumbled in the 2013 ACC tournament against seventh-seeded Maryland and went into the NCAA Midwest Region as the second seed. Carolina regrouped in the ACC tournament and reached the championship game for a third straight year, losing to Miami. The Hurricanes rose to a No. 2 seed in the East Regional, and the Tar Heels were seeded eighth in the South, where behind Hairston's 23 points they delivered Roy Williams' 700th career victory by defeating Villanova in the Kansas City pod.

But then came another matchup with third-ranked and top-seeded Kansas—and more torture for Williams. Peppered with even more questions about playing KU for the third time since leaving Lawrence, he implored the media to stop: "I'm the coach at North Carolina, pure and simple. Let's not talk about the old days so much anymore."

The Tar Heels ended the season with another double-digit loss to the Jayhawks and a 25–11 record, his third-worst record, percentage-wise, at UNC.

Before the season, Williams had gone through a cancer scare. After it, he felt just plain sick.

This postseason, at least locally, belonged to a Duke team that needed a better run after its quick ouster by Lehigh the year before. The Blue Devils had little trouble with Albany and Creighton in Philadelphia and moved on to the Sweet 16 in Indianapolis, the city where they had already won two Final Fours. So, as expected, Michigan State became the next Indy foil, with Spartans coach Tom Izzo admitting his thirteen-year-old son, Steven, had picked Duke in his bracket.

"My son's problem is whether he ever eats at my house again," Izzo said. "He's a big fan of Coach K's, so I've got real problems at my house."

Michigan State had some advantages, starting with more fans, who had less travel time from East Lansing. And the Spartans had the reputation of being bigger and tougher, as most Michigan State teams do, but also more athletic than this Duke edition.

Challenged by those minuses, fictional or not, the Blue Devils kept the rebounding relatively close, with seven each from Kelly and Mason Plumlee. Curry led all scorers with 29 points, including six 3-pointers, three of which came in a barrage to start the second half. Duke broke open a tie game with a 9–0 run, and Michigan State trailed the rest of the way, shooting 7-for-23 after halftime. The CBS cameras caught Steven Izzo smiling as the Blue Devils were running away with it.

"Seth was scoring on every possession, and it was almost like we felt like we could relax on defense," Krzyzewski said of calling a timeout after Curry's third straight 3-pointer. "And when you get a guy hot like that, and you can put a couple defensive stops with it, then you're going to get separation. And we weren't doing that. So, it was basically to remind them this kid is not going to be able to do this the whole second half. But while he is, let's pick up the intensity on the defensive end."

Duke earned its first trip to the regional final since the championship season of 2010 with the 71–61 win.

Awaiting was a rematch with second-ranked Louisville, which had dispatched 12-seed Oregon in the regional's other Sweet 16 game. Rick Pitino's Cardinals had the home crowd advantage, a 32–5 record, and were favored this time to beat the sixth-ranked Blue Devils in a duel between the Midwest's top two seeds.

What Louisville might not have needed was a psychological lift after a gruesome injury to one of its players.

With 6:33 left in the first half, Kevin Ware leaped to close out on

Duke 3-point shooter Tyler Thornton. Ware landed awkwardly on his right leg, which snapped loudly in two places between the ankle and the knee. When teammates and Pitino saw a bone protruding from the pierced skin, they began crying and shaking and were only calmed by Ware, who bravely repeated, "Go win the game! Go win the game!" as medics wheeled him off the court on a gurney.

Trailing 35–32 at the half, Duke again rallied behind Curry to tie the score at 42. But with Louisville players still yelling at one another about winning it for Ware, the Cardinals took the game to another level the Blue Devils could not match. A 13–2 run sparked them to an 85–63 victory and a second straight Final Four, where they defeated Wichita State and Michigan to win Pitino's first NCAA championship at Louisville and his second after bringing home the title for Kentucky in 1996.

"We lost to a better team," Krzyzewski said after Duke finished the 2013 season 30–6 and suffered Coach's K's second defeat in thirteen regional finals to date. How much did Ware's injury affect the outcome? No one knew for sure, but it had to give the Cardinals added incentive against the hot Blue Devils.

Louisville's championship was wiped from the NCAA's record books five years later, when the organization penalized the Cardinals for a sex scandal involving players, recruits, and prostitutes. It was the first time the NCAA had stripped a school of its title in Division I men's basketball.

Collectively, the 2014 season was arguably the most disappointing for the Blue Blood programs since 1974, when both missed the NCAA tournament in the last year only one team per conference could go.

During Duke's washout of 1995 without Coach K, Carolina made the Final Four. After the Tar Heels' disastrous 2002 season (8–20) ended, the Blue Devils advanced to the Sweet 16. In UNC's NIT season of 2010, Duke won its fourth national championship.

So, what happened to make 2014 so substandard?

For Duke, losing Curry, Kelly, and Mason Plumlee represented 55 percent of the scoring and 51 percent of the rebounding from the 2013 Elite Eight team. That put the pressure squarely on Jabari Parker, perhaps before he was truly ready despite his reputation as the most heralded recruit ever signed by the Blue Devils and the only one Coach K allowed *Sports Illustrated* to profile during his first semester in college.

Parker was the first freshman to start at Simeon Career Academy in Chicago and the second player in Illinois history to start on four state championship teams. Coming from Krzyzewski's hometown, he was considered a lock for Duke but revealed that he almost went to Michigan State because his father was on dialysis for kidney failure and East Lansing was only a three-hour drive away. Roy Williams said he had a home visit scheduled with Parker for the fall of 2012, but his doctor would not let him travel so soon after surgery to remove a benign tumor from his left kidney.

The Blue Devils, who opened at No. 4 in the polls, lost their second game with Parker and Hood to fifth-ranked Kansas and freshman star Andrew Wiggins at the United Center in Chicago, where Parker poured in 27 points in front of his parents and thousands of friends and fans. Duke later played three times in three weeks at Madison Square Garden, beating Alabama and losing to fourth-ranked Arizona in the NIT Season Tip-Off in late November, then easily defeating UCLA at the Garden six days before Christmas.

In late December, William Krzyzewski died of a heart attack after undergoing surgery for throat cancer. Traveling back and forth to Chicago to be with his older brother's family, Coach K wasn't fully engaged with his team over the next few weeks. And Parker was going through a rough patch as the coaching staff bore down on him over some fundamentals the gifted athlete had never thought about before.

After losing at Notre Dame and Clemson—both of which failed to make the NCAA tournament—the first week of the 2014 ACC season, the Blue Devils plummeted to 23rd in the polls. Wearing contact lenses for the first time since high school to correct some nearsightedness, Parker put it back together with 23 points in a home win over N.C. State and, from there, was the best player on a surging team.

Duke had won seven of its last eight games and climbed back to No. 8 before the scheduled February 12 renewal with Carolina. However, a snow and ice storm created treacherous conditions and some banter between the two programs. When Governor Pat McCrory declared a state of emergency, UNC encouraged only fans who could walk to the Smith Center to attend the game. In 2000, a similar storm resulted in open seating, and students surrounded the court as the unranked Tar Heels upset favored Maryland. Ed Cota, the senior point guard on that team, likened the atmosphere to the Cameron crowd.

Whether or not having to play in front of another Dean Dome full of *Carolina* Crazies was considered, Duke decided traveling to and from the game was too dangerous. The school informed the ACC and UNC that its team was not coming. Critics crowed chicken.

"That's the way Dean Smith always thought about things like this—what's the angle?" Duke radio and marketing man Johnny Moore said. "Honestly, no one over here is that smart. Trust me, they just couldn't get to the damn Dean Dome, okay?"

Eight days later, they played the game, but that's a story for later in this chapter.

The Blue Devils finished 13–5 for third place in the ACC and made the championship game in the ACC tournament before losing to regular-season winner Virginia. Parker scored 23 points and led the all-tourney voting. Then they went one-and-done again in the Big Dance and, again, in North Carolina, this time losing in Raleigh to experienced and underrated 14-seeded Mercer 78–71.

After combining to average better than 35 points per game, Parker and Hood shot six of 24 from the floor and teamed for just 20 against the aggressive Bears defense. Duke made runs to take the lead in both halves, but with its two best players having off games could not sustain the advantages against the senior-laden and fired-up foe.

"We're not going to win a lot of games where those kids play like that," Krzyzewski said of the bad shooting by his main duo, still rookies to big-time college basketball. "We've won a lot of games where they've been terrific, and I've loved coaching them, because you have—we all have—to live with that."

Now in his 34th season in Durham, Krzyzewski graciously walked down to the wild locker room of the celebrating conquerors to congratulate Mercer coach Bob Hoffman and his players, who shot 55.6 percent from the field (to Duke's 35.5) and made 11 more free throws. "I love the game, and you guys play it very well," Coach K told them. "If we had to lose, I'm glad we got beat by a hell of a basketball team."

The Bears were both surprised and awestruck to have the Hall of Fame coach and national TV regular in their locker room. "Coach K is one of the most famous basketball coaches ever, and for him to come in here and say we're a great team—that's pretty unbelievable," Mercer senior Daniel Coursey said.

Parker and Hood knew they were one-and-done, as well as their team. After Duke finished the season 26–9, both entered their names into the NBA draft. Parker, still unsure after such a dud of a season for Duke, made the announcement on the morning after the team's annual banquet. Hood followed the next day. Both were selected in the first round, with Parker going to Milwaukee as the No. 2 pick and Hood to Utah at No. 23. Parker signed a guaranteed three-year contract with the Bucks, worth more than $22 million.

Carolina had begun practice for the 2013–14 season engulfed in controversy over junior P. J. Hairston, whose eligibility was suspended by the university while it investigated several possible NCAA violations for driving a rental car he did not pay for. After the details unfolded in the media over the next few months, UNC announced it would not seek NCAA reinstatement for Hairston, the team's scoring leader (14.6) in 2013, who made the second-most 3-pointers during one season in school history.

"I am extremely disappointed for P.J., his family and our team as he will no longer be playing basketball at North Carolina," Roy Williams said in a statement. "P.J. made mistakes and I was very disappointed by his actions and now he is suffering the very difficult consequences. He is not a bad kid; he just made some mistakes."

A few days later, Williams added, "It is probably the most difficult and saddest thing I've ever gone through as a head coach."

He was initially furious with Hairston, then allowed him to practice with the team and sit on the bench in street clothes until the suspension was resolved. The Hairston family said in a statement it was "displeased" with UNC's decision not to apply for reinstatement but did not file legal action. With Williams' help, Hairston signed with an NBA developmental league team and played well enough to go No. 26 to Miami in the first round of the 2014 NBA draft. He was traded that night to the Charlotte Hornets and signed a guaranteed rookie contract for just under $2 million, not bad for having had one productive year of college basketball.

The 2014 Tar Heels had opened at No. 12 in the polls but began falling after losing at home to unheralded Belmont in their third game. More of an enigma with young players and future stars Brice Johnson and Marcus Paige playing alongside junior post man James Michael McAdoo, they managed the unprecedented feat of upsetting the top three teams ranked in most preseason polls—Louisville, Michigan State, and Kentucky—to climb back to No. 14. They looked like world-beaters at No. 1 Michigan State, where five players scored in double figures in the 79–65 victory, setting an NCAA record with UNC's 13th win against top-ranked teams.

But then came three straight losses to start the ACC season and rekindled thoughts of the 2010 team's collapse to the NIT.

They rallied with a great late stretch, winning 13 of the next 14 games that included Williams' 300th win at UNC, which made him the only college coach in history to reach that milestone at two schools. Paige, a sophomore, had emerged as the new go-to scorer, averaging better than 17 points a game, heading into the biggest night of the season. It came against the fifth-ranked Blue Devils in Chapel Hill on February 20 in the game originally postponed.

Trailing by seven at the half, Carolina went to a 1-3-1 zone defense with the long-armed sophomores Johnson and J. P. Tokoto at the wings, forcing a confused Parker to the bench for most of the final five minutes despite having tallied 15 points and 11 rebounds. The 74–66 upset was triggered as much as anyone by senior starter McDonald, who scored 21 points after returning from his own nine-game suspension for accepting illegal benefits totaling $1,800, which he paid back to the NCAA.

Parker thought that playing three games in New York at the Garden and in front of a sellout crowd at the Carrier Dome in Syracuse had prepared him for the wild Smith Center. But he sat in the visitors locker room with a towel draped over his head, muttering, "I had no idea."

He rebounded in the rematch at Cameron two-plus weeks later, scoring a college-career-high 30 points and tying a record held by Tyler Hansbrough and Kenny Anderson of Georgia Tech with a 10th ACC Rookie of the Week notice; Hood contributed 24 in the 93–81 win on what was the equivalent of their Senior Night, as well as for senior reserves Andre Dawkins, Tyler Thornton, and Josh Hairston. Parker also matched Tar Heel Hansbrough's feat as the second freshman to be voted unanimously to the All-ACC team.

He easily won ACC Rookie of the Year and received 25 votes for Player of the Year that went to N.C. State sophomore T. J. Warren. When Duke expanded the freshman records section of its media guide to four pages, Parker was listed first in points scored, scoring average, field-goal attempts, free throws attempted and made, double-doubles, and 20-point games, and he is second in another half-dozen categories.

Parker made assorted All-American teams, but like Irving, who also wore No. 1, his jersey might never hang in the girders of Cameron.

UNC's season also ended with a relative thud, with a loss in its ACC tournament opener to unranked Pitt and failing again to get out of the first weekend of NCAA play. The sixth-seeded Tar Heels rallied to win a game they should have lost to Providence, and then blew a late lead and lost to injury-depleted Iowa State in the Round of 32. The final record was 24–10, the second of three consecutive seasons of double-digit defeats for Carolina. Having Hairston obviously would have helped.

The week of the fourth straight Final Four that included neither Duke nor UNC, the longest such drought since 1973–76—almost forty years—Tar Heel McAdoo announced he would forgo his senior season to enter the NBA draft. He had scored 1,232 points and pulled down 640 rebounds in 108 career games, but despite a late-season scoring surge that led to second-team All-ACC notice for the second straight year, McAdoo was not projected to be drafted in the first two rounds. If that turned out to be true, he planned to pursue his dream of playing pro basketball as a free agent for the right team. That was the Golden State Warriors, with whom he won NBA championships as a reserve forward in 2015 and 2017.

Harrison Barnes, McAdoo's Carolina teammate in 2012, also won a ring with the Warriors in 2015. Kyrie Irving, off Duke's 2011 team, won the 2016 NBA title with Cleveland and LeBron after James had returned to the Cavaliers.

HOW BLUE BLOODS STACK UP NATIONALLY
IN THE TWENTY-FIRST CENTURY

Duke and Carolina have been the two premier programs of the twenty-first century. To measure that, look at the top teams and their NCAA success rate (since 2000):

NCAA championships:
3—Duke, North Carolina, Connecticut
2—Florida, Villanova
1—Michigan State, Maryland, Syracuse, Kansas, Kentucky, Louisville*
(*vacated)

Final Fours:
6—North Carolina, Michigan State
5—Kansas
4—Duke, UConn, Florida, Kentucky
3—Wisconsin, Syracuse, UCLA, Villanova

Sweet 16s:
14—Duke
13—Kansas
11—Michigan State, Kentucky
10—North Carolina, Arizona
 8—Florida, UCLA
 7—UConn, Villanova

NCAA Tournament wins:
49—Kansas
48—North Carolina
46—Duke
43—Michigan State
42—Kentucky
37—Florida
33—UConn
30—Arizona

* Duke and UNC have met 45 times when BOTH have been ranked in the AP top 10, the most for any rivalry in NCAA basketball history by a wide margin. The second most top 10 matchups in a rivalry are 11 (by UNC–N.C. State).

* Either Duke or UNC has been ranked in the AP poll for every meeting since February 27, 1960. North Carolina WAS ranked in the UPI (Coaches Poll) that week. The last time the two teams met when neither was ranked in either poll was February 25, 1955.

6

LIGHTNING IN A BOTTLE

When Mike Krzyzewski promoted Jeff Capel III to associate head coach in April of 2014, Duke was awaiting the arrival of its most ballyhooed recruiting class—led by incoming freshman five-stars Jahlil Okafor, Justise Winslow, and Tyus Jones.

Kyrie Irving, Austin Rivers, and Jabari Parker—all nationally recognized high school players in their own way—came in as solo artists and likely one-and-dones before moving on to the NBA. But the freshman class of 2015 represented a shift in recruiting philosophies that accompanied Krzyzewski's ascension as the best coach in all of basketball after guiding U.S. national teams to two Olympic gold medals and getting ready to chase a third in 2016. He had more access than any of his college peers as the face of USA (amateur) Basketball since 2005. And he could sell an impressive pathway to the NBA, having coached the world's best players through two Olympiads.

Capel replaced Steve Wojciechowski, also a former captain of the Blue Devils, who left to become head coach at Marquette. Wojo had been co-associate head coach with Chris Collins, who went to North-western as head coach in 2013, before Capel moved up to the position after three years as an assistant on the Duke staff.

As a sophomore, Capel hit the 40-footer that sent the 1995 Carolina-Duke game at Cameron into double overtime before the Tar Heels prevailed. The swish shot became a popular clip in ACC video history. He was also part of Krzyzewski's tradition of hiring former players as assistant coaches, which began with Tom Amaker in 1989 and continued a year later with part-timer Jay Bilas, who attended Duke law school while helping Coach K.

Already a major college head coach twice, Capel was the youngest in his profession during his four years at Virginia Commonwealth after having grown up around the sport. His father, Jeff Capel Jr., was a successful college coach for twelve years and an NBA assistant for nine seasons. His younger brother, former UNC player Jason, had just finished four years as head coach at Appalachian State.

And Jeff Capel III had the right pedigree besides having attended and played at Duke. He hailed from a well-known, highly respected family in Fayetteville, where he was the North Carolina High School Player of the Year for South View. He married the daughter of state senator Dan Blue, the minority leader of the North Carolina Senate and the Duke Board of Trustees' first black chair. Capel's wife, Duke alumna Kanika Réale Blue, also graduated from Yale Law School.

Capel brought a more experienced skill set to his alma mater when he returned there after nine years as a head coach, particularly the last five at Oklahoma, where he recruited and coached first-team All-American Blake Griffin and other top 100 players. After his 2009 Sooners lost in the South Regional final to Tyler Hansbrough and the Tar Heels, who were steamrolling toward the NCAA tournament championship, Griffin entered the NBA, leaving Capel a lesser team.

Then Oklahoma had to vacate its 13 victories from 2010 for NCAA violations committed by one of Capel's assistant coaches. Capel was fired after his 2010–11 team finished 14–18, though he wasn't implicated in the NCAA charges. Krzyzewski immediately brought him home.

Capel knew the full recruiting drill, from scouting and doggedly staying after his prime prospects to signing them to letters of intent and scholarships. And now he had the luxury of fronting the most recognized coach in America, the distinctly looking and sounding Coach K, who developed his own brand while rebuilding Duke into the top program in college basketball. Like Dean Smith in his heyday, Krzyzewski had become the best closer in the game.

The Duke basketball media guide boasted of Capel's "prominent role with USA Basketball during Krzyzewski's last four years as head coach of the U.S. National Team." It also called him "a force on the recruiting trail since returning to his alma mater, helping Duke secure the talents of 15 McDonald's All-Americans in the last six years," including the first- or second-rated recruiting hauls by ESPN for the last five years. "He was crucial to the signing of the 2014 class that was ranked No. 1 in the nation and featured" Grayson Allen, Jones, Okafor, and Winslow.

The promotion of Capel as a one-and-done pitchman was not subtle. Duke credited him for recruiting six of Duke's twelve first-round draft selections since 2012 (including freshmen No. 2 overall picks Jabari Parker and Brandon Ingram and No. 3s Okafor and Jayson Tatum in four consecutive years). Of course, this was all under the brilliant orchestration of Krzyzewski, who represented the best possible marriage between an outstanding, driven coach and a private university with almost limitless resources.

As the wealthiest and most powerful employee on the Duke

campus, Krzyzewski held a position that allowed him and Capel to minimize the educational part of their recruiting pitch, when necessary, and go with enticements like the influence of well-heeled alumni and former Blue Devils. These people were now called a "Brotherhood," perhaps to counter the decades-old "Carolina Family" promoted by Smith and now Roy Williams. "Come to Duke and you will be set for life," or some variation on that theme, replaced the elite educational opportunity that one-and-dones did not have after they left with guaranteed millions and were at least three years short of credits toward graduation.

James Coleman, a Duke law professor who chaired the school's faculty Athletic Council, said in 2018 that all ten of Duke's one-and-done players to that point had completed their freshman year in good standing. However, at a meeting of the Duke faculty senate in the fall of 2017, political science professor Peter Feaver had raised the issue of whether the one-and-done practice was causing a "reputational risk" to Duke's pristine academic image by adding to it the tag of basketball factory.

Dean Smith's only "one-and-done" was junior college transfer Robert McAdoo after the 1972 Final Four season. Beginning with James Worthy (1982) and Michael Jordan (1984), eight of Smith's UNC players left with either one or two years of eligibility remaining. For them, Smith insisted their rookie NBA contracts included a bonus for graduating. All but one attended summer school to complete their degrees.

Approaching his seventieth birthday (he turned seventy-one in February 2018), Krzyzewski also began ducking the constant speculation of how long his health and passion would allow him to coach—something that shadowed Smith over his last decade. A Duke degree and playing for a nationally ranked program in the ACC, no matter the head coach, was fine for most four-year athletes. But any recruit with a clear goal of reaching the NBA wanted to know the coach he signed with would be his coach for however long he stayed there. Concentrating on the very best high school players, most of whom fashioned themselves as one-and-done, Coach K merely had to say, "I will be here as long as you are."

It was a self-perpetuating policy because, as long as Krzyzewski kept coaching and remained the best pipeline to the NBA, the Blue Devils were in the running for every top high school star who never intended to stay in college. Ironically, the best predictor on Krzyzewski's retirement was how long the NBA Players Association retained its 19-year-old minimum age rule.

And, too, with so many great prospects in that category, Duke would rather have them than lose to them. That was also at the heart of the revised recruiting plan. His three goals for Parker, according to a 2014 *Sports Illustrated* feature, were *national player of the year. A national championship. First pick in the NBA draft.* No mention of a coveted Duke degree needed.

Actually, Krzyzewski's top goal was not among those three, according to those who have watched his transition to hoarding the top players, regardless of their size. "The great ones—Durant, LeBron, Kobe, Carmelo—don't have positions," Coach K told Parker, trading on his Olympic experience. "You're a great player. And at Duke you will be a player without a position." Something he said all the way back to luring Danny Ferry away from UNC in 1985.

He knew that teaching defense and building team chemistry to win a national championship took more than one year—unless you catch "lightning in a bottle"—but one marquee recruiting class would win enough games to keep Duke's profile high, which helped Capel set up the next group for Coach K to close.

His methodology was tailored to who he pursued every year. But it always included the concept of trusting the most famous coach in basketball, although a long line of players apparently never earned Krzyzewski's faith and departed for other schools. Those who stuck it out, for as long as they were there, called Coach K a father figure and left with something very important to each of them, whether a Duke degree, scores of victories, memorable championships, or first-round draft status in the NBA. Duke basketball of the twenty-first century offered something for almost everyone who chose to hang in there.

In a candid revelation for the age of ultracompetitive, high-stakes recruiting, Krzyzewski said in 2015 that he had no backup plan in case his top three prospects—Okafor (the No. 1 high school player in the prep class of 2014), Jones (No. 8), and Winslow (Texas Mr. Basketball from Houston)—did not commit to playing at Duke.

"The guilt trip that sometimes people put these kids through, I don't want that to be the basis of our relationship," Coach K told *Sports Illustrated* before any of the three signed. "We didn't recruit some other kid because we wanted to show them: You're the kid we want. I want them to trust me from the very beginning."

If true, was that the ultimate gamble for Krzyzewski in his attempt to get back to his 12th Final Four and win his fifth national championship? Maybe, but he also knew the favorable odds that at least Okafor and Jones were coming since they had bonded as teammates on the same USA Under-17 team in Lithuania in the summer of 2012 and made a pact to attend the same college.

Okafor, like Parker, was from Chicago, and Krzyzewski still had never lost a player from his hometown that he truly wanted. Okafor took official visits from coaches at Baylor, Kansas, Michigan State, and Ohio State (all of which were also on Jones' list), but the smart money was on Duke for the agile 6'11" athletic specimen with huge hands.

ESPNU televised the decisions of Okafor from Chicago and Jones, a quick 6'1" point guard, from his high school in Apple Valley, Minnesota, when both put on Duke caps. A week later, Winslow, a 6'7" small forward whose athletic ability Krzyzewski compared to that of Grant Hill, joined them (after considering UNC to play with Houston prep star Justin Jackson). With all three on the same USA team roster, other college coaches understandably groused that the playing field had tipped sharply toward Duke.

Jones was not an automatic one-and-done, more like a younger, more athletic version of senior leader Quinn Cook, a player who might stay a couple of years and help guide the next set of candidates at the lead guard position. He and Okafor had been friends for almost ten years, Midwesterners who went to the same summer camps. After meeting Winslow, all four of their paths crossed when they watched the 6'5" Allen win the slam-dunk contest at the 2014 McDonald's All-American game.

Krzyzewski might have hoped to keep Jones and Winslow for more than one year, but he admitted before Okafor's first college game, "We won't have him long."

The 2015 Blue Devils were ranked No. 4 in the preseason polls, behind the skilled-and-veteran Wisconsin Badgers; Arizona, which had finished No. 4 the previous season; and consensus pick Kentucky, which had a rare blend of new freshman faces and returnees who had lost to UConn in the 2014 NCAA title game.

A near-perfect mix comprised the youngest-ever Duke team. And Krzyzewski's cachet allowed him to start his best players from day one, not what other established coaches favored. Even UNC's Smith rarely started a freshman, no matter how highly regarded, unless a clear position was available with no returnee in line to take it. Allen was the not-ready-for-prime-time outlier and played the fewest minutes of the top nine, but he worked hard in practice and waited for his moment, which famously came.

Okafor, Jones, and Winslow started along with Cook, the shrewd senior from Washington, D.C., and Oak Hill Academy. The fifth starting spot went either to the 6'9" Amile Jefferson or the 6'5" Matt Jones, depending on matchups with the opponent, but both wound up averaging almost exactly the same minutes (21.7 and 21.3). Junior Rasheed Sulaimon, who had started 50 games in his first two seasons, was seventh man.

Having the starters and seasoned subs set from the first game gave Duke a tremendous advantage of fast-tracking chemistry and togetherness, especially among new players who were friends before they arrived in Durham. And they were all quick learners and great athletes who took to Coach K's man-to-man and zone defenses faster than most first-year kids he had before or since.

After winning their first 14 games, only one by fewer than 10 points, the Blue Devils had climbed to No. 2 in the rankings and already experienced the national stage, defeating Michigan State at the Pacers' home arena in Indianapolis, and, in the biggest early season attraction, upset then second-ranked Wisconsin in the ACC–Big Ten Challenge in Madison. "They embraced the moment and weren't scared by the moment," Coach K said of the 80-70 victory. "I knew then we had something special."

Almost shockingly, a month later they lost two early ACC games at N.C. State and at home to Miami, both unranked opponents.

They also found themselves down by 10 points in the second half to St. John's on the biggest stage, Madison Square Garden, as Krzyzewski was coaching for an unprecedented 1,000th career victory. In his 35th season at Duke, Coach K had come a long way from his last, 9–17 team at Army and his first three Duke also-rans, which missed the NCAA tournament and almost got him fired. Krzyzewski wanted to get past this milestone and feared a loss to the unranked Red Storm would hurt Duke's chances for a high seed in the NCAA tournament.

Going to the zone he had pulled out after losing those two ACC games with a solvable man-to-man, the Blue Devils denied any 3-pointers that would have widened the deficit and, on the other end, managed to sucker St. John's into foul trouble. They then got hot, outscored St. John's 26–7 behind Tyus Jones' 22 points, and delivered the 77–68 victory to their coach, who wanted no part of winning it in the next game at Notre Dame against his onetime assistant Mike Brey.

Barely audible over a dozen family members and other partisan Duke fans chanting and waving "1K" signs behind him, Krzyzewski half-smiled and said, "I'm a lucky guy, been at two great institutions, never had a day to worry about my back. I'm glad it's over."

The Blue Devils had ten scholarship players, but it turned out they didn't need that many after sophomore Semi Ojeleye transferred at midseason and Coach K jettisoned the sulking Sulaimon after 20 games. Duke was left with only eight primary players, including junior 7-footer Marshall Plumlee, the third brother.

That a disgruntled Sulaimon had played the seventh-most minutes spoke to how far he had fallen into Duke's doghouse. However, his removal gave the Blue Devils the short rotation Coach K preferred for most of his career with everyone knowing his role. Plumlee got fewer than 10 minutes per game, Allen less than that until the very end.

"Eight is enough," Krzyzewski told them, as long as he had the battle-tested and unselfish Cook, savvy sophomore Matt Jones, and junior big men Jefferson and Plumlee to go along with the four freshmen, all McDonald's All-Americans.

Following a loss at Notre Dame and the dismissal of Sulaimon, Duke had a hangover and a 4–3 conference record.

Although the circumstances were different, Sulaimon's family reacted much the same as P. J. Hairston's did when UNC suspended him in 2013. Angela Sulaimon criticized Krzyzewski for saying her son "has been unable to consistently live up to the standards required to be a member of our program." She told the *Baltimore Sun*, hinting that academics didn't matter as much as winning to the head coach, "He said on TV when he let Rasheed go, 'It's a privilege to go to Duke.' He needs to take that back. It's a privilege to go to college—period. It was a privilege to have Rasheed. I promise you that not all of his players have the GPA that Rasheed had."

The Blue Devils, 17–3 overall and still fourth-ranked, faced a daunting stretch—a home game against Georgia Tech and rematch with the Fighting Irish, road trips to old nemeses Florida State and Syracuse, and the first game against North Carolina. The Tar Heels were playing under the radar of Duke's young guns, but they soon showed their own signs of a potential national run, with a hint of staying power that might be more lasting than Duke's.

The 2014–15 team had the third-worst record in Roy Williams' first 15 seasons at UNC, better than only his first team (2004) and the 2010 NIT runners-up that had one starter back from the 2009 national champions. But the secret sauce of the 2015 squad was that it had Justin Jackson, Joel Berry, Isaiah Hicks, Brice Johnson, Kennedy Meeks, Marcus Paige, and Theo Pinson—all of whom went on to start in a national championship game before they left Carolina.

Paige, despite his frail frame, was the new star and preseason ACC Player of the Year after his breakout All-ACC sophomore campaign. But a case of plantar fasciitis in his right foot contributed to periodic shooting slumps and relegated him to third-team All-ACC, although he actually ended up with his best statistical season.

At the same time, Williams was beginning to feel the effects of the ongoing investigation into an academic scandal and negative recruiting that kept some five-star prospects from his door. Until the NCAA finally ruled on the academic classes in October 2017, Carolina's last quality freshman class had arrived in that fall of 2014—Berry, three-time Mr. Basketball in Florida; Texan Jackson, the McDonald's All-American game co-MVP; and Pinson, a Mr. Basketball in North Carolina—three signees whom Williams later called "the most important" in Carolina basketball history.

Despite the accolades, the 6-foot Berry had gotten by more with his speed and shooting in high school than his work ethic. After not starting a game and averaging the eighth-most minutes on the team as a freshman, he bought in to what Williams wanted of him. Berry improved his diet and began sculpting his body in the weight room while becoming a tough-nosed competitor. The 6'6" Pinson was always a free spirit whose skills had to be reined in, and when he finally got past the injuries that cost him 14 games as a freshman and 19 as a junior he was one of the most versatile and colorful players in the country. Jackson was a 6'8" talent who had a natural feel for the game, and from early practices his freshman year he communicated on the court like an upperclassman. As his shooting percentage improved, his future became even brighter.

Paige and fellow juniors Brice Johnson and J. P. Tokoto, sophomore Meeks, and freshman Jackson started most of the games in 2015, and this unseasoned group stood 6–3 after a one-sided loss at top-ranked Kentucky. The originally sixth-ranked Tar Heels fell all the way to No. 24 in the rankings but worked their way back to No. 13 after an 11–1 spurt that began with a win over UNC-Greensboro, coached by former Tar Heel Wes Miller. One highlight of the streak was a striking comeback upset of fifth-ranked Louisville on Paige's sweeping left-handed bank shot over two Cardinals big men, shades of his dramatic coast-to-coast driving layup in a last-second overtime win at N.C. State the year before.

BLUE BLOOD II

The streak ended when Carolina blew a big lead in the rematch at 10th-ranked Louisville and then lost to Virginia in Chapel Hill. The home loss might have marked the low point of the season because of how the third-ranked Cavaliers broke open a close game after halftime and defended the Tar Heels in their own building. After shooting 52 percent in the first half, Carolina went just 11-for-29. "They kicked our rear ends," Williams said. "That's the bottom line."

In contrast, perhaps the impetus for Duke's late-season surge began at ACC leader Virginia, where the Blue Devils missed their first nine 3-pointer attempts, 11 of their first 13, and trailed by eight points with just under five minutes to play. Almost out of nowhere, they exploded with a barrage of 3-pointers and a 16–5 scoring run. Cook made three 3s without a miss, including the go-ahead shot, and Tyus Jones hit the final bomb as Duke stunned the capacity crowd at John Paul Jones Arena, where the fans were expecting the kill shot from one of the Cavaliers. But the zone defense Krzyzewski had put in flummoxed the usually unflappable Wahoos.

"There were a few possessions where I thought we were a little stagnant and didn't get the looks we wanted against their zone," Virginia coach Tony Bennett said after the unexpected outcome and 69–63 defeat. "I thought there was enough offense there to win that game. At the end, you've got to come up with some tough stops."

The dramatic rally seemed to send Duke into overdrive. The Blue Devils won their next four, including road wins at FSU and Syracuse, heading into the post–Super Bowl headliner at Cameron with UNC. The Tar Heels' own season had been suddenly interrupted by the news that the legendary Smith had passed away on the evening of February 7, 2015.

Though most knew of his decline from dementia, Smith's death still stunned the sports world. Accolades poured in by the hundreds from those who knew him and thousands more from people who did not but admired his life of service to mankind and his competitive zeal.

On Thursday morning, February 12, Krzyzewski planned to attend Smith's private funeral at Binkley Baptist Church in Chapel Hill. He wanted to wear a light blue tie but did not own one, so he sent an associate to a men's store in Durham. Coach K slipped in and out of the standing-room-only eulogy with Carolina blue glaring out from his white shirt and dark suit. A week earlier, he had passed Smith for all-time ACC victories with 423.

"I love Dean and understand him," Krzyzewski said for a Showtime special on Smith, "and I developed immense respect for what he accomplished. A lot of the things we have gone through and sustained excellence [in], the expectations are very, very similar. It's like brothers in arms.

"When you walk in the room and you're the best guy, probably most of the people in that room are not going to like you. Everyone in that room wanted to be him. I know people would not think we became really good friends, but we did."

Six days after the funeral service, the 15th-ranked Tar Heels, who had lost their last outing at Pitt, went to Cameron for a game that showed their promise and their fragility. Before the tip-off, both squads gathered at midcourt for a silent tribute to Smith. Similar to what they had done seven years earlier after UNC student body president Eve Carson was slain, Krzyzewski and his assistants put on the "DES" stickers worn by thousands of Carolina alumni and fans, a version of the round logo sewn onto every UNC uniform for the rest of the season.

The ensuing game was a classic that Smith would have loved for the grit of the players on both sides. The Tar Heels fell behind early by 12 points and angered Williams so much he later called them "brain dead." But these teams almost always came back and did this time, too. Carolina started it by cutting Duke's lead to seven at the half on a flying dunk by Tokoto.

In the second half, the Tar Heels' size and Okafor's sprained ankle turned the game around inside, where the visitors wound up scoring 62 points in the paint. Carolina had built a 77–67 lead with 3:56 remaining on sophomore guard Nate Britt's brazen drive right through the lane. Krzyzewski called a timeout and, instead of scolding his team, said, "Just play. Follow your instincts and play."

With the UNC bench and coaching staff imploring their guys to dig in on defense, Duke went on its typical late-game run, triggered by Tyus Jones. He fed Winslow for a 3-pointer; after a Winslow dunk on a pass from Okafor, Jones scored nine straight himself in just over a minute on three free throws, an inside jumper, and two layups, the last one tying the score with 29 seconds left. Paige had a jumper to win, but the ball bounded away.

The Blue Devils remained hot in overtime, hitting four of six shots and Tyus Jones and Cook each finished with 22 points. After Duke took the lead for good, Carolina had two shots that could have forced a second overtime, but both missed and the horn sounded with Duke surviving a classic blue-blood battle 92–90.

"It's tough for this game to always live up to the hype, but I think tonight exceeded it," Krzyzewski said, who added that Smith "was looking down. He might not have liked the result, but I'm sure he liked the way both teams played."

During a celebration of Smith's life four days later that filled the lower bowl of the Smith Center, Roy Williams spoke last and led everyone in a patented finger point that was Smith's way of thanking the passer and others for their help. "Everyone has minuses and everyone has pluses," Williams said. "Coach Smith had more pluses than anyone I have ever known. So let's all raise our hands and point and thank him for the assist."

LIGHTNING IN A BOTTLE

Duke stayed on a roll through the end of the ACC season, still trailing first-place Virginia. The Blue Devils won two more times on the road, including the 84–77 rematch in Chapel Hill, where Tyus Jones again controlled the game late in the typical dogfight. Jones scored 17 of his 24 points after halftime, and the Blue Devils recovered from shooting 33 percent in the first half to shoot almost 60 in the second.

"They believe in me to have the ball in my hands and to be the point guard of this team, and Coach K believes in me," said Jones, an emerging star. "We believe in one another, and if you kick it to somebody, one of your brothers, you trust them to make the shot and they trust in me."

Williams was not as upset over losing UNC's Senior Game (for Desmond Hubert and Jackson Simmons) to the third-ranked team in the nation, saying, "We played pretty doggone well except for a four- or five-minute stretch there, which you can't do against a very good basketball team."

The Blue Bloods had another instance of pregame rivalry reverence, which was a kumbaya moment compared to the days of Danny Ferry and J. R. Reid banging on each other while their coaches pointed and yelled back and forth from the benches.

With the teams having gathered at midcourt to honor Smith's passing in the first meeting, Williams wanted to recognize Krzyzewski for having reached 1,000 career victories and did so by giving him a small plaque before the introduction of lineups. Duke officials had worried about a negative reaction from the Carolina fans, whose initial boos were quickly drowned out by applause. Afterward Coach K said, "What happened in Durham and what happened here were great examples of an intense rivalry having intense respect."

Both teams went to the ACC tournament in Greensboro with high hopes for the postseason.

After a first game romp over N.C. State, Duke discovered its Achilles' heel again against Notre Dame, which pulled off the 74–64 upset in the semifinals and had Krzyzewski saying, "I didn't recognize my team tonight; it was like they had an out-of-body experience." Duke still received a No. 1 seed for the NCAA tournament, and the loss actually gave the Blue Devils a full week's rest to nurse nagging injuries, including Okafor's tender ankle he first sprained against Carolina on February 18.

The Tar Heels brought a 21–10 record and No. 19 national ranking to the ACC tournament and were positioned for a probable NCAA at-large invitation. After dispatching Boston College, they upset No. 14 Louisville for a second time that season, stunned the same third-ranked Virginia team that had drilled them in Chapel Hill, and led the 14th-ranked Fighting Irish by nine points midway through the second half of the championship game.

Ten minutes away from becoming the first team to win the expanded ACC tournament with four victories in four days, they ran out of gas and into a "lightning strike," according to Mike Brey, the Irish coach. His team blistered its pooped opponent 26–3 in seven quick minutes to cut down the ACC nets for the first time.

Although the Tar Heels lost their fourth ACC championship game in five years, their tourney run and strength of schedule resulted in a No. 4 seed in the NCAA West Regional, and Williams vowed to advance past the first weekend for the first time since 2012. In Jacksonville, Florida, the Tar Heels blew a big lead and barely hung on for a 67–65 victory over 13-seed Harvard, coached by former Duke star and assistant Tom Amaker; two nights later, they edged five-seed Arkansas in a track meet of a game and continued on to Los Angeles for the Sweet 16.

Hansbrough's first game against Duke was a close loss, as Blue Devils senior Shelden Williams (23) had four blocks.

Williams had 18 points and 15 rebounds in rematch at Cameron, but UNC shocked No. 1 Duke, spoiling Redick's Senior Night.

In 2007, Crazies mocked UNC DA who botched Duke lacrosse case, but Tar Heels had a chance and won again at Cameron, 79-73.

Wanda Williams hugs her man after freshman Brandan Wright paced
Tar Heels with 19 and 9.

Gerald Henderson broke Psycho T's nose in 2007 rematch at the Dean Dome, forcing Hansbrough to wear mask for two weeks.

Danny Green's flying dunk in 2008 win at Duke captures iconic moment in rivalry (photo © by Jim Hawkins).

Deon Thompson flashes four-peat after 2009 runaway victory at Cameron, while three Crazies refuse to leave hallowed hall.

Duke was glad to see Hansbrough go, albeit after Tar Heels' 2009 NCAA championship, their second in five years.

Jon Scheyer said farewell to Duke as a player, scoring 20 points in 2010 blowout, 82-50, the Blue Devils' biggest home win ever over UNC; eventual NCAA champs went 17-0 at Cameron.

Kyrie Irving never played against Carolina but had his college high game with 31 points, edging Draymond Green and Michigan State in 2010 ACC-Big Ten Challenge at Cameron.

Austin Rivers' 2012 buzzer-beater at UNC was one of six 3-pointers he made to also finish with his college high of 29 points.

John Henson and Reggie Bullock fired up in 2012 rematch at Cameron, when the No. 6 Tar Heels routed fourth-ranked Duke, 88-70.

Harrison Barnes was once going to be on Crazies' side before he opted to play two seasons for the Tar Heels.

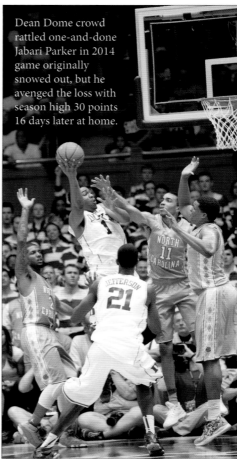

Dean Dome crowd rattled one-and-done Jabari Parker in 2014 game originally snowed out, but he avenged the loss with season high 30 points 16 days later at home.

In first year as associate head coach, Jeff Capel helped Coach K land their first multi one-and-done class. In all, four freshmen and four veterans won 2015 NCAA championship, Duke's fifth.

Senior Quinn Cook (2), and freshmen Okafor (15), Winslow (12), and Tyus Jones (5) were regular starters; Matt Jones (13) and Amile Jefferson (not pictured) alternated as fifth starter.

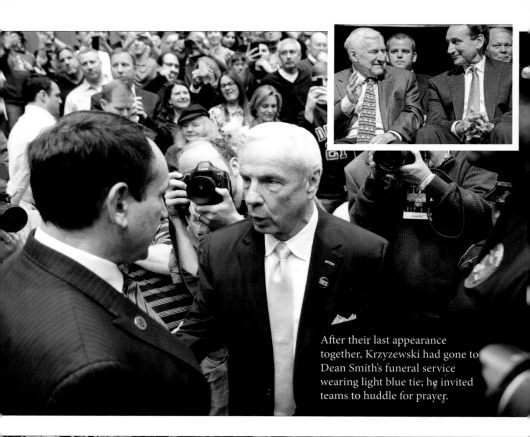

After their last appearance together, Krzyzewski had gone to Dean Smith's funeral service wearing light blue tie; he invited teams to huddle for prayer.

Guards Tyus Jones (5) and senior Cook (2) drove offense that allowed Blue Devils to shoot 50 percent from field and outscore opponents by better than 15 points per game.

ust because ACC Player and Rookie of he Year Okafor did not attempt a 3-point shot didn't mean he couldn't celebrate with the Crazies when Duke made one of he 732 it launched for the season.

(Above left) Justin Jackson helped Carolina reach back-to-back Final Fours before he turned pro as a junior. (Above right) Senior Kennedy Meeks went on a roll to end his Carolina career, averaging a double-double over last nine games of the NCAA championship season.

Jayson Tatum started the comeback against UNC in 2017 ACC tournament, and MVP Luke Kennard finished it. Tatum, Kennard, Harry Giles, and Frank Jackson all turned pro after the season.

In 2018, Williams beat Blue Devils at home wearing checkered coat and light blue tie; he wore same garb at Duke, where he brought along his two grandsons for good luck

Coach K said "Marvin went nuts for a while" so Duke could win rematch on Allen's Senior Night.

Carolina handled Duke's big men and zone for a second time in 2018 ACC tournament; Brooks dunked on Carter, Luke Maye's one block was on Bagley, who had 19 and 13.

"Theo, you just dropped the dad gum ball out of bounds!"

Berry's jersey is heading for Dean Dome rafters after he was Most Outstanding Player in 2017 Final Four and completed his career with more than 1800 points, 400 assists, 400 rebounds.

Waiting in L.A. was Wisconsin, now third-ranked, and Carolina led the Big Ten champion Badgers 43–36 midway through the second half before getting hit with a 19–7 run by the region's top seed. National player of the year Frank Kaminsky and his sidekick forward Sam Dekker combined for 42 points in the eventual 79–72 victory and a regional final date against No. 2 seed Arizona.

While disappointed, Williams was proud of the Tar Heels' marked improvement and the shooting of Jackson, Paige, and Berry, who made eight of their nine 3-point attempts while the outcome was still in doubt. Along with the steady progress of Brice Johnson, which would put him among the ACC leaders in scoring, rebounding, and blocked shots as a senior, they were building the toughness that looked like a legitimate breakthrough was possible for the next season.

Closer to home, Duke was easily handling Robert Morris and San Diego State in the first two rounds of the South Regional in Charlotte before moving on to the Sweet 16. The Blue Devils benefited from hot shooting and a rejuvenated Okafor in Charlotte, but their 31–4 record did not intimidate No. 19 Utah when the teams met in Houston.

Playing in his hometown, Justise Winslow caught fire the day after his nineteenth birthday and in front of hundreds of family and friends on the raised floor of Reliant Stadium, home of the NFL Texans. Considered by Krzyzewski one of the smartest freshmen he had ever coached, Winslow had gradually grown into the leader and best communicator on a defense that struggled early in the season.

"Coach never treated us like freshmen," he said of Krzyzewski. "There was never a moment where we felt like freshmen. He gave us his trust and just believed in us."

Utah did not score for the first four-plus minutes, while Winslow's free throw was Duke's only point before Okafor's layup gave the Blue Devils a 3–0 lead nearly four minutes into the game. They showed

maturity beyond their years by working through their offensive dol-
drums while keeping Utah in check. Coach K loved that.

"That's what my team has done this year, been able to adapt while
the game is going on," he said later. "They've gotten a bum rap really
for not being able to play defense. We wouldn't win over 30 games
unless we're playing good defense."

When the Utes closed a 15-point deficit to 49–43 with a little more
than four minutes left in the game, Duke needed a basket. Winslow
came through in front of his screaming throng. "It's just really special when you can look beyond our bench and see your mom and sib-
lings," Winslow said after recording 21 points and 10 rebounds in
the 63–57 victory.

Tyus Jones had 15 points, but Okafor scored only six, making
Winslow's and Duke's defense that much more important. "He was
the best player on the floor," Okafor said. "Maybe because he's in
Houston, maybe because he's 19 now."

The hometown advantage held against No. 7 Gonzaga for a trip
to the Final Four. Most of the Zags and neutral basketball fans sat
far from the court, which allowed the Duke contingent, including
Winslow's immediate family behind the bench, to continue being
heard by the players.

Gonzaga held a short-lived lead at 38–34 early in the second half,
the Blue Devils' largest deficit in the tournament, and the Zags almost forged a tie with less than five minutes left. But Kyle Wiltjer, the
team's leading scorer, blew a wide-open layup. "He makes that 499
times out of 500," coach Mark Few said. "When that happens, just
shake your head, it's not your night."

Duke remained in range with three minutes remaining before
Winslow hit a 3-point dagger to send the Blue Devils back to the
Final Four for the first time in five years. Krzyzewski's 12th left him

even with UCLA legend John Wooden for most Final Four appearances, but he had tunnel vision about his current team.

"We have eight guys, four freshmen," he said after the 66–52 victory. "It's the youngest team we've ever had. No one would ever say that because we're Duke or because it's me. There are eight guys. There's not somebody hiding in the locker room that's going to come out and appear."

Eight was enough, as the five starters combined to score all 66 points, from 16 each by Winslow and Matt Jones down to nine by Okafor.

"I'm not saying this because we won," Krzyzewski added, "I've said it the whole year. I love my team, they are a pleasure to be with and, as a result, they are taking me to Indy, which is kind of neat."

It was also an omen. Duke had already won half of its four NCAA titles in the Crossroads of America city.

Dean Smith got the expression from Frank McGuire, his old boss at North Carolina: "To win a championship, you have to be both lucky and good."

Duke was plenty good getting back to the Final Four in Indianapolis, where the 1991 and 2010 Blue Devils had won NCAA championships in different indoor football stadiums. And they had luck on their side both times.

Duke notched its first title for both the university and its coach at the old Hoosier Dome by defeating young Roy Williams' Kansas Jayhawks two days after the Blue Devils shocked top-ranked and undefeated UNLV. The year before, the Rebels had routed basically the same Duke team in the 1990 championship game in Denver. In the rematch, with a full week to prepare, the Blue Devils kept it much closer. They trailed UNLV by five points with 2:15 to play when sophomore guard Bobby Hurley started the rally with a 3-pointer that some have called the biggest shot in school history.

Then, nineteen years later, Duke earned its fourth national championship at Indy's new Lucas Oil Stadium, beating a rugged West Virginia team and edging sentimental favorite Butler in the closing seconds. Like the first NCAA champs, the 2010 team had veteran leaders who overcame the odds against them all season.

The freshman-laden 2015 team won neither the Atlantic Coast Conference regular season nor the conference tournament, but its 29–4 record and wins over seven ranked teams had given Duke a No. 1 NCAA seed for the 13th time, one shy of UNC's 14. The Blue Devils played up to it by impressively handling two more ranked opponents in the regional, giving Krzyzewski one more Final Four appearance than Smith (another outstripping that was significant for some fans of both schools).

Luck was awaiting them again in Indianapolis.

Seventh-seeded Michigan State, Saturday's semifinal opponent, had 11 losses and got hot at the right time, upsetting second seed and ACC champion Virginia, third-seeded Oklahoma, and No. 4 seed Louisville in the East Regional. No. 1 seed Villanova had already been knocked out by N.C. State, leaving Duke to face the Spartans, whose coach, Tom Izzo, had a career record against Krzyzewski of 1–8.

Duke's underrated defense held Michigan State to nine points over the last 10 minutes of the first half and, behind 54 points from Winslow, Okafor, and Cook, the Blue Devils rolled to an 81–61 victory. They then got another big break in the second semifinal, where third-ranked Wisconsin ended No. 1 Kentucky's undefeated season with a stunning 71–64 upset.

Duke had already beaten the Badgers on their home floor back in

December and was understandably confident it could beat them again. Despite the easy win on Saturday and his youngsters facing their biggest game of the season on the largest stage in college basketball, Krzyzewski said he discounted the possibility that his team would be nervous.

"Every night when I'm watching tape or I'm getting prepared, I never worry about attitude," he said on Sunday. "I never worry my guys aren't going to come, so you can be a little more creative."

He needed all the creativity and influence he could muster against the Badgers, whose frontcourt tandem of senior Kaminsky and junior Dekker were on a scoring rampage in the tournament. They had combined to average 42.8 points in five games, including 36 in sending Kentucky home with a 38–1 record. Plus, Wisconsin presented the challenge as one of the most disciplined teams in America, committing the fewest turnovers and limiting opponents to the fewest free throws in Big Ten conference play. The game tipped off about 9:20 p.m. before more than 71,000 fans and a massive CBS television audience.

The first half had 13 lead changes, but Krzyzewski did not like the foul differential in what he considered an aggressive game. Wisconsin was called for two fouls and his Blue Devils for seven, putting the Badgers in the bonus with 4:47 left in the half. Duke had made 4-for-4 free throws and Wisconsin only 3-for-7 when the first half ended in a 31–31 deadlock.

Coach K hated stopping on the way to the locker room for a halftime TV interview, but he did it occasionally in the NCAA tournament because, his assistant coaches joked, "that's where the big money comes in."

Before the Final Four, Krzyzewski said of the halftime interviews, "That stinks, that shouldn't be, it's horrible.

"That's why I never do [them]. I want my team to know that the only people I am talking to from start to finish is them, and sometimes the referees."

This time he did it and was almost too candid. "We're driving, but we couldn't get them to foul," he told Tracy Wolfson of CBS.

In the second half, with the entire Duke bench animated, Krzyzewski talked to the officials a lot. Wisconsin was called for three fouls before the under-16 TV timeout and committed its seventh with 11:43 left in the game, putting Duke in the bonus. Despite losing Okafor, their prime inside threat, to his fourth foul with 9:18 remaining, the Blue Devils continued taking the ball right at the Badgers and made 12 of 16 from the foul line in the second half, compared to Wisconsin's three of three. Duke's 13 more total free throws were one difference in the game.

Another was Grayson Allen, who played the least of the top eight Blue Devils all season, but uncharacteristically went in the game during the first half and scored six points. When Kaminsky's layup gave Wisconsin a 48–39 lead with 13:23 remaining, Krzyzewski called timeout and put Allen back in. The epic rally began as Allen hit a 3-pointer to cut the deficit to six points.

Allen then dove head long for a loose ball and came up screaming, "Let's Go! Let's Go!" The outburst was infectious and the whole team came alive behind Allen's rant.

His steal, old-fashioned three-point play, and two free throws—followed by a Tyus Jones three-point play—cut Duke's deficit to one in a little more than two minutes. Jones—whose teammates called "Tyus *Stones*" for his willingness to take the big shot—tied the score at 54 with a jumper, and Allen's layup gave Duke a two-point lead. Jones' two 3-pointers and two free throws down the stretch helped the Blue Devils put the game away for good in a dramatic 68–63 victory and the sixty-eight-year-old Krzyzewski's fifth national championship, tying Adolph Rupp for the second most.

"He wasn't focused on getting his fifth, he was focused on us getting our first," said captain Quinn Cook, who endured two one-and-dones in the NCAA tournament before the four freshmen showed up for his senior year.

"We had one of the smallest teams, I think, in the history of this championship on the floor. But not in heart," Krzyzewski said. "We were dead in the water without Grayson. We won it because of that kid. We don't win without him."

Or Tyus Jones, who earned Most Outstanding Player recognition with 23 points, 19 in the second half. Winslow (11 points, nine rebounds) and Allen (16 points) also made the All-Final Four team with Kaminsky and Dekker, who missed 18 of their 31 attempts as the Badgers shot 41 percent, their lowest in six postseason games. Okafor was saddled by foul trouble in the final, played only 22 minutes, and did not make all-tourney.

For the third time, Duke left Indianapolis with the NCAA championship trophy and had its fifth raucous homecoming celebration at Cameron Indoor Stadium.

Five months later, after three of the freshmen were already the 3rd, 10th, and 24th first-round picks by NBA teams, and two seniors had graduated, the Blue Devils reassembled for a return visit to the White House on September 8, 2015, deep into Barack Obama's second term. It was more presidential than five years before, with Obama and Krzyzewski entering the East Room after the team, a mini-procession that included Duke president Richard Brodhead, athletics director Kevin White, and Board of Trustees chairman David Rubenstein.

The University of North Carolina, whose basketball team had not made it beyond the NCAA Sweet 16 in the last three seasons, was not specifically mentioned, but a couple of good-natured barbs found their way into the words that followed.

Upon congratulating the new NCAA champions, a more polished

and comfortable Obama said, "If folks didn't like this year's Blue Devils, they were just being haters . . . or they lived in Chapel Hill."

After introducing the various dignitaries, POTUS added, "We also have an up-and-coming coach named Mike Krzyzewski. We think he has some potential.

"So it's good to see the Blue Devils again. This is the second time I've hosted them here at the White House. And I can relate to this program . . . won twice in the last four years [actually five for Duke] . . . know what it's like for people to oppose you, no matter what you try to do."

The mood was more festive than in the Rose Garden in 2010. The well-briefed president praised Quinn Cook for "providing senior leadership and setting a Duke record for best assist-to-turnover ratio . . . Most Outstanding Player of the Final Four Tyus Jones—or Tyus *Stones* . . . soft-spoken center Jahlil Okafor, whose size and footwork bent defenses the way people hadn't seen in a very long time . . . Justise Winslow for flying all over the place, dominating some games in the tournament . . . and Grayson Allen, who just went crazy and clearly didn't know any better and scored eight straight points." In summary, Obama noted that "in the championship game against Wisconsin, the four freshmen scored every [Duke] point in the second half."

He praised Krzyzewski for earning his 1,000th career victory and his fifth national championship. "And somehow, he did it without ever saying a bad word to a referee," Obama teased. To which Coach K jovially responded, "It's true . . . only what they deserved."

In the face of Duke's one-and-done notoriety, Obama said the players not only excelled on the hard court but in the classroom, where five "made the all-conference academic squad this year—Tyus, Justise, Grayson, Amile Jefferson and Marshall Plumlee . . . that is worth applause."

Krzyzewski, who did not speak in 2010, stepped to the podium and delivered a gentle needle to Obama, who had visited UNC more than once and scrimmaged with the Carolina team in 2008 before he was elected. "Mr. President, thank you for opening up your home. You know, we've been to your house twice, but you have never been to our house." Coach K paused with perfect timing to let the murmurs grow into laughter at the president's expense.

A slightly embarrassed Obama shrugged, raised his arms, and said, "We'll have to correct that."

"We'll have to correct that in a little over a year after your term is over," Krzyzewski countered, offering Obama a scholarship to his thirty-five-and-over basketball fantasy camp. Somehow, Coach K seemed to know that, with this one-and-done class all but gone, he had caught lightning in a bottle and would not be back at the White House for the one season left of Obama's presidency.

As it turned out, Carolina missed that chance by a buzzer-beater.

COACH K VS. ROY

The 15 seasons since Roy Williams became UNC's coach (2004–18):

- Overall record: Duke 433–104; UNC 424–131
- Average wins: Duke 28.3 and 6.9 in the ACC; UNC 26.9 and 8.7
- 30-win seasons: Duke 7, UNC 7
- No. 1 finishes: Duke 1, UNC 1
- Top 10 finishes: Duke 13, UNC 9
- Top 25 finishes: Duke 14, UNC 13
- Head-to-head: Duke 19, UNC 14
- Duke wins in Smith Center: 8
- UNC wins in Cameron: 6
- ACC regular-season championships: UNC 8 (1 shared), Duke 3 (1 shared)
- ACC tournament championships: Duke 6, UNC 3
- NCAA titles: UNC 3, Duke 2
- Final Fours: UNC 5, Duke 3
- Sweet 16s: Duke 10, UNC 9
- NCAA wins: UNC 43, Duke 34
- NCAA tournaments: Duke 15, UNC 14
- First-round NCAA tournament losses: Duke 3, UNC 0

■ NOTE: Either Duke or UNC has reached the ACC tournament championship game every season since 1996 (when Wake Forest beat Georgia Tech).

■ NOTE: Duke and/or North Carolina reached the NCAA Sweet 16 in 14 of 15 years from 2004 to 2018. The only season neither advanced that far was 2014.

7

CAROLINA'S COMEBACK

In late May 2015, Roy Williams attended the funeral service and reception for Bill Guthridge, the thirty-year assistant to Dean Smith and head coach of the Tar Heels for three seasons. Guthridge had died at age seventy-seven from an inoperable tumor on his heart, a rare condition complicated by dementia not dissimilar to Smith's.

A few days before the funeral, the University of North Carolina received a notice of allegations from the NCAA that came after an investigation into academic irregularities. They involved athletes who took approved-but-aberrant classes in the department of African and Afro-American Studies in the College of Arts and Sciences.

According to Williams, the two-year-old probe had cost him the chance to sign several recruits, the most noteworthy being 6'9" forward Brandon Ingram of Kinston, North Carolina, a basketball hotbed that had produced close to fifty major- and small-college players through 2018. Among them were Reggie Bullock, who left UNC after his junior season in 2013 and was a first-round NBA draft pick, and Jerry Stackhouse, a Tar Heels All-American in the 1990s and

18-year NBA veteran for eight teams after being the third selection in the 1995 NBA draft.

In 2018, ESPN called Kinston "most surely, per capita, the greatest producer of NBA players in America." And Kinston players usually attended in-state schools.

Williams once told a local news station, "If I hear there's a player in Kinston, I am going to go there quicker than I would go to New York City."

Charles Shackleford went to N.C. State in Raleigh in 1985 and led the ACC in rebounding as an all-conference player his junior year. In 1973, lesser-known Kinston High alum Cedric "Cornbread" Maxwell had gone to up-and-coming UNC-Charlotte and, as a senior All-American, led the 49ers to the 1977 Final Four in Atlanta, where eventual national champion Marquette, North Carolina, and UNLV also made it.

Stackhouse had briefly flirted with Mike Krzyzewski and Duke before joining Rasheed Wallace and Jeff McInnis in North Carolina's highly rated recruiting class of 1993, the year Smith won his second NCAA championship. Stackhouse knew Ingram and his family and tried to push them toward Carolina despite the growing doubt about the immediate future of Williams' program; the best they could all agree on was waiting until the 2015 spring signing period to see if the NCAA had cleared UNC.

However, by April, the NCAA was still investigating and the Ingram family had grown so comfortable with Brandon playing for Krzyzewski that he signed with Duke, a huge "get" for the Blue Devils and an equally devastating loss for the Tar Heels.

"I've been in the Ingram home, and they all wanted Brandon to come here," Williams said after Guthridge's service. "I promised them that we weren't going on probation, but so many other schools had told them that we were, Brandon's father said they just couldn't risk it. They wanted him to get the most exposure possible in his first year so he could go on to the NBA."

Krzyzewski and Jeff Capel, whom Donald Ingram called Duke's "main recruiter," visited Kinston twice the last week, once at 6:45 a.m. before school started, and Brandon committed on April 27. "They've always been on me hard," Ingram said of the Blue Devils. "They even took me through some plays they would use me in."

Ingram's father told the Raleigh *News & Observer,* "We are looking to go into a system where he can make an immediate impact. They have four guys that are leaving this year, Quinn Cook and three freshmen. With Brandon's skill set and his upside . . . we feel like he should be able to go in and make an impact without being on the bench to start with.

"And with four players gone—four starters—it's cut and dry. It's a no-brainer, so to speak."

Both Ingram and his father admitted the uncertainty surrounding UNC, where they made more unofficial visits than to any other school over the last three years, did play a significant role in his decision.

Like most of the Duke one-and-dones in the decade, there was no mention of academics as the reason Ingram chose Duke, the respected private school where its revered head basketball coach was asked to deliver the 2016 commencement address. Coach K did and ended with a standing ovation.

And like with some signees before him, Ingram used a line that came right out of the clever Coach Krzyzewski's recruiting playbook as to why he did not follow other Kinston players to Carolina. "Today, I created my own path," he said.

After a slow start with the Blue Devils, Ingram went on to average 17.3 points and 6.8 rebounds and ran away with ACC Freshman of the Year honors. He entered the NBA draft and was the second overall pick by the Los Angeles Lakers, signing a three-year contract for a guaranteed $16,558,200. In retrospect, that path to pro basketball might have been enhanced by playing for Duke, with the depletion of its 2015 national champions, rather than joining the veteran Tar Heels, who had four starters and eight of their top nine players back from the 2015 Sweet 16 team.

Another Duke freshman who had been recruited by Carolina was 6'5" shooting whiz Luke Kennard, an Ohioan who had leaned toward playing for the Blue Devils for two years. With Tyus Jones joining Jahlil Okafor and Justise Winslow in the 2015 NBA draft, Krzyzewski was left without a pure point guard; so he dipped into his bag of tricks by getting 6'2" Derryck Thornton of Findlay Prep—a private, accredited high school in suburban Las Vegas, founded by businessman and auto dealer Cliff Findlay—to reclassify after his junior season and jump right to college basketball. Thornton turned out to be a one-year rental when 6'3" five-star Frank Jackson committed to Duke in the fall of 2016 before Thornton ever played a game as a freshman.

Ingram, Kennard, and Thornton weren't the simpatico trio that led the Blue Devils to their national championship the season before, and the return of three players who became starters made the 2016 roster look more like Carolina's mix of young and older.

Fifth-year senior center Marshall Plumlee was the only one to start all 36 games; sophomore Grayson Allen, whose eight-minute spectacular stretch against Wisconsin in the 2015 NCAA title game made him a preseason All-American, started 35 games. Senior Amile Jefferson and junior Matt Jones were the two other designated starters with Ingram, before Jefferson suffered a broken foot in the ninth game and opted for a medical redshirt and return in 2017. That forced freshmen Kennard and Thornton to play more minutes than expected.

Duke jumped out to a 14–2 start against an early schedule mixed with tough opponents (Kentucky, Indiana, Utah), easy home games, and two ACC road trips to doormats Wake Forest and Boston College, which combined for a 2–34 conference record. The pollsters only lowered the Blue Devils from No. 5 to No. 6 the week after they lost to second-ranked Kentucky in Chicago. But they wised up after unranked Utah sprang a 77–75 upset at Madison Square Garden, and Duke dropped all the way to No. 15.

After winning its first three ACC games, Duke lost four of the next five and fell out of the rankings altogether but climbed back into the polls by upsetting No. 13 Louisville and No. 7 Virginia at Cameron. Allen triggered the important wins with five 3-pointers against the Cardinals and an acrobatic basket at the buzzer to beat the Cavaliers. The Blue Devils went to Chapel Hill for the first UNC game on the high of those upsets and a four-game winning streak.

The fifth-ranked Tar Heels had been No. 2 after starting 17–2 before losing close road games at Louisville and Notre Dame, and were battling Virginia and Miami for first place in the ACC. They were also looking like one of the best teams in the country with senior stars Brice Johnson and Marcus Paige, improving junior Kennedy Meeks, and sophomore scorers Joel Berry and Justin Jackson in a potent starting lineup.

In a game eerily similar to the Austin Rivers buzzer-beater four years earlier, bigger, better, and deeper Carolina led Duke most of the way but could not deliver the knockout punch. The Blue Devils were hampered by Plumlee's foul trouble and Matt Jones' sprained ankle, but they stayed close enough to crawl back within two points with less than four minutes left against the uptight home team suddenly feeling game pressure in its own building.

After Roy Williams called for a 1-3-1 trapping zone, Kennard found the open spot in the right corner, and the smooth southpaw drilled his third 3-pointer for Duke's first lead since midway through the opening half. Meeks scored to put UNC back ahead before Allen sank two free throws with 1:09 left. After confusion over whether to call a timeout on the Tar Heels' last possession, Berry hurriedly drove the lane for an off-balance shot that was blocked by Thornton, and the elated Blue Devils ran off the court with a 74–73 victory and their fourth straight win in the rivalry.

"We're a bunch of fighters," Thornton said in the jubilant Duke locker room.

Krzyzewski broke another record of Dean Smith's, albeit an obscure one—most road wins (15) against top five teams in NCAA history.

Williams called it a "tough one to swallow" and apologized for not calling a timeout on UNC's last possession. "I should have gotten us a better shot at the end," he said. His wasn't the only late lapse.

Despite 29 points and 19 rebounds, the 6'10" Johnson managed only two shots in the final 13 minutes and had trouble getting open against Plumlee, who played the last 14:06 with four fouls. After starting only two games in each of his first two seasons due to poor defensive effort—when Williams often kidded about just how bad his young big man was on defense—Johnson gradually grew into one of the best rebounders and shot-blockers in college basketball. Always a dangerous scorer, he had a career-high 39 points and 23 rebounds in a January 4 win at Florida State. Since then, the team relied on Johnson for big plays in the clutch, which made his disappearance late in the first Duke game so crucial.

After losing at third-ranked Virginia, Carolina came back to beat Syracuse on a teary-eyed Senior Night send-off for Johnson, Paige, and Joel James. But the Tar Heels had to get even with Duke at Cameron to win the ACC regular season for the first time in four years; it was the same scenario as in 2012, when they avenged the loss at home and edged out the Blue Devils for first place by winning on their Senior Night.

And, like four years ago, Carolina was the better team and proved it by holding on for a 76–72 victory, disappointing another 2,000 tent-dwelling Crazies who had camped out for two months in Krzyzew-skiville. A 64–29 rebounding advantage, including 27 offensive boards, won it for the Tar Heels, who shot 28 percent in the second half and 35.6 for the game. All five starters finished in double figures, led by Johnson's 18 points and 21 rebounds, which solidified his unanimous selection to the All-ACC team with Virginia's Malcolm Brogdon, who won Player of the Year. Duke's Allen also made first-team All-ACC and Ingram second-team.

Allen, who had 29 points and hit six 3-pointers on Plumlee's Senior Night, was the second-highest scorer (21.6) in the ACC behind N.C. State's Cat Barber, but he likely lost some all-conference votes for two tripping fouls called on him against Louisville and Florida State, which began his downward spiral for two seasons. As in the year before, Duke lost to Notre Dame in its second game of the ACC tournament in Washington, D.C., and carried a No. 19 ranking into the true postseason as a fourth seed in the NCAA West Regional.

Carolina had routed Pitt and Notre Dame in the tournament, then broke open a taut ACC championship game against Brogdon and the fourth-ranked Cavaliers for a 61–57 victory. The Tar Heels became the third team in four years (Miami in 2013, Virginia in 2014) to win both ACC titles, and it was the Tar Heels' first sweep since 2008. UNC was the sixth different tournament champion over the last six years, following Duke, Florida State, Miami, Virginia, and Notre Dame.

During Carolina's run to an 18th ACC tournament championship, Berry leaped onto the national stage by scoring 51 points in three victories, all televised on ESPN. He was the first UNC sophomore to earn the Everett Case MVP award and the school's first point guard to do it since freshman Phil Ford in 1975. Berry was joined on the all-tournament team by Johnson and Marcus Paige.

The Tar Heels received their 15th NCAA No. 1 seed, the most by any program in the country, and were assigned to the East Regional.

Duke's two close games in Providence forecast a rough journey through the 2016 NCAA tournament. The Blue Devils struggled against lower seed UNC-Wilmington, coached by Kevin Keatts, whom N.C. State would hire within a year. Unranked UNCW was primed to upset No. 19 Duke, and the 13-seed Seahawks startled the Blue Devils with their tenacious defense, taking a 43–40 lead into halftime. The 7-foot Plumlee started wearing a plastic mask after having suffered a broken nose in the ACC tournament, but he threw it off after scoring just four points in the first half. Before Krzyzewski's locker room tirade, Plumlee told his teammates, "I got you."

Once buried on the Duke bench early in his career, Plumlee lived up to Coach K's declaration that he was "our most valuable player," by scoring 10 quick points to help seize control of the game. He finished with a career-high 23 despite picking up his fourth foul with just over six minutes left in the game. Plumlee, a four-star recruit and McDonald's All-American, got the most out of his college career and relationship with Krzyzewski. As a senior, he finished second behind Christian Laettner for highest field goal percentage (.688) in one season.

"I'm a product of my environment here at Duke," said Plumlee, who worked through the ROTC program and became a commissioned second lieutenant in the Army National Guard after graduation. He also won a gold medal with the senior U.S. national team at the 2017

FIBA Americas Cup. Undrafted by the NBA, Plumlee signed two-way contracts with the New York Knicks, LA Clippers, and Milwaukee Bucks and their developmental G League teams in his first two seasons after leaving Duke. (His older brothers, Miles and Mason, were already NBA veterans.)

The 93–85 victory over UNCW sent the Blue Devils on to their second-round game against upstart Yale. The Ivy League–champion Bulldogs had upset taller-and-talented Baylor, the No. 5 seed in the West Regional, in the first round.

Duke raced to a fast start, leading Yale 48–25 at the half and then by 27 points when the Bulldogs began a furious rally that had them on the brink of the biggest NCAA tournament comeback in history. Yale's 15–0 run cut the deficit to seven points with 11:38 left, and eventually to three, and it was a devil of a dogfight to the end. Ingram and Allen finally salted away the 71–64 victory from the foul line for the Blue Devils.

"Our house is on a cliff, and we hope it doesn't rain," Krzyzewski offered as a metaphor after the game. "That's who we've been, so I really have an appreciation of that."

More foul trouble for Plumlee mitigated the most astounding statistic, a 42–28 rebounding advantage for smaller Yale, which had lost only once previously that season when winning the backboard battle. Duke's offense—with Allen, Ingram, and Kennard scoring 67 of Duke's 71 points—proved enough to send the Blue Devils back to the Sweet 16 and keep their shaky hopes alive to repeat as NCAA champions.

Besides Krzyzewski, Nate James was the only member of the coaching staff left from the 2011 Blue Devils, who ended their season—and chance to repeat as NCAA champs—at the West Regional in Anaheim, California. That team, which won 32 games and finished ranked third in the nation, was certainly worthy with ACC Player of the Year and ACC tournament MVP Nolan Smith and All-ACC forward Kyle Singler, joined by freshman point guard Kyrie Irving. But after Irving missed most of the season with an injured toe, he could not comfortably reintegrate with the Duke lineup. The Blue Devils lost to 17th-ranked and fifth-seeded Arizona.

Now Duke was back in Anaheim for the Sweet 16, again as the defending national champion, but with the tables turned. The 2016 Blue Devils were 25–10, ranked No. 19, and since losing Jefferson's leadership and defense had struggled for consistency. Their opponent was another Pac-12 team (like Arizona), and this time the top seed in the regional. The Oregon Ducks were No. 5 in the polls with a 30–6 record after winning their conference regular-season and tournament titles for the first time in the same season. Now they faced the game's biggest brand with the Olympic coach and huge reputation. Could the Ducks' relentless running game take a toll on Duke's lack of depth?

Oregon's star was 6'5" sophomore Dillon Brooks, a Canadian who had attended Findlay Prep in Las Vegas with Duke's Thornton. Like five years ago against Arizona, the score was close at the half, with the Ducks holding a 36–31 lead. But, again, the game got away from the Blue Devils in the second half. Brooks scored 11 of his team-high 22 points, including his fourth 3-pointer with 10 seconds left as the passive Duke defense waited for the final buzzer. Brooks celebrated the methodical 82–68 victory, Oregon's first over the Blue Devils, causing the only controversy of the otherwise ho-hum night.

As the teams exchanged their customary handshakes, Krzyzewski used his familiar left-hand pat to Brooks' chest and appeared to be more than congratulating him. Brooks told the media that Coach K had "lectured me" about sportsmanship, which the Duke coach strongly denied at his press conference. Krzyzewski's own occasional poor sportsmanship after tough losses came back to bite him when televised replays with audio confirmed Brooks' side of the story.

For his part, Oregon coach Dana Altman was respectful toward Duke and Krzyzewski after the game.

"Duke is a household name," Altman said. "Coach K, I have a great deal of respect. So yeah, our guys knew the significance of playing Duke, defending national title, all the Final Fours, all the national championships that their program has been able to win. It was a different feel to it."

Upon returning to Durham, Krzyzewski fessed up that he had fibbed and released a 118-word apology to Brooks and Altman, saying he "did not react correctly" to the media's questions. He signed the statement after his name with "Duke University Head Coach and United States National Team Coach." The story died quickly with a few back-and-forth barbs from bloggers. Duke finished 25–11, its fewest victories since the 2007 season and second fewest in nineteen years.

Ingram, who led all scorers with 24 points against Oregon, capped off a splendid three-game tournament with 69 points, strengthening his NBA draft status and fulfilling the goal he and his father had laid out when he signed with Duke.

After Ingram turned pro, as expected, Thornton announced he was transferring, and the third Plumlee graduated, the Blue Devils faced another mini-rebuilding job. Fortunately, Krzyzewski and Capel had secured a new sterling recruiting class that included five-star freshmen Jayson Tatum and Harry Giles. The 6'8" Tatum from St. Louis was in the top five of every recruiting ranking and had known Krzyzewski since playing for the U.S. teams in the FIBA Under-17 and Under-19 World Championships. A 6'10" forward from Winston-Salem, North Carolina, Giles was thought to be ticketed for UNC before the academic scandal turned him away.

———

Carolina opened the 2016 NCAA tournament in Raleigh, where the Tar Heels had suffered their only loss in 32 NCAA games played in North Carolina. That defeat came in 1979 and was part of a Sunday doubleheader with Duke at Reynolds Coliseum on the N.C. State campus. After brash No. 3 UNC and banged-up No. 6 Duke fell to unranked Penn and St. John's, respectively, the media dubbed the shocking defeats Black Sunday. Both winners advanced to the Sweet 16 in Greensboro, and the blue bloods missed a possible chance to play each other a fifth time that season for the right to join Indiana State (with Larry Bird) and Michigan State (with Magic Johnson) at the Final Four in Salt Lake City. A Black Sunday for them and the entire ACC, it was.

From 1960 through 2015 first- and second-round victories in Charlotte, Duke had won a total of 34 NCAA games in North Carolina (including two in Chapel Hill in 1988) and lost six, counting Black Sunday. The Blue Devils played in the 1994 national championship game at the Charlotte Coliseum, losing to Arkansas, but only twice had advanced from a regional in the Tar Heel state to one of their 16 Final Fours (1964, 1966 from Raleigh).

Carolina's record in NCAA games played in North Carolina through 2015 was 31–1, which included regional sweeps in Raleigh in 1968 and 1982 at Reynolds Coliseum, 1998 in Greensboro, and 2008 in Charlotte. In 2008, UNC had won its first two tournament games at PNC Arena, N.C. State's new home court that the Wolfpack shared with the Carolina Hurricanes of the National Hockey League.

The top-seeded 2016 Tar Heels were heavy favorites at PNC Arena to defeat No. 16 seed Florida Gulf Coast and the winner of the 8–9 game between Southern Cal and Providence in the first two rounds of the East Regional. The placement in Raleigh gave Carolina a massive home court advantage, engendering overconfidence.

Florida Gulf Coast was a Cinderella story of the 2013 postseason by advancing to the Sweet 16 as a No. 15 seed. The Eagles led UNC early in the game and trailed 41–40 at halftime. From there, the bigger Tar Heels ran away to an 83–67 victory with five players finishing in double figures. Isaiah Hicks, the 6'8" junior, played more minutes than erratic starter Kennedy Meeks and scored 12 points.

A similar consequence unfolded in the second round with Hicks, who had been the North Carolina High School Player of the Year for Webb High School in Oxford. He came off the bench and scored 13 points, joining four starters in double figures. Led by Brice Johnson's 21–10 double-double, the Tar Heels blew out Providence, whose foul-plagued stars Kris Dunn and Ben Bentil combined for 50 points in the 85–66 loss.

The Sweet 16 in Philadelphia brought together familiar foes. Fifth-seeded Indiana of the Big Ten, which seemed like a semiregular on the Tar Heels schedule, played tough man-to-man defense and worked hard to get open shots, many of them by All-Big Ten guard Yogi Ferrell. The Hoosiers drained 13 3-pointers, but Marcus Paige made six of UNC's 11 outside attempts and led five starters in double figures with 21 points. Paige had recovered from a broken bone in his right (non-shooting) hand and a 3-point slump to pace the torrid Tar Heels, who hit 51.6 percent from the floor while holding IU to 41 percent in the 101–86 runaway.

Notre Dame defeated Wisconsin in the other Sweet 16 matchup and had a chance to avenge a 31-point drubbing by Carolina in the ACC tournament. UNC led the well-played game at the Wells Fargo Center at halftime 43–38, with both teams making better than 58 percent of their shots. The Irish rallied from 11 down by scoring 12 straight points to go ahead with 13:04 remaining. A 12–0 run from Paige, Berry, and sixth and seventh men Hicks and Theo Pinson regained control of the game, and the eventual 88–74 victory sent the Tar Heels to the Final Four for the first time since 2009.

"Never in my life have I wanted something for someone else as I wanted to get these guys to Houston," Roy Williams said, holding a bandage to the hand he sliced open while cutting down the nets.

Johnson recorded a school-record 23rd double-double of the season with 25 points and 12 rebounds, winning MVP of the East Regional. Paige scored 13 points as five starters again reached double figures while shooting better than 60 percent. Carolina had won its first four NCAA tournament games by an average of 16 points and was on the way to Texas as one of the Final Four.

"It took us four years to do this, but we're finally there," Johnson said.

Carolina caught a huge break when Virginia, the top seed in the Midwest Regional, blew a 15-point lead with 9:20 left in its Elite Eight game and lost to ACC mate Syracuse. Thus, the Tar Heels faced the 10th-seeded Orange, whom they had already beaten twice during the regular season, instead of giving the fourth-ranked Cavaliers a chance to avenge their ACC tournament loss to UNC.

Final Four Saturday featured two laughers at massive Reliant Stadium. Villanova, the second seed in the South Regional, routed Oklahoma 95–51, the biggest blowout in Final Four history. The game was essentially over after the Wildcats led the Sooners by more than 20 points midway through the second half.

Carolina then easily solved the Syracuse zone with 31 2-point baskets and cruised past the Orange 83–66, giving the ACC an NCAA record 19 of tournament victories in 2016. Despite missing 13 of 17 attempts from the 3-point line, the Tar Heels still shot 53.8 percent overall, and only Joel Berry's eight points kept the starters from scoring in double figures for the third straight game.

So the 2016 championship game was set for Monday night, with the college basketball world hoping for at least one close contest on the last night of the season. Carolina and Villanova produced it.

CAROLINA'S COMEBACK

The Tar Heels were a 2½-point favorite over Villanova, probably because Roy Williams had already won two NCAA championships and was making his eighth appearance in the Final Four—four each at Kansas and UNC. The Naismith Hall of Famer won more than 300 games each at schools that had the second- and third-most victories in college basketball history.

Carolina was in its 47th NCAA tournament and had 117 NCAA tourney victories, second to Kentucky in both categories. The Tar Heels' 19 Final Fours to date were an all-time high, two more than Kentucky and UCLA. Williams' 70 NCAA tournament wins trailed only Duke's Krzyzewski (90), who had been a head coach for thirteen years longer than Williams.

This was Jay Wright's 15th season coaching Villanova of the Big East Conference, but in comparison only his second Final Four. His first was in 2009, when No. 2 UNC out-scrapped Wright's 11th-ranked team in the national semifinals in Detroit. By 2016, the Big East had been realigned as a basketball-only league and played most of its games on Northeast regional television. Carolina was considered a weekly national TV show.

Villanova was a bigger basketball name than its fifty-four-year-old coach. The Wildcats were in their 35th NCAA tournament and fourth appearance in the Final Four, not including their 1971 berth, which was vacated by the NCAA for rules violations. Nova won a national championship in 1985, stunning top-ranked and heavily favored Georgetown in the best-known upset in eighty years of March Madness, one of the trademarked monikers owned by the NCAA. That was two years before Wright joined coach Rollie Massimino's staff at Villanova; he stayed five seasons as an assistant coach and obviously made a positive impression on the university.

Wright's first head coaching job was at Hofstra, which he led into the postseason for three straight years. In 2001, he was named head coach at Villanova to bring back the glory days of Massimino, who had moved on to UNLV in 1992. Wright returned the Wildcats to the NCAA tournament in his fourth season and every year since except one. His star was just beginning to shine.

The 2016 UNC and Villanova teams were eerily even on paper, even though one was more celebrated, with its most famous alumnus, Michael Jordan, among the thousands of blue-clad Carolina fans in the stands. But the darker blue opponent, called grinders and guys no one else wanted, had the eighty-one-year-old Massimino sitting behind its bench and an equally rabid Philadelphia fan base in Houston.

The Tar Heels had begun the season ranked No. 1 in the Associated Press poll, dropped as far as No. 11 in mid-December, and, after winning both the ACC regular-season and tournament championships, reached the NCAA final at No. 3 in the AP rankings. Their 33–6 record came against the sixth-toughest schedule in the country.

Villanova arrived as the No. 6-ranked team but had spent most of February at No. 1 before losing to Seton Hall in the Big East tournament championship game. After blowing out Oklahoma, the Wildcats were 34–5, the best winning percentage in the country, and it came against the 17th-hardest schedule. Their Simple Rating System (which computes overall statistics) was No. 1. UNC's SRS was No. 3.

Carolina still started seniors Paige and Johnson, junior Meeks, and sophomores Berry and Jackson. The Tar Heels were shooting just under 52 percent from the floor and 35.3 percent from 3-point range in the tournament. For the season, they were fourth nationally in assists per game, seventh in offensive rebounds, ninth in scoring margin, and 10th in rebounding margin.

Villanova also started two seniors, point guard Ryan Arcidiacono and 6'11" Daniel Ochefu, junior swing forwards and leading scorers Josh Hart and Kris Jenkins, and freshman shooting guard Jalen Brunson. The Wildcats shot the ball better from the 3-point line and free throw line than Carolina, but they were nowhere near the rebounding team. The final two were close in overall field goal percentage and turnovers.

Thus, who would have expected anything else but a tight game?

The first half mirrored those team statistics, with Villanova shooting better overall and Carolina getting more rebounds and assists. After six ties and eight lead changes, the Tar Heels led 39–34 because Berry, Jackson, and Paige had made seven of eight 3-point shots. A potential four-point swing occurred in the final seconds, when Jackson's fast break layup was blocked by Hart, and Nova sixth-man Phil Booth hit a jumper at the other end as time expired. UNC assistant coach C. B. McGrath thought Hart had fouled Jackson and started chasing the officials off the court but pulled up and walked into the runway.

America had its close game, and the second half would be even closer.

The score was tied three times, but there was only one lead change. It came on Villanova's 21–11 run over nearly eight minutes that gave the Wildcats a 10-point advantage and control of the game with 5:29 remaining. Arcidiacono (nine), Booth (seven), and Jenkins (five) combined for the 21 points, as Carolina went cold, missing 13 of 16 shots from the floor on the way to a 34.3 percent shooting half.

The Tar Heels countered with a 12–3 run of their own behind Berry, Johnson, and Paige, which closed the deficit to 70–69 with 1:06 remaining. Villanova still led 72–71 when Hart stepped to the free throw line for two shots with 13 seconds left. He made both, after which Wright called a timeout to set up his defense for what he knew would be a 3-pointer by UNC to tie. Berry got the ball to Paige, who was determined to take the shot in his last college game. But Arcidiacono ran at him as he was about to let it go from the right side. It caused Paige to double clutch to avoid Arcidiacono. Then lefty Paige, while airborne, almost shot-putted what, momentarily, was the greatest shot in UNC basketball history to tie the score with 4.7 seconds left.

"How did he do that?" CBS announcer Bill Raftery said in amazement after the ball rattled in.

Amidst the panic and pandemonium of Paige's miraculous tying basket, Villanova called another timeout. Wright and Williams both had a few extra minutes in their huddles, as hundreds of seat cushions heaved into the air from the Carolina section had to be cleared from the bench and court areas.

Wright knew exactly what to call, a play he said his team worked on every day in practice. "I didn't have to say anything," Wright said. "We have a name for it, that's what we're going to do. Just put everybody in their spots."

The Carolina huddle was less calm, as Paige kept yelling, "We're going to win this game!" The Tar Heels were 4.7 seconds from overtime in what already had become a classic in NCAA tournament history. Williams set up his defense, knowing the ball was going into Arcidiacono, who would try to race it up court.

But they made it too easy for the fast point guard to catch the ball on the run, and then the scramble was on. Carolina had two big men under the basket guarding against the long lob, so Arcidiacono dropped it off to the trailing Jenkins on his right. The adopted brother of UNC reserve guard Nate Britt, Jenkins was already squared up to the basket and had a clean look. By the time Isaiah Hicks got to him with a hand up, Jenkins had released the long 3-pointer. It went in cleanly as the horn sounded, firecrackers exploded, and confetti fell from the sky. Villanova 77, UNC 74. Paige's spectacular shot no longer mattered except for the record book.

That the last two baskets were 3-ponters was symbolic. The Tar Heels and Wildcats combined to make 19 of their 31 3-point attempts, Villanova hitting 57.1 percent (eight of 14) and Carolina setting an NCAA championship game record in the 3-point era by shooting 64.7 percent (11 of 17) from behind the arc.

Williams and his team appeared disoriented as they waited to shake hands with the celebrating champions. They gathered in the hushed locker room, where Jordan came in and told the players how proud he was of them. It didn't take away the pain or stunned feeling of losing that way. Paige pulled a chair away from his locker and put it in the middle of the room, knowing what was coming.

The heartbroken Iowan, who was the two-time ACC Academic Athlete of the Year and perfect ambassador for UNC in troubled times, sat in the middle of the almost funereal atmosphere, patiently answering every question from the encircling media. He and Johnson, Paige's best buddy and opposites in height and public persona, had scored the last 10 points to give their team that was on the brink of defeat a last chance at the championship.

They were graduating after arduous up-and-down four-year careers in which the news was almost never-ending about the academic scandal. But they had played the first of at least three straight seasons when Carolina had two seniors starting for a nationally ranked team. That was almost unheard of in the so-called one-and-done era.

"I'm not very good because I can't take away the hurt," Williams said at his press conference. "I told them I loved them. I told them I wish I could have helped them more."

For the returning Tar Heels, there would be another chance.

BLUE BLOOD II

Tom Butters, the retired athletics director at Duke and the man who both hired Krzyzewski and backed him when the wolves were at Coach K's door, died on April 1, 2016. Krzyzewski spoke at Butters' memorial reception on April 10 at the Washington-Duke Inn, limping to the podium on crutches from having his second knee replacement.

About three months later, Roy Williams had his left knee replaced after the bone-on-bone pain got so bad that he often ran practices sitting down during the prior season.

When the next season rolled around, Williams was still not walking smoothly. Asked why he didn't have his operation earlier in the summer, Williams said he wanted to continue scouting and visiting high school prospects during the entire recruiting period. Reminded that Krzyzewski had spent most of the summer rehabbing his surgery, Williams smiled before limping away and said, "He doesn't have to recruit."

How these archrivals approached recruiting was one of several major story lines of the 2017 season, some before the first games were played, and into 2018.

Duke was picked No. 1 in 2017 preseason polls for the first time since 2011 and the fifth time in the last nineteen years—based primarily on its third straight top three freshman class of Giles, Frank Jackson, and Tatum. However, the Blue Devils' one-and-done recruiting hadn't worked as well on the court, except at the end of the 2015 championship season.

Three days before Giles committed to Duke in November 2015, he had torn his right ACL in the first game at his new high school, Oak Hill Academy in Mouth of Wilson, Virginia. It cost Giles his entire senior season and called into question his medical history.

Equally serious ACL and MCL tears to his left knee caused Giles to miss his sophomore season at Wesleyan Christian Academy in High Point, North Carolina, where as a freshman he teamed with UNC commit Theo Pinson to win the North Carolina independent school 3A championship. As a testament to Giles' injury-free junior year and the potential of the smooth power forward in the mold of former all-pro Kevin Garnett, ESPN kept him rated No. 1 in its recruiting Class of 2016. But Giles arrived in Durham still limping, hardly ready to play.

The Tar Heels had lost their two best players, Paige and Johnson, but it could have been worse. After the 2016 agony in Houston, Justin Jackson and Kennedy Meeks entered their names into the NBA draft, but did not hire agents and hoped to get honest feedback from coaches and general managers at the NBA Combine in May. If the news wasn't promising, they could still return to UNC and play the 2017 season.

Jackson, who had been homeschooled, wasn't accustomed to crowds like he found at the sold-out Smith Center and the rabid fans who both cheered and jeered Carolina away from Chapel Hill. He had attended UNC's summer basketball camp as a grade-schooler, and his natural ability even at that age attracted Williams and his staff. A consistent shooter in practice, Jackson never fully relaxed in games and shot about 30 percent from 3-point range his first two seasons. At the Combine in Chicago, Golden State Warriors general manager Bob Myers and the team's advisor, legendary NBA star Jerry West, bluntly told Jackson he needed to improve his shooting and get stronger in order to become a fixture on NBA draft boards. Feelings hurt, Jackson called Williams and told him he was coming back to school for his junior year.

For Meeks, who battled weight and conditioning problems since his high school days in Greensboro, it was more one-sided. He wasn't among the approximately seventy-five players invited to the Combine. So, instead of trying the free agent route, he also returned to UNC for his senior year. Some personal incentives, combined with the lingering pain of losing to Villanova, made the returning Tar Heels highly motivated as summer workouts commenced and fall practice began for the new season.

The players started using "Redemption" as the name of their social media messaging to each other. A lineup of stars Berry and Jackson plus Meeks, Pinson, and Hicks—all three from North Carolina—didn't appear as strong as the 2016 starters, but they had added promising 6'10" freshman Tony Bradley and reserves who were working hard to earn more minutes. During their first get-together at his home, Williams said, "In this room is a team capable of winning the national championship."

Despite all the motivation that had carried them from the heartbreak in Houston through the off-season, five long months of basketball still separated them from a chance at redemption. Dozens of teams had their sights set on Phoenix and the Final Four.

The Tar Heels opened the season ranked No. 6 and climbed to third after sweeping the Maui Classic—their head coach's favorite holiday trip—over Thanksgiving. They dropped out of the top 10 with losses at No. 13 Indiana in the ACC-Big Ten Challenge, to sixth-ranked Kentucky at the CBS Sports Classic in Las Vegas, and at Georgia Tech in their ACC opener.

Berry, who suffered the first of several ankle sprains that would plague him all season, missed two games and almost two weeks but returned and scored 23 points against Kentucky. The 6'6" Pinson, who was UNC's best defender, had broken the fifth metatarsal in his right foot in preseason practice and sat out the first 16 games. He might have helped on Kentucky freshman Malik Monk, who scored 47 points, including the go-ahead 3-pointer with 22 seconds to play in the 103–100 thriller on network television, which was the most watched regular-season game of 2016 by far. Carolina would see Kentucky again on the road back to the Final Four.

On the last day of 2016, UNC did not resemble the ninth-ranked team in its ACC opener at Georgia Tech, which finished 11th in the league. The Yellow Jackets spanked the Tar Heels 75–63, sending Williams home to a miserable New Year's Eve. He watched the tape of dreadful 33.3 percent shooting against Tech's zone and 19.2 percent (five of 26) from 3-point distance. It was Carolina's worst combined shooting game of the season, plus 20 turnovers didn't help Williams ring in 2017.

"Early, we took too many 3-point shots," he lamented later in the week. "We lost confidence and they gained confidence. Their zone got stronger."

It was not a harbinger of things to come, however. The Tar Heels won seven in a row against unranked teams except No. 9 Florida State, a 96–83 victory that featured Pinson's first basket of the season after returning from the foot injury. It was a coast-to-coast dunk that drove the Smith Center wild and stopped a late rally by the Seminoles.

Two nights later, Williams won his 800th career game (second-fastest coach to reach that plateau behind Adolph Rupp) with an 85–68 victory over Syracuse and coach Jim Boeheim, who with Krzyzewski was among the eight coaches with 800-plus wins. After the game, the players presented a framed jersey with No. 800 to Williams, who deadpanned, "The best news is I'm not dying; we're going to coach a few more."

Then Carolina laid another egg, this time at Miami. Jackson was the lone starter in double figures (21), and Berry shot 0-for-8 and made only two free throws. The Hurricanes' Bruce Brown lit them up for 30 points, 10 from the foul line, as the helpless Heels sent Miami to the stripe 30 times trying to cut into the early double-digit deficit. They never did and lost 77–62.

Carolina clung to first place in the ACC by winning six of the next seven (losing at Duke) and actually wrapped up a second straight regular-season title despite a stone-cold loss at Virginia, scoring a season-low 43 points and just four points in the last 9:26 of the horrid performance. The Tar Heels, who had pounded 14th-ranked Virginia at home nine days earlier by 24 points, fell to 13–4, but closest pursuers Duke, FSU, Louisville, and Notre Dame all had six losses.

They came back to life and scored 48 in the first half against Duke on Senior Night for Hicks, Meeks, Nate Britt, and Stilman White. Berry responded to the bad game in Charlottesville with 19 first-half points on 5-for-5 3-pointers. Carolina could not shake determined Duke, which shot 54.2 percent in the first half, making four of eight from the 3-point line, and led only 48–46 at the break.

This was the halftime where Michael Jordan accompanied UNC football coach Larry Fedora and several of his players to midcourt to announce that his Nike Jumpman brand was now going to adorn their uniforms, as well. Saying there was no limit to how far Carolina football could go, Jordan used "The Ceiling is the Roof" phrase that has since made it from merchandized goods to the roof of the runway to the Tar Heels' locker room in Kenan Stadium. Asked what he thought Jordan meant, Roy Williams responded, "If Michael Jordan said it, I'll go with it."

Back at the basketball game, Justin Jackson's top-of-the-key 3-pointer after he had missed his first six broke a 71–71 tie and sparked a late push that allowed the Tar Heels to hold off the Blue Devils. Five late points from Berry gave him 28 for the game and helped seal the 90–83 victory.

"You know what? Big-time players have got to make big-time plays in big-time games," Roy Williams said of his tough junior point guard.

Hicks saved his best college game for Senior Night, with 21 points and nine rebounds. Fellow senior Meeks, who had gotten into the best shape of his life, finished his home career with a quiet eight points, eight rebounds, and two blocks.

It was also the last home game for junior Justin Jackson, who made All-ACC for the first time in his college career, nine votes short of unanimous. Still, he was voted ACC Player of the Year, and his plans to enter the NBA draft were no secret.

"You saw a game where a lot of guys played well," Krzyzewski said after his team finished the ACC regular season in fifth place at 11–7. "And that's it. Sometimes it's not nuclear science. It's that easy." Luke Kennard led Duke with 28 points and was named unanimous first-team All-ACC as a sophomore the next week. And he was to validate that honor in the ACC tournament that followed.

Krzyzewski had recruited more depth but still played basically six men for most of the 2017 regular season.

The Blue Devils returned seniors Amile Jefferson (back for his redshirt fifth year) and Matt Jones, junior Allen, and sophomores Kennard, Chase Jeter, and Antonio Vrankovic. They also had freshmen Tatum, Giles, Jackson, 6'11" Marques Bolden, and 6'10" Javin DeLaurier in Krzyzewski's latest highly rated recruited class. Adding freshman 6'7" Australian Jack White and redshirt Justin Robinson, the 6'8" son of former Navy All-American and NBA All-Star David Robinson, gave Coach K a rare full complement of thirteen scholarship players. He wanted that more for competitive practices after finishing the 2016 season with just seven recruited members of the team.

That depth didn't last long after Giles underwent further knee surgery, missed the entire preseason and the first 11 games. He made his college debut in late December 2016 against Tennessee State, playing only four minutes. He wound up his freshman year getting into 26 games, starting six, and averaging 3.9 points and 3.8 rebounds in 11.5 minutes.

Duke started 12–1, its loss coming at Madison Square Garden against seventh-ranked Kansas. The Blue Devils led into the second half before Frank Mason and Josh Jackson powered the Jayhawks to a 12-point lead with 8:06 to play. Allen, Kennard, and Frank Jackson rallied their team to tie the score, but Mason's late jumper won it for KU 77–75.

Still ranked No. 5 before Christmas, Duke's 72–61 victory over Elon in Greensboro was tarnished by the worst meltdown of Allen's career. After getting tangled up with Elon's Steven Santa Ana on the baseline, Allen threw out his right leg and tripped Santa Ana to the floor. After another flagrant foul was assessed, Allen lost control in the bench area and had to be restrained by assistant coach Jon Scheyer. ESPN analysts, including former Virginia Tech coach Seth Greenberg and former Duke player Jay Williams, called for Krzyzewski to suspend Allen until Duke was able to truly diagnose the player's emotional problems.

Krzyzewski suspended Allen for the ACC opener at Virginia Tech, which the Blue Devils lost. Allen was reinstated for the next game, prompting further media criticism, but was cast in the role of sixth man coming off the bench to energize the team. Duke lost three more ACC games, two on the road to top 20 teams, and a home loss to unranked N.C. State continued the Blue Devils' fall to No. 21 in the polls. Three consecutive wins put them at No. 18 before the February 9 game against eighth-ranked Carolina at Cameron.

The Tar Heels were favored to win their second straight at Duke, dating back to last season, but wound up playing without Hicks, who had strained a hamstring in practice the day before and his absence allowed the Blue Devils to stay even on the boards with the best rebounding team in the ACC in another classic encounter.

Both teams shot extremely well, better than 52 percent, but 13 3-pointers—seven by Allen—helped Duke pull away to the 86–78 victory. Allen (25), Kennard (20), and Tatum (19) led the scoring in their coach's second game back from taking a month off for minor surgery to clean up a herniated disk. Assistant Jeff Capel had taken over as acting head coach and, presumably with Coach K's approval, reinserted Allen into the starting lineup, where he still was for the Carolina game.

"We had more interruptions than six teams," Krzyzewski said.

Frank Jackson made all four field goal attempts, scored 11 points, had three rebounds, and no turnovers in 20 minutes. It was a springboard to his starting the last eight games, when Allen returned to the sixth-man role, playing well enough to become a borderline first-round draft pick. Jackson had taken the roster spot of point guard Derryck Thornton, who transferred to Southern Cal after his freshman year; so he, too, might have seen the writing on the wall with 6'3" five-star guard Trevon Duval coming from IMG Academy in Florida to be part of the next freshman class. After the season, Jackson entered the NBA draft and was the first pick in the second round, 31st overall.

Duke's victory over Carolina came in the midst of a seven-game winning streak, and the Blue Devils soon climbed to No. 10 in the polls. But losses at unranked Syracuse and Miami knocked Duke out of the ACC race before the regular-season finale at Carolina.

The Blue Devils went to the ACC tournament as the fifth seed at the Barclays Center in Brooklyn, and for the second straight year they had to play four games to win it. Carolina had to win three and opened with a second-half blowout over Miami. Williams upstaged his team's victory when asked about the importance of holding the tournament in the media capital of the world, New York City.

"Now everybody's got social media, and we don't need the *New York Times* to find out what in the dickens is going on in the country," he said. "You know, our president tweets out more bullshit than anybody I've ever seen. We've got social media."

After defeating unranked Clemson and 10th-ranked Louisville, Duke was on the brink of losing its second game to UNC in six days, trailing in the second half of the ACC semifinals by 13 points with 13:53 to play while being beaten up by the bigger Tar Heels. More than halfway through its third game in three days, Duke looked tired. But after Tatum scored on a breakaway dunk, Krzyzewski called for a timeout and revved up his team for one last push.

It happened swiftly, while UNC's Berry sat on the bench with four fouls. "We knew they were coming at us, but I wanted to save Joel a little longer," Williams said.

Over the next eight and half minutes, Duke erupted on a 27–9 scoring run, triggered by a Kennard corner 3-pointer and being fouled by Britt. Allen, Jackson, and Kennard buried 3-pointers during the surge in which the Blue Devils also scored in the paint and at the foul line. The tsunami ended with a flying dunk by Giles, who scored six points, pulled down seven rebounds, and blocked four shots in 15 minutes—the best game of a shortened college career.

By the time Williams got Berry back in with just under five minutes left, Duke had a seven-point lead and all the adrenaline it needed to finish off the 93–83 stunner. Blue Devils fans in the sections behind the Duke bench, who seemed resigned to defeat moments earlier, were in pandemonium over the electrifying rally.

Tatum, who started the comeback, led all scorers with 24 points, further elevating his pro stock on national television. But Kennard, with his four-point play, 10-for-10 from the free throw line, and 20 points, was the catalyst. Allen scored 18 and Jackson 15. The Blue Devils shot 50 percent for the game and made 10 of 17 3-pointers, critical to their comeback.

"It was brutal. I hate that I was on the bench; I put the blame on me," said Berry, who was limited to 24 minutes and missed all three of his 3-pointers as the Tar Heels made only five of 22 from behind the arc.

Williams was mad at his players, and told them so, for not wanting it as much as Duke. But, as he was wont to do after losses, he shouldered the blame and said, "The most-disciplined, the best-coached team, the most-focused team won the game tonight. I didn't do as good a job as Mike did." Questioned about not calling a timeout during Duke's run, Williams noted that he had two media breaks to talk to his team, and that didn't work.

Carolina, which was favored to win its second straight ACC tournament, left New York shell-shocked. Two promising takeaways were Meeks' 19 points and 12 rebounds against the Blue Devils, which was a precursor to a sensational NCAA tournament for the 6'9" forward, and Hicks, who totaled 38 points and 13 rebounds in the quarterfinal win over Miami and loss to Duke, making the all-tournament team.

Duke found the legs for one more game and held off Notre Dame 75–69 for its record 20th ACC championship and first since 2011. The Blue Devils were also the first team to win the tournament with four victories in four days.

Kennard, confirming his unanimous All-ACC selection the week before, took home the Everett Case MVP trophy. Tatum, with 19 points and eight rebounds in the title game, joined him on the all-tournament team. Allen, Frank Jackson, and Amile Jefferson made second team in support of Duke's unprecedented accomplishment.

BLUE BLOOD II

The Blue Devils, 27–8 and ranked No. 7, earned a second seed in the NCAA East Regional. The first two rounds in the Greensboro pod had been moved to Greenville, South Carolina, due to the controversial bathroom bill passed by the North Carolina legislature, which required that individuals use public bathrooms based on their gender at birth. The NCAA viewed the law as discriminatory against the LBGTQ community. The NBA had taken its 2017 All-Star game out of Charlotte for the same reason.

Even though the Tar Heels had lost two out of three games to Duke, their ACC regular-season championship and higher rankings in the polls and various ratings indexes gave them the top seed in the South Regional. They were also sent to Greenville, which turned out to be the perfect venue for another Carolina.

FIRST-ROUND NBA DRAFT CHOICES

Duke (45)

Dick Groat, 1952
Art Heyman, 1963*
Jeff Mullins, 1964
Jack Marin, 1966
Tate Armstrong, 1977
Jim Sparnarkel, 1979
Mike Gminski, 1980
Mark Alarie, 1986
Johnny Dawkins, 1986
Danny Ferry, 1989
Alaa Abdelnaby, 1990
Christian Laettner, 1992
Bobby Hurley, 1993
Grant Hill, 1994
Cherokee Parks, 1995
Roshown McLeod, 1998
Elton Brand, 1999*
Trajan Langdon, 1999
Corey Maggette, 1999
Will Avery, 1999
Shane Battier, 2001
Mike Dunleavy, 2002
Jason Williams, 2002
Dahntay Jones, 2003
Luol Deng, 2004
Shelden Williams, 2006
J. J. Redick, 2006
Gerald Henderson, 2009
Kyrie Irving, 2011*
Nolan Smith, 2011
Austin Rivers, 2012
Miles Plumlee, 2012
Mason Plumlee, 2013
Jabari Parker, 2014
Rodney Hood, 2014
Jahlil Okafor, 2015
Justise Winslow, 2015
Tyus Jones, 2015
Brandon Ingram, 2016
Jayson Tatum, 2017
Luke Kennard, 2017
Harry Giles, 2017
Marvin Bagley III, 2018
Wendell Carter Jr., 2018
Grayson Allen, 2018

UNC (49)

Lennie Rosenbluth, 1957
Pete Brennan, 1958
Lee Shaffer, 1960
Billy Cunningham, 1965
Charlie Scott, 1970 (ABA)
Robert McAdoo, 1972
Bobby Jones, 1974
Mitch Kupchak, 1976
Walter Davis, 1977
Tom LaGarde, 1977
Phil Ford, 1978
Dudley, Bradley, 1979
Mike O'Koren, 1980
Al Wood, 1981
James Worthy, 1982*
Michael Jordan, 1984
Sam Perkins, 1984
Brad Daugherty, 1986*
Kenny Smith, 1987
Joe Wolf, 1987
J. R. Reid, 1989
Rick Fox, 1991
Pete Chilcutt, 1991
George Lynch, 1993
Eric Montross, 1994
Jerry Stackhouse, 1995
Rasheed Wallace, 1995
Antawn Jamison, 1998
Vince Carter, 1998
Brendan Haywood, 2001
Joseph Forte, 2001
Marin Williams, 2005
Sean May, 2005
Raymond Felton, 2005
Rashad McCants, 2005
Brandan Wright, 2007
Tyler Hansbrough, 2009
Ty Lawson, 2009
Wayne Ellington, 2009
Ed Davis, 2010
Harrison Barnes, 2012
Kendall Marshall, 2012
John Henson, 2012
Tyler Zeller, 2012
Reggie Bullock, 2013
P. J. Hairston, 2014
Brice Johnson, 2016
Justin Jackson, 2017
Tony Bradley, 2017

(*) **First Overall Picks**

8

REGRET AND REDEMPTION

The move of an NCAA tournament site across state lines made a significant difference in which teams had a home crowd in 2017, and it seemed unfair to place the seventh-seeded basketball team from the University of South Carolina in Greenville. Seeds that low usually don't play so close to their home base in the early rounds, and the Gamecocks had thousands of alumni and fans living in the Palmetto State.

Duke, the No. 2 seed in the East, and top-seeded UNC in the South had earned placement closer to home, but they found a full house with mostly hostile fans waiting for them at the relocated venue in Greenville. The Bon Secours Wellness Arena, home of a minor league professional hockey franchise, had a seating capacity of more than 17,000 for basketball.

Both schools had bitter rivalries with South Carolina when the Gamecocks were in the ACC for the first eighteen years of the conference's existence—1953 through 1971.

While that was more than forty years ago, some rabid South

Carolina fans could recite chapter and verse about how their school was considered an outcast by the Big Four (Duke, UNC, N.C. State, and Wake Forest) in North Carolina, especially the Blue Devils and Tar Heels.

Duke's powerful athletic director Eddie Cameron led an investigation into the signing of 6'9" high school All-American Mike Grosso by South Carolina coach Frank McGuire in 1965. Grosso had not made the minimum 800 ACC score required to receive an athletic scholarship. McGuire claimed that Grosso's uncle in New Jersey was paying the tuition and other expenses so Grosso could attend South Carolina. The ACC ruled that was also a violation and banned Grosso, who transferred to Louisville (which was not in the ACC at that time). He played three seasons for the Cardinals, averaging 16.2 points and 14.3 rebounds for his career.

The bitterness grew so virulent between the two basketball programs that the ACC canceled the Duke–South Carolina home-and-home series for the 1967 season. They did play in the ACC tournament semifinals at the Greensboro Coliseum; Duke won 69–66 before the defending champion Blue Devils relinquished their title to UNC the next night.

The dislike for North Carolina was more incestuous. McGuire had been the Tar Heels' coach in 1957, when they won all 32 games and captured the NCAA championship by defeating Kansas and 7'1" All-American Wilt Chamberlain in triple overtime in Kansas City. McGuire left UNC in 1961 to coach the old NBA Philadelphia Warriors, whose star was the same Chamberlain. But that lasted one season. When the Warriors were sold and the team moved to San Francisco, McGuire resigned. After taking two years off from coaching, he was hired by South Carolina in 1964. His goal was to build the same kind of powerhouse he had in Chapel Hill, recruiting mainly from his native New York City and throughout the Northeast.

REGRET AND REDEMPTION

When McGuire's successor at UNC, his former assistant coach Dean Smith, rebuilt the Tar Heels into a top 10 program and won three straight ACC championships from 1967 to 1969, the two Carolinas began a rabid, almost vicious, rivalry. Upsets, near-fisticuffs, and racial epithets hurled at Charlie Scott, the Tar Heels' first back scholarship athlete, were commonplace when their two basketball teams played.

McGuire and Paul Dietzel, South Carolina's football coach at the time, were behind the school's withdrawal from the ACC in 1971. Both coaches believed that playing as independents would help them get bowl bids and NCAA tournament at-large invitations more easily than having to win the conference championship, which was the only way to qualify in those days. After South Carolina withdrew, the ACC operated with seven schools until it began gradual expansion with Georgia Tech in 1979. The conference grew to fourteen members in football and fifteen in basketball by 2014.

South Carolina joined the Southeastern Conference in 1991 and fielded nationally ranked teams that made the postseason under football coaches Lou Holtz and Steve Spurrier and basketball coach Eddie Fogler. In recent years, such success was more elusive, and the basketball coach in 2017, Frank Martin, finally had put together a formidable foe for any opponent. His latest team finished tied for third in the SEC (12–6) and was 22–10 when invited to the NCAA tournament.

The Gamecocks were built in the mold of taskmaster Martin, the son of Cuban exiles and a former nightclub bouncer, and they used defense as their mantra. South Carolina was among the stingiest teams in the country against shooters and ball handlers, fifth in 3-point percentage defense and in forcing turnovers. Martin's players were also in superb condition and prided themselves on wearing down teams in the second half with their aggressive play.

215

First-round games in the afternoon session in Greenville featured eighth-seeded Arkansas vs. No. 9 Seton Hall, and No. 1 seed North Carolina versus 16th-seeded Texas Southern. To that point in NCAA tournament history, a No. 1 seed had never lost to a No. 16 seed, a record of 126–0.

The only story line before UNC's game was Texas Southern head coach Mike Davis, a college basketball lifer who fifteen years earlier guided Indiana University to the 2002 NCAA championship game, losing to Maryland. Davis had been thrust into that job when Indiana president Myles Brand fired Hall of Fame coach Bobby Knight for "a persistent and troubling pattern of behavior." The dismissal came after Knight grabbed a student by the arm and lectured him about manners. It was the last of several controversies at IU engulfing the outspoken and fiery Knight, who eventually finished his career at Texas Tech in 2008 with the most all-time victories among Division I coaches.

Knight's abrupt departure led to a decision that benefited North Carolina. Sean May, a 2002 McDonald's All-American and son of former Indiana All-American Scott May, turned away from his father's alma mater and eventually signed with UNC. That was largely due to Scott May's relationship with Dean Smith and former Tar Heels star Phil Ford. Scott May, the leading scorer on Knight's 1976 unbeaten NCAA championship team, had played for Smith on the '76 U.S. Olympic team, which won the gold medal at the Summer Games in Montreal. Ford was the starting point guard on that team.

After Davis resigned under pressure at Indiana in 2006, he spent six years as head coach at Alabama-Birmingham and was in his fifth season at Texas Southern. The Tigers made the NCAA tournament in 2017 for the third time under Davis. They played in the small Southwestern Athletic Conference and were outmatched by Carolina from the opening tip.

REGRET AND REDEMPTION

The fifth-ranked Tar Heels led 52–27 at the half and cruised to a 103–64 victory, with six players scoring in double figures. Joel Berry wasn't one of them, going 1-for-8 shooting and suffering the first in a series of sprained ankles that would test his resolve through the tournament. Justin Jackson made five 3-pointers in the first half and tied former Tar Heel Shammond Williams with 95 in one season. (Jackson broke the UNC record in the next game against Arkansas and finished the season with 105.)

Jackson was coming off a 3-point shooting slump of 7-for-31 over four games, including two against Duke. He admitted to feeling pressure to prove he deserved the ACC Player of the Year award over the Blue Devils' Luke Kennard, a seemingly popular choice who actually finished fourth with only five votes compared to Jackson's 24. After heart-to-hearts with his mother, a former college basketball player, and Williams, the teammate known as "JJ" relaxed and made eight long shots in the first two NCAA games.

In the evening doubleheader, Duke handled 14-seed Troy by draining 10 3-pointers and shooting 52.8 percent in the first half to lead 52–38. The Blue Devils cooled off after halftime but were sent to the free throw line 16 times by the pursuing Trojans and won easily 87–65 for their fifth straight victory, a stretch that included the ACC tournament title. Grayson Allen led all scorers with 21 points, continuing to hear boos from all but Duke fans every time he touched the ball. He had become a villain in the minds of many because of his tripping incidents over the last two seasons.

The following game pitted South Carolina against 10th-seeded Marquette, which was coached by former Duke player and Krzyzewski assistant Steve Wojciechowski. The Gamecocks were trying to earn their first NCAA tournament victory in forty-four years to the day (since McGuire was there), and the Golden Eagles (né Warriors) were trying to reach the second round against a Duke program they had heard so much about from their own head coach, who was in his third season at the Milwaukee school.

After Marquette made eight 3-pointers in the first half and jumped out to a 26–16 lead, and was still ahead 40–39 at the break, South Carolina's defense turned the game around. The Gamecocks allowed only three 3-pointers in the second half and forced 12 of Marquette's 19 total turnovers. Afterward, Wojciechowski called the escalating physical play the difference.

"I thought the better team won tonight," he began. "They're a team that plays very hard and is incredibly physical. They were allowed to play really physical tonight."

When asked if he thought the officials permitted too much contact, Wojciechowski replied, "I'm not an official. I don't want to speak for them. I thought the game was really physical. That's how Frank's teams play."

That raised the distinct possibility that the former Duke lieutenant would advise Krzyzewski, his coaching mentor, that a big factor on Sunday would be how closely the Duke–South Carolina game was called.

At the press conference after Saturday's practice, Krzyzewski immediately picked up that theme when asked about South Carolina. "They're men and they're coached by a man," he said of Martin's team. "And so we're going to have to be men tomorrow night in order to beat them."

Coach K addressed two other links between Duke and South Carolina, one dating back to playing for Knight at the U.S. Military Academy. At the 1969 NIT in New York, Army upset McGuire's nationally ranked Gamecocks, and Krzyzewski was credited for holding South Carolina sophomore All-American John Roche to six points in the Cadets' 59–45 victory. "I did defend John Roche," he said, smiling. (An irony of that game: South Carolina went to the NIT after being knocked out of the ACC tournament by Duke in the last season for Hall of Fame coach Vic Bubas, who died in 2018 at age ninety-one.)

And there was another connection. When Coach K got the Duke coaching job in 1980, he replaced Bill Foster, who left for South Carolina.

"Bill was . . . one of the innovators about promotion," Krzyzewski said, then mused about Foster, who died in January 2016. "It would be unbelievable if he was a coach in this era to see what he would do with social media—he was just really innovative."

Inevitably, questions followed about Allen, the controversial junior who was still coming off the bench as the Blue Devils' sixth man. Recently, Allen's hometown newspaper, *The Florida Times-Union*, had published the story of a Duke coed, Savannah Goodman, also from Jacksonville, who suffered from a congenitally compromised immune system. Allen had befriended her at Duke and corresponded with her when she returned to Jacksonville for treatment. She had died on December 19, two days before Allen tripped an Elon player and received a one-game suspension. Krzyzewski was asked why Duke did not use that story to explain Allen's emotional state at the time.

"There's a lot of things all these kids do on all teams that go unnoticed," he said. "But it's called using your platform the right way, and not just for bringing attention to yourself, but bringing maybe comfort, some help to people and not everyone needs to know it. And he did that and he's done more. But we're not going to say, well, now it's okay that he tripped [someone]. We're not. That was wrong. But there's a lot more to it than that."

While he did not pardon his player's behavior on the court, Krzyzewski mildly chastised the media for taking the easy way out regarding

Allen's latest flagrant foul and not finding the story about his terminally ill friend, which apparently was no secret on the Duke campus.

"We live in this quick-judgment, shallow-analysis world really because of Twitter and all of this stuff to get something out," he said. "And we don't have to document anything. We don't have to investigate. We can hear something and we put it out. And then we're not held accountable for whether it was true or not. And it can take on a life of its own. And that's for any player. If someone wanted to look deeper, it wouldn't ruin their story."

By beating Seton Hall 77–71 in the other first-round game Friday afternoon, Arkansas advanced to its second NCAA game against North Carolina in three years and the schools' sixth postseason matchup in history. In three of those games, the Tar Heels faced Nolan Richardson, the first major college black head basketball coach in the South and in the old Southwest Conference, which broke up in 1996. Mike Anderson, who was in his sixth season at Arkansas, had brought back Richardson's famous philosophy of fast break offense and intense defense nicknamed "40 Minutes of Hell." In 2017, the unranked Razorbacks had developed a reputation as a second-half team.

That eventually spelled trouble for Carolina, which raced to a 30–13 lead in the first half, lost most of it by halftime, and fell behind the relentless Razorbacks by five points with under four minutes to play. The arena was alive with panicky Carolina fans and Duke supporters, many of whom were pleasantly surprised upon arriving for the second game to find their archrival on the brink of elimination.

During a television timeout with 3:43 left, Williams told his players:

"We haven't had this kind of game; we need to experience it. If we can get through this, it will be really good for us. All we have to do is play; we've done this in practice so many times."

The Tar Heels came back out refocused and after an Arkansas basket went on a stunning 12–0 run to finish the game. They wound up scoring on six of their last seven possessions, while shutting out Arkansas on its last seven trips down the court.

After Berry's two free throws cut the deficit to three points, their biggest baskets came from the two native North Carolina big men. Isaiah Hicks, who just had a shot blocked by Arkansas forward Moses Kingsley, slipped by him, took a pass from Jackson, and slammed home a dunk that made it a one-point game.

Two Hicks free throws gave the Tar Heels a 66–65 lead, and Kennedy Meeks got his hand on a Razorbacks 3-pointer and Carolina took possession. Berry found himself on the right wing with the ball and the shot clock winding down. He started to drive, got bumped, and, hoping for a foul, threw up a prayer. Meeks boxed out Kingsley and tipped in the missed shot with his left hand for a three-point lead with 44 seconds to play.

After forcing Arkansas' 19th turnover that resulted in a breakaway dunk by Jackson, Carolina went on to win 72–65, erasing the biggest deficit with less than three minutes to play in its long NCAA tournament history. The Tar Heels had somehow survived and moved on to the Sweet 16 in Memphis to play Butler.

Meeks finished with 16 points and 11 boards, the first of five straight double-digit rebounding games at the end of his college career. Jackson bounced back from a poor ACC tournament with another solid performance—15 points, eight rebounds, five steals, and five assists. A gimpy Berry shot only 2-for-13 and scored eight of his 10 points in the first half.

"He makes 40 percent of his 3-pointers, but he didn't do that today," Williams said. "Now we've got to rest his ankle. We feel very fortunate to still be playing."

As the exhausted Tar Heels boarded the bus for Greenville airport and a flight back to Chapel Hill, Duke had taken the court against South Carolina in a raucous building filled with fans from both Carolinas, pulling for an upset by the underdog Gamecocks. In comparison, there were relatively few Blue Devils rooters. After about five minutes, a heated Krzyzewski took off his jacket. The game wasn't being called to his liking.

South Carolina shot a dismal 20 percent (7-for-35) in the first half but trailed by only seven points at the break. Even after Duke went ahead 35–25 early in the second half, foul trouble and shaky shooting kept the Blue Devils from pulling away. The Gamecocks caught fire behind SEC Player of the Year Sindarius Thornwell, who led five players in double figures with 24 points. They shot 71.4 percent in the half while holding Duke's 3-point shooters to five of 19, including one of four from leading scorer Kennard. Duke's best overall performance came from senior Amile Jefferson, who finished with 14 points and 15 rebounds in his last college appearance.

The officials called 48 fouls in the game, and each team made 27 free throws. But the Blue Devils' 18 turnovers cost them in what was otherwise a statistical stalemate.

"I wish we had some of that tape that doesn't let water into the boat. . . . The game was very complex in the second half with the fouls," Krzyzewski said after the 88–81 defeat that ended Duke's season at 28–9. "We got worn down. It's the most physical game we've been in all year."

After the NCAA tournament, Kennard surprised Coach K and his staff by entering the NBA draft. He had averaged 19.5 points as a sophomore that season and improved his 3-point shooting by more than 100 percentage points from his freshman year to 43.8, setting a Duke record by going 6-for-6 at Wake Forest. He went to the Detroit Pistons as the 12th pick in the first round.

But freshman Jayson Tatum's pro stock was the highest in the entire ACC. Tatum, Duke's second-leading scorer with a 16.8 average, also turned pro and was the No. 3 overall pick by the Boston Celtics. He finished behind N.C. State one-and-done Dennis Smith Jr. for ACC Freshman of the Year. Smith went to the Dallas Mavericks as the ninth overall selection.

As further proof of his upside, Harry Giles entered the draft as a projected first-round selection and was taken by the Portland Trail Blazers with the 20th overall pick and then was immediately traded to Sacramento. Despite playing only two full seasons since his freshman year in high school, Giles' potential trumped his two injured knees.

All three players—plus second-round pick Frank Jackson—were assured to make millions. Tatum's contract, worth $5,645,400 in his first season, guaranteed him more than $12.3 million for two years and could be worth another $17.7 million if team options were picked up in the third and fourth years. Kennard made $2,759,280 as a rookie and was guaranteed more than $6 million for two seasons, with team options worth $9.1 million more in years three and four. Giles' deal guaranteed him more than $4 million, including $1,859,400 in his first season. Two years of team options could pay him more than $6.5 million more. Jackson, drafted by the Charlotte Hornets with the first pick in the second round, and then traded to the New Orleans Pelicans, was paid $815,615 in his rookie season. With a team option, he could make $3.8 million for three seasons, and even without the option, his guaranteed pay was almost $2.7 million.

Grayson Allen came back to Duke for his senior year. But with freshmen Tatum, Giles, and Jackson, and sophomore Kennard turning pro, plus Jefferson and Matt Jones graduating, the Blue Devils had lost six of their top seven. They had another No. 1 recruiting class in the country coming in, however.

The 2017 Sweet 16 in Memphis featured nine players who were in the NBA the next season, seven drafted in the first round. Most of their names were familiar to basketball fans, including UCLA's Lonzo Ball, Kentucky's De'Aaron Fox and Malik Monk, and North Carolina's Justin Jackson.

Although he had great athletic bloodlines, UNC sophomore Luke Maye was not considered more than a role player for the Tar Heels. He was 6'8" but without the requisite quickness and leaping ability for stars in big-time college basketball. With Duke out of the NCAA tournament and the local North Carolina coverage doubling-down, and the national media converging on Memphis, Maye was the surprise story of the weekend.

Having played in all 31 games, starting only one, Maye was known more for his gene pool than for his skill set. He earned Academic All-ACC honors, as did his father, Mark, a star quarterback for the football Tar Heels in the 1980s. His mother, Aimee, was a high school basketball star, and his younger brother Cole pitched for Florida's national championship baseball team in 2017.

Nice story but, until Memphis, nothing to write home about. Then Maye came off the bench against Butler in the South Regional semifinals, played 25 minutes, and recorded career highs of 16 points and 12 rebounds in Carolina's 92–80 win over the Bulldogs. The media was all over Roy Williams after the game, asking why this kid was only offered a scholarship after Brandon Ingram chose Duke.

"Shows you how dumb I am," Williams said.

Asked if Maye was better than he thought, Williams snapped,

"No!" The fastest way to get under a coach's skin was to suggest he couldn't recognize talent. Williams said he always believed Maye had potential and that he advised the Maye family to be patient; Luke would get his opportunity.

As a freshman, Maye got into 33 of the 40 games Carolina played during its national championship runner-up season. Most of his minutes were mop-up, 5.4 per game. None of his statistics forecast a great college career, and in 2017 he still averaged fewer than five points per game going into the NCAA tournament. The stats that stood out were roughly four rebounds and 39 percent 3-point shooting in 14 minutes per game. Those were signs that Maye could deliver under duress.

But nothing before or after the regional came close to matching what he did in Memphis. He made three 3-pointers against Butler and was the first Tar Heel to come off the bench and finish with a double-double in 12 years, since freshman one-and-done Marvin Williams, a first-round NBA lottery pick. By halftime against the Bulldogs, Maye had scored more points (14) than in any full game of his college career.

Despite Butler's persistence, UNC was never seriously threatened. Carolina was comfortable in Memphis, where in 2009 Tyler Hansbrough's team had advanced to the Final Four by beating Gonzaga and Oklahoma, which had All-American Blake Griffin. Roy Williams recruited in Memphis during his fifteen years at Kansas and had friends all over the hometown of Elvis Presley and birthplace of rock 'n' roll. He again kept his team at the famous Peabody Hotel and, as he had eight years earlier, walked the ducks to the lobby one morning, this time with his two grandsons as helpers. He had taken his players to eat pork ribs at his favorite barbecue haunt, the Rendezvous restaurant, the night before the Butler game, where reserve Shea Rush presented each teammate with a fedora hat he had made for them.

Two days later, the Tar Heels faced a rematch with No. 6 Kentucky, which had beaten Ball and UCLA in the other regional semifinal. The Wildcats had defeated UNC 103–100 at the CBS Sports Classic in Las Vegas in December. Like that one, this was a Final Four–type game, but only the winner was going on to Phoenix.

The Tar Heels never trailed in the first half, led by as many as nine points, and were ahead 38–33 at the break, even though Berry sprained his *other* ankle and still scored nine points in 15 minutes. Carolina shot 50 percent, and Maye made the only 3-pointer.

The second half had three dramatic swings of momentum over the last eight minutes. After Kentucky rallied to go up by five points with 5:10 remaining, Williams called a timeout and reminded his players they had come back from the exact same deficit against Arkansas, and that game would help them do it again. After another 12-point run, Carolina led by seven before the Wildcats made one more charge.

Maye was about to join Michael Jordan in Carolina's history of last-minute heroics, but he was playing his finest college game before that. In 20 minutes off the bench, he now had made five of eight field goals and two of three from 3-point range. He dove on the floor with 2:26 remaining to come up with a key defensive rebound as Carolina clung to a three-point advantage over the surging Wildcats.

In the last 34 seconds, Maye lofted a long pass to Jackson for a breakaway dunk and then stole the ball to preserve the Tar Heels' tenuous lead, as a sold-out arena and national television audience held on to see which of these blue bloods would join Gonzaga, Oregon, and South Carolina at the 2017 Final Four.

With the thousands of Kentucky fans roaring, Monk worked through a double-team by Jackson and Maye and hit a contested 3-pointer from the top of the key with 0:7.2 left to tie the game 73–73. Roy Williams disdained a timeout, which would have let Kentucky set up its defense; Meeks jumped out of bounds and threw the ball in to Theo Pinson, who was already on the move up the floor. Pinson was galloping, using up one of the fleeting seconds with every bounce. The junior, whose off-court antics had injected personality into the UNC program, thought he could take the ball to the basket for the winning shot, but two Kentucky defenders blocked his path.

"I'm about to make a play and win the game for us," Pinson said. "But making a play isn't just scoring."

Pinson looked over his left shoulder and saw Maye wide open on the left wing—Jordan territory—facing the basket. At that moment, it was a mirror image of Villanova's last play of the 2016 season, with Pinson as Ryan Arcidiacono and Maye as Kris Jenkins behind him but getting ready to spot up. Jenkins, ironically, was at the FedEx Forum to cheer on UNC's Nate Britt, his adopted brother, after the defending NCAA champion Wildcats were upset by Wisconsin the prior weekend.

Pinson dropped the ball to Maye, who went up from 19 feet with the cool of a hardened veteran. The ball had perfect loft and rotation and found the net without touching the rim; the clock showed 0:0.3 seconds left in regulation. Mayhem for Maye and his teammates and Tar Heels fans across the country, anguish for Big Blue Nation.

This obscure, onetime walk-on became the third player since 1985 to send his team to the Final Four with a buzzer-beater, joining Duke's Christian Laettner (who did it twice) and Villanova's Scottie Reynolds. Maye seemed stunned to be in such a bright spotlight, wearing a championship shirt and cap and surrounded by the media. And then hearing his name called as the Most Outstanding Player of the South Regional, the first Tar Heel off the bench to win MVP honors in the NCAA tournament. His 17 points, three rebounds, and game-winner outdid Jackson's 19 points, five rebounds, and four assists.

Berry, now nursing two sore ankles, missed all five of his 3-point shots and combined with Jackson in shooting 1-for-10 from outside, making Maye's marksmanship so critical.

"I just shot it, and luckily it went in," Maye said after the Tar Heels kept alive their chance for redemption. "Yes, it has to be the biggest moment" of his young life.

Thirty minutes later, after the nets had been stripped, Mark and Aimee Maye were outside the arena, trying to get back in. They had left to tend to a family member and heard the players were still on the court celebrating, but the doors were locked. The Mayes were ecstatic, of course, with one weekend still left to the season and their son helping his team get there.

But they had no idea what lay ahead for Luke and his basketball career.

The University of Phoenix Stadium in Glendale, Arizona, was prepared to welcome the second-largest crowd in NCAA Final Four history. The expected attendance for 2017 national semifinals Saturday wouldn't equal the 79,444 who showed up at AT&T Stadium in suburban Dallas for the 2014 Final Four. But it was going to be close.

This represented the best (attendance) and worst (seats) in college basketball.

The first Final Four played at a football stadium was in 1971, when UCLA won the title by beating Villanova in the Houston Astrodome. The next came in 1982, when UNC defeated Houston and Georgetown at the Superdome in New Orleans to win Dean Smith's first national championship. But the move to a domed stadium began with a regular-season game on January 20, 1968, a made-for-TV matchup between No. 1 UCLA with Lew Alcindor and No. 2 Houston with Elvin Hayes at the Astrodome. The attendance for that game was

52,693, primarily because the court sat at the 50-yard line and there were no spectator seats on the field.

In 1982, official attendance at the Superdome was 61,612 for the championship game. The basketball configuration for Final Fours in domed stadiums through 2008 placed the court in one end zone close to the permanent stands, with temporary bleachers moved in to cover the other sideline. Final Fours continued to sell out, with some fans paying premium prices to sit in the upper levels where they watched most of the game on the video boards. But they had their ticket stubs to prove they were there!

If it was an experiment by the NCAA, it worked. Only seven more Final Fours (1983, Albuquerque; 1985, Lexington, Kentucky; 1986, Dallas; 1988, Kansas City; 1990, Denver; 1994, Charlotte; and 1996, East Rutherford, New Jersey) were played in basketball arenas. And then the NCAA got real greedy.

In 2009, Ford Field became the experiment to do, sort of, what they did at the Astrodome almost forty-one years earlier.

To get more paying customers in, the NCAA placed a raised floor in the middle of the Detroit Lions home field and surrounded the court with more rows of chairs than the old configuration could accommodate. At a modest estimate of the average ticket for the 2009 Final Four being $100, the NCAA was looking at $15 million for the Saturday and Monday night sessions. And that average ticket price grew exponentially over the next eight years, along with the NCAA tournament revenues.

The announced attendance for the 2009 NCAA semifinal games was 72,456, and it was more than 70,000 for the next eight years— from Indianapolis twice, to Houston twice, to New Orleans, Atlanta, Dallas, and Phoenix. Only the 2018 Final Four in San Antonio at the slightly smaller Alamodome, which did not have an NFL tenant, kept the attendance down to 68,257.

So when the Tar Heels talked about getting back to the big stage, they weren't kidding. Between his Final Four teams of 1972 and 1977, Dean Smith was amazed at how much the last weekend of the NCAA tournament had exploded with interest.

In 1982, he did not like taking the game James Naismith invented to a cavernous domed stadium, but at least the third-place consolation game that Smith had lobbied for years to abolish was finally gone. Within five more years, the 3-pointer was added to the college game, and Carolina teams were knocked out of three Final Fours on Saturday with bad, some very bad, shooting performances in domes.

In 1991, the Tar Heels were ousted by Williams' Kansas Jayhawks after missing 15 of 18 3-pointers, including 0-for-7 by All-ACC guard Rick Fox, at the old Indianapolis Hoosier Dome. In 1995, 50 percent 3-point shooter Dante Calabria also went 0-for-7 in a loss to Arkansas at the Seattle Kingdome. And back in Indy in 1997, Carolina shot 4-for-21 from the arc in losing to Arizona. After Smith turned the team over to Bill Guthridge, the 1998 Tar Heels shot their way out of the Final Four in San Antonio by going 3-for-23 from "3" against Utah.

But at least in Smith's second national championship back in New Orleans in 1993, Donald Williams won Most Outstanding Player by making 10 of 14 3-pointers combined in the semifinals and final.

Still, Smith hated the lengthy walk from the playing floor to the locker rooms and the bigness of it all. That same year, he took a cab to the Superdome after the team had bused over from the hotel. The security guards did not recognize him and wouldn't let him in, and Smith threatened to leave and have Guthridge coach the Tar Heels against Michigan's Fab Five in the championship game. True story.

Smith was at the Edward Jones Dome in St. Louis to watch Williams win his first national championship in 2005, and he groused about how long it took him and Michael Jordan to reach the locker room to congratulate the team. Smith had grown ill before the 2009 Final Four; by all accounts he would have not liked a basketball game played in the middle of a football field.

For Williams, his goal every season was to make the Final Four. If he did and the games were scheduled on Mars, he and his team would be booking the first spaceship out. Their 2017 appearance was especially important to him because it erased part of the bad taste from losing to Villanova in what he termed a gut-punch. Brice Johnson and Marcus Paige were gone, but Williams wanted it badly for the other guys who had come so close the year before. He also wanted it for his school, which was still in the middle of a seemingly never-ending fight with the NCAA over whether any bylaws had been violated.

Williams received nasty letters calling him a cheater and could hardly watch a game tape without some announcer referring to what he called the "junk" that had been permeating UNC for more than three years. He believed his players had done nothing wrong, and he said coaching them at practice every day was his salvation.

Getting to Phoenix and working out Friday with thousands of people watching renewed Williams and made him more determined to go home with the championship trophy this time.

But Joel Berry was now dealing with two sprained ankles and was under the constant care of the team trainers. The Tar Heels were not good enough to win it all without their motor and quarterback, as witnessed in the ACC tournament when Berry fell into foul trouble against Duke.

Saturday's semifinals opponent Oregon, known for its length and speed, had not been to the Final Four since winning it in 1939, the inaugural year of the NCAA tournament. In the other semifinal, neither team had been to a Final Four. Gonzaga, coached by respected colleague Mark Few, was always among the best prepared, most underrated teams in the country. And South Carolina was a Cinderella with knee pads, having scraped its way through the East Regional in New York City.

The other Carolina—the one in Chapel Hill—would have to adjust to the weird depth perception in this particular dome and again depend on the veterans Williams was so lucky to have in the mercurial world of college basketball. They would set the tone and get them all to Monday night.

The Final Four featured no bigger poster child, literally, for staying in college all four years than Carolina's Kennedy Meeks.

The senior from Charlotte enrolled at UNC in the summer of 2013, and as a freshman was listed on the Tar Heels roster at 6'9" and 290 pounds, far more of it soft tissue than muscle mass. Meeks was something of an athletic phenomenon, always battling his weight but good enough to be a five-star recruit and McDonald's All-American who also lettered in tennis for three years at West Charlotte High School.

A starter since midway through his freshman season, Meeks was one half of the post tandem with Brice Johnson constantly being called soft by critics; at times that included their head coach. Williams knew he had two talented big men but remained frustrated over their level of intensity, especially on the defensive end.

"I've told them both they can play at the next level, if they will just work harder at it every day," Williams said early in the 2015 season.

Going into the 2017 NCAA tournament, Meeks' best season statistically was as a sophomore, when he played more than 23 minutes a game and combined with Johnson to average better than 24 points and 15 rebounds. Meeks regressed slightly as a junior and was often labeled a disappointment by Tar Heels fans, compared to Johnson, who blossomed into a first-team All-American and projected first-round NBA draftee.

With Johnson graduated, Meeks became the first inside option as a senior and delivered by starting all 40 games. He averaged close to a double-double during the regular season but did not appear regularly on NBA mock draft boards. However, the Tar Heels were successfully countering Duke's one-and-done approach by starting upperclassmen, including Meeks, on consecutive Final Four teams.

Meeks arrived in Phoenix with the 2017 Tar Heels a sculpted senior having grown one inch and having lost 30 pounds from that freshman roster. His shoulders, which had become broader than his waist, actually formed a "V" with his toned buttocks. That's what four years of pumping iron and running sprints did for him.

Tyler Hansbrough was the most famous four-year player during the one-and-done era. Posting consistent numbers over his entire career, he could have turned pro as a first-round NBA draft pick after his first three All-American seasons at Carolina. Hansbrough stayed because he liked being a college athlete and, perhaps, he had an inkling that his in-between size (6'9" and 250 pounds) would not allow him to be the dominating banger in pro basketball that he was as an amateur. He left Chapel Hill as the most decorated Tar Heel in history and was a marginal pro and eventually among the internet's "15 most forgotten NCAA stars."

Meeks' only hope of playing in the NBA was to stay in college until his eligibility ran out and he could improve his conditioning and his game. He tested the waters after his junior season and barely got his big toe wet, not being invited to the NBA Combine to get evaluated by pro coaches and general managers. His choices to turn pro were trying to make a team as a free agent, after already being rejected at first glance, or go to Europe, where his size, skill, and alluring smile could have resulted in a nice career with little hope of ever being signed by an NBA team.

The best alternative was to return to UNC for his senior year and help lead his team back to the Final Four and bask in the spotlight one last time. His career statistics were not dissimilar to his last three college seasons, but he had warmed up for the NCAA tournament with those 19 points and 12 rebounds in the ACC tournament semifinals against Duke. Despite the defeat, it was Meeks' best career game in nine against the archrival Blue Devils.

In the second-round game against Arkansas, his 12th double-double of the season (16 and 11) was punctuated by the crucial tip-in with less than one minute left. It gave Carolina a three-point lead and helped the Tar Heels avoid elimination in the tournament. Meeks did it by combining his trimmed-down body and improved dexterity with the coaching of Williams, who harped on Meeks for four years about fighting to get inside position when the shot went up.

"He always says to try to get in front of the defender, because you have an easier rebound that way," Meeks said, "so that's what I did." The game was on national television, and that was one of the plays Meeks made over the next three weeks that likely changed the minds of some NBA coaches about his potential to play in the league. Suddenly, his decision to stay in school looked like the right move.

Meeks continued to be a beast on the boards with 11 rebounds against Butler in the Sweet 16 and a career-high 17, plus four blocks, against Kentucky in the South Regional championship game. He also started the winning play by adroitly inbounding the ball to Pinson as the Wildcats were caught momentarily celebrating Monk's 3-pointer, which tied the score. The victory meant that Meeks' four-year record would include starting in two straight Final Fours—and much more.

REGRET AND REDEMPTION

The Saturday semifinals at University of Phoenix Stadium proved to be a showcase for Meeks. He matched another career high with 25 points and finished with 14 rebounds against Oregon, his 13th double-double of the season. The last of his eight offensive rebounds came in the closing seconds. Berry was at the free throw line for two shots, and the Tar Heels' lead had been cut from nine points to one in less than six minutes. After Berry missed both free throws, Meeks slipped around Oregon's Jordan Bell, the game's leading rebounder with 16, to snatch the ball away. He whipped it back out to Pinson as the Tar Heels ran off the final four seconds of the 77–76 victory and advanced to the championship game against Gonzaga.

Meeks made 11 of 13 shots against Oregon and joined an elite list of owning one of the top five field goal percentage performances in the Final Four. UCLA's Bill Walton made 21 of 22 shots against Memphis in 1973. UNC's Sean May tied Jerry Lucas of Ohio State and Billy Thompson of Louisville for second on the list, hitting 10 of 11 against Illinois in the 2005 NCAA title game. Meeks was fifth, tying Walton's 84.6 percent shooting against Louisville in the 1972 Final Four.

As it turned out, Meeks wasn't the only late bloomer starting in the post for Carolina. Isaiah Hicks was more highly touted than Meeks when he arrived in Chapel Hill but suffered even greater early struggles. Hicks had 34 points, 30 rebounds, and seven blocked shots for Oxford Webb in the 2013 North Carolina 3A high school championship game, won by the Warriors over Statesville. He was named the state's Associated Press High School Player of the Year as a senior and earned *Parade* and McDonald's All-American honors. With that résumé, most 6'8" freshmen would be some kind of factor in college basketball. Playing only 7.3 minutes a game, Hicks averaged 1.2 points and one rebound and did not reach double figures in either category in any of the 34 games he played.

With James Michael McAdoo, Johnson, Meeks, and Joel James rotating in the post, Hicks played mostly small forward as a freshman and had trouble guarding quicker players. As a sophomore, and McAdoo having turned pro, Hicks moved into the post and doubled his playing time. He averaged 6.6 points and 3.0 rebounds per game but, by far, led the team in personal fouls per minutes on the court. That became a constant problem throughout his career.

As a junior, Hicks played in all 40 games and started three when Meeks was injured, improving enough to be named the ACC's Sixth Man of the Year. His statistics were similar to Meeks' numbers, averaging slightly fewer points and rebounds but shooting high percentages from the floor and free throw line. Villanova's Jenkins hit the winning shot over Hicks' outstretched arm to win the 2016 national championship, but Williams pointedly said at a press conference after the season that Hicks' defense did not cost Carolina the game.

After Johnson graduated and Hicks moved into the starting lineup as a senior, the expectations had been lowered by his first three seasons. He did not post a single double-double and fouled out of five games while continuing to lead the team in personal fouls per minutes played. His averages rose to 5.5 rebounds and 11.8 points per game, and he scored 19 or more six times. But he was never more important to his team than in his last college game, when he played 30 minutes, had 13 points, nine rebounds, and two blocked shots against Gonzaga and scored, arguably, the biggest basket of the season.

Nigel Williams-Goss, the Zags' leading scorer with 15 points in the game, gave his team the lead three times with jumpers in the final five minutes, the third putting Gonzaga on top 65–63 with 1:55 to play. Justin Jackson took a bullet pass from Pinson, made a layup, and was fouled, completing the three-point play that pushed the Tar Heels ahead by a point with 1:40 left to play. In a game when both teams shot poorly and Carolina missed 23 of 27 3-pointers and 11 of 26 free throws, the score remained 66–65 in UNC's favor until 27 seconds were left.

With the shot clock under five seconds, Hicks drove the lane on Williams-Goss, warded him off with his left arm, and made a right-handed hanging banker to give his team a 3-point lead. At the other end, Meeks leaped to block Williams-Goss' shot in the lane, and Jackson took the outlet pass for a redemptive dunk for the Tar Heels, who would not be denied the title a second straight time. They finished the 2017 season with a 33–7 record and the school's sixth NCAA championship.

This time, the confetti fell on Carolina. Berry was named Most Outstanding Player in the Final Four after finishing with 22 points against Gonzaga and becoming the first player since Walton in 1972 and '73 to score at least 20 points in consecutive NCAA championship games. The award, which came with Berry's jersey headed for the rafters at the Smith Center, easily could have gone to Meeks, whose 34 points, 24 rebounds, three blocks, and five steals put him on the All-Final Four team with Berry and Jackson.

Seniors Meeks and Hicks, who hadn't quite met their lofty high school reputations, saved their best for last. Meeks, one of six Tar Heels to start in two national championship games (joining Berry and Jackson and Jimmy Black, Sam Perkins and James Worthy in 1981 and '82), had key rebounds and blocked shots throughout the tournament, including the last rejection, which made the cover of *Sports Illustrated* with the headline REDEEM TEAM. Hicks, one of twelve Tar Heels to *play* in two NCAA title games, had difficulty scoring consistently and avoiding foul trouble during his career, but he made the victory-preserving basket against Gonzaga.

Although neither was drafted, both signed two-way NBA contracts as free agents, Meeks with the Toronto Raptors and Hicks with the New York Knicks. They had a chance to make the NBA rosters but were expected to start the season with the G League teams of each franchise and try to play their way up.

Justin Jackson entered the draft after averaging 18.3 points as a junior and shooting 37 percent from 3-point range, an increase of more than 70 percent from his sophomore season. The Portland Trail Blazers took him with the No. 15 overall pick, then traded his rights to the Sacramento Kings. Jackson signed a contract that paid him $2,365,560 in his rookie season and guaranteed him more than $5 million for two seasons. Including two more years with a team option, the contract could be worth more than $13.4 million. He also got engaged and, in August before NBA training camps opened, married University of Florida basketball player Brooke Copeland.

Tony Bradley, the 6'10" freshman from Bartow, Florida, played in 38 out of 40 UNC games in 2017 but did not start in any of them. He averaged 14.6 minutes per game, and his 7.1 scoring and 5.1 rebounding numbers showed enough potential to make him a projected late first- or second-round NBA draft pick. Williams told Bradley's family that, if he returned for his sophomore season, Bradley could be a lottery pick (first 14) in the 2018 draft. But his father apparently had final say.

At the team hotel in Phoenix before the players boarded the bus, Tony Bradley Sr. told his son, "Go play your game and then cash a check." In two Final Four games, young Bradley combined for seven points and 13 rebounds in 28 minutes, slightly below his season averages. Bradley entered the 2017 draft and, even though no team guaranteed Williams it would pick Bradley in the first round, stayed in when the deadline passed to opt out and return to school. The Lakers selected Bradley with the 28th overall pick and then traded him to Utah. Bradley signed a two-year contract worth a guaranteed

$3,094,440 with two more years at a club option that could make the deal worth more than $8.5 million.

On the sixtieth anniversary of UNC's 1957 NCAA basketball title, its first of the six, the Tar Heels held their third national championship celebration with Roy Williams as their head coach. Thousands of fans greeted the team at the Smith Center, and the players and coaches were feted by celebrity fans that included North Carolina governor Roy Cooper, a UNC graduate and Morehead Scholar who was elected the previous November.

Williams received an invitation for the team to visit the White House and President Trump. He asked for a list of days when the new POTUS would be available to host the Tar Heels. It wasn't clear why it happened—and whether it was a result of Williams' relationship with former President Obama and/or his needling of Trump during the ACC tournament about the president's tweeting fetish—but the Tar Heels never went. They didn't go after winning in 2005, when George W. Bush was president, but did after the 2009 title, when Obama was in the White House.

"We couldn't find a date that worked for both parties," UNC spokesman Steve Kirschner said. "We tried about eight or nine dates and between them, we couldn't work out that date, so—we would have liked to have gone, but not going." Kirschner added that the "players were fine with going."

ONE-AND-DONE PLAYERS

Duke (17)
Corey Maggette, 1999
Luol Deng, 2004
Kyrie Irving, 2011
Austin Rivers, 2012
Jabari Parker, 2014
Rodney Hood, 2014
Jahlil Okafor, 2015
Justise Winslow, 2015
Tyus Jones, 2015
Brandon Ingram, 2016
Jayson Tatum, 2017
Harry Gilles, 2017
Frank Jackson, 2017*
Marvin Bagley III
Wendell Carter Jr.
Gary Trent Jr.*
Trevon Duval**

UNC (4)
Robert McAdoo, 1972
Marvin Williams, 2005
Brandan Wright, 2007
Tony Bradley, 2017

(*) Second-round draft pick
(**) Undrafted

NOTE: Duke had 14 transfers during the twenty-first century; UNC had 6.
NOTE: UNC had 26 early departures for the NBA in the twenty-first century; Duke had 24.

9

BAD ENDINGS

Except for a shocking federal investigation into college basketball that touched the ACC in big and small ways, the fifteenth season of the Blue Blood rivalry—circa Mike Krzyzewski versus Roy Williams— began just the way one expected.

Duke started four brand-new freshmen and one senior, who could have and probably should have gone to the NBA earlier. Carolina, for the third straight season, started two seniors on a nationally ranked team—almost unheard of in the full-blown era of one-and-dones.

Both had good seasons, but neither got where it wanted to go.

The Blue Devils were trying to validate their controversial recruiting strategy of bringing them in and pushing them out. Krzyzewski looked somewhat like the Bill Belichick of college basketball, maneuvering his roster from season to season rather than building a unit for the long term as he had for years.

The Tar Heels were left with three freshmen big men who weren't ready and the team lacked experience inside, ironically, because UNC lost only its third one-and-done player in twelve years. Had Tony

Bradley returned for his sophomore season, Carolina would have been among the favorites to reach a third straight Final Four.

Coach K succeeded again with one of his goals. His thirty-eighth Duke team had captured the headlines since he signed his latest five-star class and was immediately installed as a Final Four pick to win the 2018 national championship, with a preseason ranking of No. 1. Keeping the Blue Devils in the news and high in the polls helped solidify Krzyzewski's next recruiting class, and it wasn't long before fans and the media were talking as much about the 2019 team as the one about to play that season.

Marvin Bagley III, the No. 1 forward in the high school classes of 2017 and '18, pushed a recruiting haul already near the top over it when he reclassified from a junior in high school to a graduating senior and, presto, committed to Duke in August 2017. He wanted to wear his favorite number, 35, which had been retired since All-American Danny Ferry wore it from 1985 to 1989. "I think it's great for Marvin to have 35 if he desires," Ferry said, "and we'll warmly welcome him to the Duke family."

The bearded 6'11" southpaw with the 7'1" wingspan joined three top 20 prospects—6'10" Wendell Carter Jr., 6'6" Gary Trent Jr., and 6'3" Trevon Duval—and top 100s Alex O'Connell and Jordan Tucker and three-star recruit Jordan Goldwire. Because Bagley, Carter, Trent, and Duval were superior talents, they and senior Grayson Allen were anointed as the first five from the day they stepped on campus, the first time four freshmen started for the Blue Devils since 1983, when they had yet to become a national power under Krzyzewski. This gave the Duke coaches a jump on building team chemistry, if not the kind of man-to-man defense they wanted.

Bagley, who was eighteen and the age of most college freshmen, said Duke had been recruiting him for more than three years and was among the schools that offered him a scholarship as a 6'8" fourteen-year-old in Phoenix. That relationship was enhanced by Jerry Colangelo, the former owner and president of the NBA Suns and managing director of USA Basketball. Colangelo had hired Krzyzewski in 2005 as the U.S. national team coach for the Olympic Games.

Perhaps more important than the Phoenix connection was Bagley's father, who grew up in Durham and was a football star at North Carolina A&T in Greensboro; and his grandfather, "Pogo Joe" Caldwell, pro basketball's renowned leaper who played for the Carolina Cougars of the old ABA after he won a lawsuit for his release from the NBA. "We knew about Marvin through Jerry but also 'Jumpin' Joe,'" Coach K said.

"I really trusted the coaching staff over there," Bagley said after signing with Duke. "They told me if I went there, it would go smooth and make me better. I'm very happy with my decision."

Sophomore Marques Bolden, a 6'11" five-star recruit who missed 13 games as a freshman due to injuries, considered transferring closer to his home in Texas but decided to stay when he thought he might start next to Carter, the No. 5-ranked recruit in his high school class from Atlanta. Then Bagley committed and Bolden went back to the bench, got hurt again, and missed eight games and averaged 13 minutes when he was healthy enough to play.

Javin DeLaurier, one of the best pure athletes on the team, also lost his chance to start when the superstuds signed. But the 6'10" sophomore and 6'6" O'Connell, the son of former 1970s Blue Devil Dave O'Connell, and 6'2" backup point guard Goldwire gave Duke more depth than it had the season before. For Tucker, a 6'7" forward whom Krzyzewski had stolen from Syracuse at the eleventh hour, there was too much depth and he joined the more than one dozen scholarship players to flee Coach K's program when he left at the semester break and transferred to Butler.

The newcomers meshed with the returnees, as they had in years past, but there was still too much defense to learn and too little time and interest for freshmen already with one eye on the NBA. So Krzyzewski made zone part of the practice plan from day one. And when asked about it by the media, he used the old analogy that "there are so many zone principles in man-to-man." Indeed, when playing man-to-man and the players constantly switched whom they were guarding, wasn't that in essence a zone defense?

"When we have a majority of guys more than one year—a good crux of guys—you are able to teach man-to-man at a level that is incredibly adaptable to the opponent you are facing," Coach K said during the 2018 season. "We have not been able to do that with all these young guys. We also have a lot of bigger guys, and it fits better in what we do in zone."

Duke improved statistically on defense as the 2018 season wore on, climbing from No. 116 nationally in defensive efficiency in early January to No. 22 in early March after going all zone in February. "You said we were really bad on defense early in the season, and now you say we're really good," Krzyzewski chided the media in March. "So which is it?"

Coach K said that early in the season his team did not always do what he asked of them in games. "Not necessarily, have you been in some of our huddles?" he pondered to the media. "Holy mackerel."

Bad defense didn't keep the Blue Devils from winning their first 11 games of the 2018 season and maintaining their top ranking. That included an 88–81 victory over No. 2 Michigan State at the United Center in Chicago, where Bagley played only 10 minutes before suffering an eye injury. Allen erupted for a career-high 37 points (seven of 11 3-pointers), Carter had a 12 and 12 double-double, and Duval, the top point guard in his recruiting class, dished for 10 assists.

BAD ENDINGS

They were tested twice at the PK80 tournament in Portland but came back to erase second-half deficits against Texas in overtime and seventh-ranked Florida, which led by 17 points with about 10 minutes remaining. Bagley was dominant with 30 points and 15 rebounds. Despite closing November at 9–0 and sill ranked No. 1, Duke had shown some serious flaws in defense, intensity, and bench scoring, which was almost nonexistent.

The Blue Devils went to Boston College for an early ACC opener on December 9, 2017. Continuing to mix man-to-man and zone, they were burned by BC's Jerome Robinson, Jordan Chatman, and Ky Bowman, who combined for 13 3-pointers, in a shocking 89–84 upset. Duke had rallied to lead by four points late and, perhaps thinking another comeback win had been pulled off, then let the Eagles take back the game. Bowman, who once had committed to play football at North Carolina, finished with 30 points, 10 rebounds, and nine assists. The team picked 14th (out of 15) in the ACC was in first place, and the heavy favorite to win the conference regular season was alone at the bottom of the league standings for three weeks until the ACC schedule resumed.

After beating Florida State in Durham, the Blue Devils opened January with a short trip to N.C. State, which had a measure of Duke's number at home. The Wolfpack upset the now second-ranked team at PNC Arena 96–85, the fourth time in six games over the prior nine years the Blue Devils had lost on State's home floor. Bagley's 31 points were poorly supported by their three-of-15 shooting from the arc, and Duke fell to seventh in the polls and 13–2 for the season.

A subsequent five-game winning streak ended with a loss to Virginia, Duke's third ACC defeat and first at home to the Cavaliers in twenty-three years. The Blue Devils played zone the entire second half, rallying from a double-digit deficit to take the lead before the second-ranked Cavs showed why they eventually won the ACC regular season, stealing the 65–63 win at Cameron, which had gone from chaos to comatose at the end.

From almost the beginning of time, UNC basketball had been an inside-out program. From Frank McGuire to Smith and Guthridge to Williams, Carolina guards came down the court and looked for a big man at the low post before starting a play on the perimeter or going to the team's freelance offense. Now, seniors Joel Berry and Theo Pinson didn't have Brice Johnson, Kennedy Meeks, or Isaiah Hicks down on the low block. Instead there were three freshmen— Garrison Brooks, Sterling Manley, or Brandon Huffman—all close in height as well as inexperience.

At one preseason practice, Williams jumped all over his guards during a scrimmage for not throwing "the damn ball inside. You may not think they can score, but they can get fouled trying if they have the ball!"

The 6'9" Brooks, from Lafayette, Alabama, originally signed with Mississippi State, where his father, George Brooks, played and was an assistant coach. Bulldogs head coach Ben Howland granted Brooks' full release, saying he did not want to "put him in a situation that causes further family hardship." Apparently, Brooks' mother wanted him to go farther away to college. He started the first 16 games for UNC, averaging about 18 minutes. Brooks was considered the best defensive player of the three freshmen but averaged only 5.8 points and 4.6 rebounds as a starter. His minutes and numbers decreased when he came off the bench, after being replaced by graduate school transfer Cameron Johnson.

Manley missed most of his junior and senior high school seasons in Ohio after breaking each of his legs, dropping him down the recruiting rankings to the 267th prospect in his class and 64th power forward. His coaches sent a tape to UNC assistant Steve Robinson, who showed it to Williams. They decided to take a look at the 6'11" Manley, who had athletic bloodlines; his great-great-uncle Willie Thrower was the first black quarterback in the NFL, joining the Chicago Bears in 1953. Despite displaying the best offensive moves of the three young post men, conditioning remained a problem for Manley; he had trouble making his required time for the mile run and wound up averaging 5.4 points and 3.6 rebounds in 10 minutes per game, plus blocking the second-most shots on the team with 24, behind Luke Maye's 38.

The 6'10" Huffman, from Goldsboro, North Carolina, was the least skilled but bulkiest big man at 250 pounds. He was a ferocious dunker who didn't show much more offensive skill. As the ACC season and tournaments progressed, Huffman got less time and did not play at all against the smaller, quicker opponents.

UNC's most talented freshman, 6'3" Jalek Felton, the nephew of 2005 star Raymond Felton, dropped out of school in late January after being suspended for an undisclosed violation of university policy and wound up playing in Slovenia the next year. Asked if Felton was guilty of any charges, Williams said, "He was guilty of being dumb," and added he could not elaborate for privacy reasons. Before that, Felton had made four of five 3-pointers in an 86–72 win over Ohio State in New Orleans, even though opponents refused to double the post, making it difficult for Carolina to beat them from outside.

This came three days after the Tar Heels suffered a surprising second loss of the season to tiny Wofford College at the Smith Center. Up to that point, they had lost only to fourth-ranked Michigan State at the PK80 tourney, shooting 24.6 percent in a 63–45 defeat. After that, UNC won five straight, beating eventual Big Ten champion

Michigan at home and rallying in Knoxville to edge No. 20 Tennessee and coach Rick Barnes, a former Dean Smith antagonist but now a good friend of Williams from their days coaching in the Big 12 Conference.

Carolina began ACC play on December 30 with an unimpressive home win over Wake Forest, except for Maye's eighth double-double of the young season. Knowing he would be a starter, Maye worked tirelessly over the summer to change his body and improve as a scorer and rebounder. He already had 28 points and 16 rebounds against Arkansas in Portland and 24 and 17 against Davidson, with a huge hometown following from neighboring Huntersville leading the Carolina cheers in Charlotte.

The No. 12 Tar Heels went to Florida State on January 3 with a 12–2 record. They trailed the 24th-ranked Seminoles 51–40 at the half but came all the way back and had a shot to win before Berry's drive to the basket to steal the game in his home state was thwarted. Carolina left Tallahassee an 81–80 loser with a trip to Virginia scheduled next. After getting a combined six points and 13 rebounds from his freshman bigs in the team's dreadful shooting performance (29.6 percent) and 61–49 loss in Charlottesville, Williams made the lineup change.

He wanted his five best scorers on the court to ramp up Carolina's running game. Cameron Johnson, who had transferred after winning a fight with his undergraduate school, Pitt, to play his two remaining seasons of eligibility at UNC, had come off the bench as the sixth man since missing the first 11 games recovering from a sprained neck and minor knee surgery. He was supposed to fill the spot, and much of the role, Justin Jackson had played for the prior three years. Both were 6'8" and could hit the 3-pointer, but they had different nuances to their game, and the returning Tar Heels needed time to grow as accustomed to Johnson as they had been to Jackson.

BAD ENDINGS

Junior Kenny Williams, who missed the 2017 championship run with knee surgery, had come back with renewed confidence as a shooter and defender and showed remarkable aptitude as an offensive rebounder for a 6'4" guard. Up to this point in the season, however, Maye had been the biggest story.

After surfacing from near-obscurity at the 2017 South Regional in the Sweet 16 victory over Butler, then hitting the winner against Kentucky to send Carolina back to the Final Four, Maye inherited the power forward position from Hicks. He turned out to be more of a "stretch 4" who could hold his own in the paint and go outside to hit the medium- and long-range jumper. Still, few expected his 3.4 career scoring average to quintuple and his 2.8 rebounding average to more than triple as a junior.

From the first week of the season, Maye went from a popular sub fans serenaded with calls of "Luuuke" when he did *anything*, to a Larry Bird–type player who never looked like he did as much as his stat sheet showed. In his first five games as a starter, Maye averaged 21.2 points and 10.8 rebounds. Realistically, he couldn't keep it up once ACC play started, but he did even better in some games.

Maye scored more than 30 points three times and in all of those games had double-doubles with 18, 12, and 17 rebounds. Yet Maye, or his fellow starters with more experience, could not save Carolina from losing three straight games at Virginia Tech, at home to N.C. State, and at Clemson, which left the Tar Heels 5–5 in the ACC by late January and jeopardized their NCAA tournament chances.

UNC had its basketball "family" and Duke's former players called themselves a "brotherhood." Like many other college athletic teams, both programs have dozens of unpublished stories on how they have helped former players with personal problems or rejoiced in their off-court accomplishments long after they were out of school.

Roy Williams was big on celebrating family ties, and the weekend

of the home loss to State, Dean Smith's first three ACC championship and Final Four teams assembled in Chapel Hill for a fifty-year
anniversary celebration. The group included Larry Miller, the only
two-time ACC Player of the Year in UNC history, and Charlie Scott,
the first black scholarship athlete at Carolina and the first African
American basketball *star* in the ACC and the South.

The Tar Heels got back in the victory column by routing last-place
Pitt, and now they faced Duke in Chapel Hill, a visit to N.C. State,
and a home game against Notre Dame in five days—the only ACC
team to have that scheduling challenge in 2018.

But with the other starters, especially Theo Pinson emerging as a
scorer, Carolina turned its season back in the right direction.

Some teams knew how to stretch the monstrous Duke zone better
than others, and when that happened the Blue Devils left holes that
were easily filled by opponents who screened, cut, and drove to get,
and make, easy shots.

Carolina was one of those teams, and the Tar Heels' success against
Duke continued the metamorphosis of Williams as a pure basketball
coach, not just a relentless recruiter at a school, like Duke, that attracted interest from the best high school players almost organically.

Ol' Roy claimed to work harder than most coaches, keeping track
of how many times he watched a kid he wanted versus how often the
opposition coaches did. And, too, Williams was lucky to have split
his thirty years as a head coach between Kansas, the king of the Midwest, and Carolina, the best public school program in the Southeast
not named Kentucky.

Williams needed perhaps the best leadership he ever had to help
cover the Tar Heels' obvious weaknesses, just as Krzyzewski needed
Grayson Allen to be a mature senior and no longer the volatile player

who had been stripped of his captaincy as a junior for committing another tripping foul.

Duke arrived at the Smith Center on Thursday night, February 8, having lost to Virginia at home and unranked St. John's at Madison Square Garden in two of its last three games after winning five in a row. Krzyzewski called the 81–77 loss to the Red Storm, which was winless in the Big East at that time, "disgusting," among other adjectives. But after five days of rest, meetings, and practices, the Blue Devils were ready to beat their archrivals for the sixth time in the last nine years on their home court.

Carolina knew Duke was taller and more talented, if greener. The Tar Heels hoped to hit some early 3-pointers against the 2-3 zone, opening the middle for Maye and Pinson to operate as facilitators from the high post, where their passing and driving skills could create opportunities to draw fouls close to the basket. When the Blue Devils shot 56.8 percent in the first half, made five of 11 of their 3-pointers, and once led by 12 points, the roaring home fans almost willed their team to a late run that cut the halftime deficit to four points, 49–45.

This was another breakout game for Johnson, who scored 32 points in the 82–78 loss at Clemson, and Kenny Williams, who had fallen into a scoring slump by not looking for his shot more aggressively. Williams came out firing and hit four 3-pointers in the first half and two more in the second half, which Carolina opened with a 16–2 run. Johnson's fourth 3-pointer with 3:12 remaining broke a five-and-a-half-minute scoring drought for the Tar Heels and gave them a 77–71 lead. The Dean Dome crowd, which came *hoping* for a win more than expecting one, exploded in appreciation.

With the Blue Devils using a rusty full-court press in the final 15 seconds, both Bagley and Carter were caught in no-man's-land as Pinson took a pass from Johnson and blew by both of them for a

two-handed dunk that sealed the 82–78 victory. "What a performance by North Carolina in the second half!" ESPN's Jay Bilas bel-
lowed twice as the first meeting came to an end. Neither team shot
well in the game, but the Tar Heels dominated the offensive rebounding with 20 and committed only two turnovers, exhausting Duke's
young and thin team on defense.

"Everybody crashed the boards," Pinson said afterward. "We told
them at halftime: Me and Luke are going to do everything we can to
keep Carter and Bagley off the boards. You have to come in and rebound."

"The start of the second half, they played great," Krzyzewski said,
"and we were awful."

"We went from a 12-point lead to a four-point loss," lamented
Grayson Allen, who was held to nine points on three field goals.

Maye then scored 27 of his 33 points in the second half at N.C.
State to help avenge the defeat two weeks earlier when he had 31 and
12 in Roy Williams' second home loss to State. The victory in Raleigh
gave Williams a 28–4 record against the Wolfpack in his UNC tenure. Worn down after two emotional wins over their primary rivals,
the Tar Heels did not give in to Notre Dame after they had stolen a
win at South Bend earlier in the season. Maye just missed another
double-double with eight points and eight rebounds, but Pinson
picked him up with 16 and 10 and five assists in the second of what
would be eight straight double-figure scoring games for the defensive
ace and pass master from Greensboro whose career average was six
points per game.

Carolina was now 9–5 in the ACC and found itself battling Duke
for second place and, more important, a top four finish in the regular season and double-bye in the ACC tournament, which returned
to Brooklyn for the second straight year. After UNC lost at home to
a Miami buzzer-beater on Senior Night for Berry and Pinson, the Tar

Heels had to win at Duke on Allen's Senior Night to finish second and avoid slipping to a four-way tie for third place and sixth seed in the tournament.

The Blue Devils remained somewhat of an enigma with the rawest talent in their storied history. Bagley had become a double-double machine, setting a school freshman record of 22 for the season. Yet he personified Duke's defensive woes, and the fact that he eventually won so many national and conference awards and rewrote the Duke freshman record book indicated that voters didn't consider, or care much about, anything but statistics. Bagley was such a dominant scorer that he never learned or bothered to play defense in high school, and more than anyone else caused Krzyzewski to go away from the variations of man-to-man that had been his trademark for four decades.

Bagley missed four games with a sprained knee he suffered late in the loss at Carolina, and the Blue Devils won them all by at least nine points. Carter, Trent, and über-athlete Duval were more engaged and more effective, and Allen went back to leading the team in scoring with just under a 24-point average in those four victories. In Bagley's first game back, he scored 19 points and Allen had six. Several columnists and commentators wondered if Bagley was a selfish player, chasing his own numbers, and holding down the other four starters.

Krzyzewski said the critics "have a right" to say and write whatever they want, adding, "There are always two sides to every story, maybe more."

The Blue Devils had stayed with the zone they implemented because of Bagley and, in his absence, perhaps should have been running and pressing to force turnovers and showcase skills of the other great players on the roster like Trent, who nevertheless broke J. J. Redick's freshman 3-point record.

Duke's highest-percentage play was the lob or dump inside to Bagley, who rarely passed the ball and averaged a paltry 1.5 assists per game. But he was a transcendent talent headed for the NBA, where he hoped to have better success than Coach K's only other one-and-done big man, Jahlil Okafor, the No. 3 pick by Philadelphia in the 2015 NBA draft. Okafor made the All-NBA rookie team for the terrible 10-win Sixers in 2016. But as the team improved, he got branded as lazy and a defensive liability and was traded in December 2017 to Brooklyn, where he averaged a little more than 12 minutes a game in his first season with the Nets.

Bagley wasn't even his team's best rim protector, averaging less than one block per game compared to Carter's 2.1. And Bagley was almost glib about it when asked after the season why he hadn't blocked more shots. "We had Wendell," he said.

But Bagley had spectacular stretches when he controlled both ends of the court. He had nine points, nine rebounds, and three assists in the first half at UNC and seemed either tired or bothered by the knee sprain in the second half. In the rematch at Cameron on Saturday night, March 3, Bagley's second-half explosion helped the Blue Devils erase a 16-point deficit.

Duke was fortunate not to be behind by more than 10 points at halftime, having shot 1-for-10 from 3-point range and missing 10 of 14 free throws. The Tar Heels shot only 38.2 percent, including five of 17 from behind the arc. And they extended their lead early in the second half before the Blue Devils brought a quiet Cameron to life.

"At halftime, I said, 'Look, take the pianos off your back,'" Krzyzewski recounted, "'quit playing with all the pressure in the world. Get a smile on your face, just play.' I said I'm not gonna call any plays. You hit, cut, everybody touches the ball. You see a play to make, make it. Get comfortable in the game. And they did that. Obviously, Marvin went nuts for a while and put us on his back."

Bagley made eight of 11 shots, including a 3-pointer, for 18 points and had 11 rebounds in the second half. He finished the game with 21 and 15. Allen played all 40 minutes and ended his home career with 15 points and an emotional send-off from the Crazies. Trent scored 13, including three 3-pointers in the second half, which helped Duke take control. Carter played second banana with nine points and nine rebounds, and Duval had seven points, six assists, no turnovers, and two steals. All of them had played their last game at Cameron, a satisfying 74–64 win over the ninth-ranked team in the country and their Blue Blood rival.

The Tar Heels were led by Cam Johnson's 16 points. Pinson and Maye had 13 each. Berry, who had been on a scoring tear, averaging better than 21 points over the last eight games, finished with six points and went 0-for-7 from the 3-point line.

"Needless to say, that's not Joel Berry," Williams said. "I think some aliens crept up into my guys' bodies in the second half, because that wasn't the North Carolina team that I've seen all year, and that wasn't the North Carolina team that I love."

Six nights later, they got to do it all over again in Brooklyn, and for the second straight year the underdog won the rubber match in the ACC tournament semifinals.

Bagley matched Okafor as the second to win ACC Player of the Year and Rookie of the Year and make the all-conference team unanimously. He was the third to lead the league in scoring, rebounding, and shooting percentage, joining Horace Grant of Clemson and Tim Duncan of Wake Forest. Carolina's Maye and Berry also made the 2018 All-ACC first team, and Maye was named the ACC Most Improved Player. Duke's Carter made the all-freshman team and second-team All-ACC, and Allen was on the third team after missing altogether as a junior. Pinson was one of ten players who received at least 12 All-ACC votes and earned honorable mention.

When the fifteen teams convened in Brooklyn for the ACC tournament, news had died down that Carter and Tar Heel one-and-done Tony Bradley were mentioned in the FBI's investigation into sports agents and shoe company executives who allegedly paid high school recruits to attend certain schools. Duke quickly released a statement saying "no eligibility issues" were pending with Carter, and UNC pretty much ignored the report since Bradley was already in the NBA. A bigger concern to the Tar Heels came before the season, when five-star commit Nassir Little from the high school class of 2018 was cited in the probe; he and his father agreed to sign sworn statements that neither had taken money from any third party. The scandal hit the ACC hardest at Louisville, which fired Hall of Fame coach Rick Pitino after a federal indictment of some other people hovering around college basketball suggested he was aware of a scheme in which Adidas paid six figures to recruit Brian Bowen before he signed with Louisville, an Adidas-sponsored school. Bowen wound up transferring to South Carolina and having to sit out the season.

Duke, the second seed in the tournament, and sixth-seeded Carolina were in the same bracket and met in the semifinals for the second year in a row. The Blue Devils had beaten Notre Dame in their first tournament game, and the Tar Heels had defeated Syracuse and Miami in their two games. Duke was still ranked No. 5, but UNC had fallen to 12th in the polls after losing its last two regular-season games to Miami and Duke.

For the third time in a month, the Blue Bloods battled on national TV in a game that meant more for pride and NCAA tournament seedings than anything else. "Everybody and their mama will be watching," Pinson quipped after the Thursday night quarterfinals.

Virginia had already won the ACC race, the first team to go through an 18-game schedule with just one loss, and wrapped up a No. 1 NCAA seed. Duke, which was 26–6 and had finished 13–5 in the ACC regular season, still had a chance for a top seed, but Carolina seemed no better than a No. 2 with a 24–9 overall record, 11–7 in the ACC.

Like the year before, the Tar Heels controlled the first half and led the Blue Devils at the break, this time by 36–31. Seven players scored, including Brooks and Manley off the bench for a combined 12 points and five rebounds while competing with Duke's size. Two of Brooks' points came after being hip-checked by Allen at midcourt, another flagrant foul that kept boos raining down on the Duke senior. While Brooks was making his two free throws, Allen and Berry stood side-by-side chatting and smiling. As kids growing up in Florida, they had played against each other for years.

"It's always a joking thing with me and Grayson," Berry said after the game. "We're good friends. But I told him that you've just got to watch yourself because anything you do like that you know they're going to get on you about. That's why we laughed it off."

Four Blue Devils scored all 31 of the team's points in the first half, and they got nothing from their bench. However, in the first two matchups of the season, the team leading and seemingly having its way at the half eventually lost.

It looked different this year when Maye hit a jumper with 5:34 remaining to give Carolina its biggest lead, 72–56. Duke was on its way to committing 18 turnovers and shooting 6-for-23 from 3-point range.

Clearly trying to milk the clock with each possession, Carolina got careless with its own turnovers and tentative shots, allowing Duke to make a 13–0 run. Trent's 3-pointer with 0:51 on the clock brought the Devils within three at 72–69. Two more turnovers by the Tar Heels put them in a position to lose the game or let it go to overtime. One of the turnovers was by Pinson, who when trapped on the sideline dropped the ball out of bounds. Williams looked exasperated on the UNC bench.

Allen controlled Duke's last two possessions, charging into Kenny Williams on the first and then trying to draw contact while shooting a 3-pointer that missed on the second. Pinson redeemed himself by icing the 74–69 win with a pair of free throws.

"I made a big-time turnover that I needed to make up for, and I'm going to be honest, I was like, you're making these two free throws," Pinson said. "Like you just almost blew the game for your team, so you have to make them."

Trent with 20 points and Bagley's 19 and 13 rebounds led the Blue Devils, who got no points from their bench. After playing so well in Durham the week before, Duval went scoreless and turned it over five times, though he did make seven assists.

The Tar Heels put five players in double figures, led by Maye's 17 points (plus 10 rebounds) and Berry's 13, including three 3-pointers. Pinson had 10 points and seven assists, most of them from inside the Duke zone that Carolina exposed as well as any team had. UNC won the season series, which was more important to its fans than winning the conference championship.

At that moment, the all-time ACC tournament records for both Duke and Carolina stood at 100–45. But the Tar Heels lost the next night in the final game to Virginia and went home to await their NCAA assignment.

A year before, they had lost to the Blue Devils in the conference tournament and won the national championship, and Duke went out in a second-round NCAA loss to South Carolina. "I think we're much better prepared for the NCAA tournament than we were a month ago, and these two games will help us even though we lost tonight and could have played better," Krzyzewski said before leaving Brooklyn.

It was a foregone conclusion, as with most years, that Duke would make the NCAA tournament field. But this was the 23rd consecutive bid to the Big Dance for Krzyzewski, who tied Dean Smith and Lute Olson for the all-time high among coaches. The Blue Devils gathered at Cameron late Sunday afternoon to find out their seed and regional assignment.

As a tradition, Williams' players met at his home for dinner and dessert and watched the NCAA pairings show. They had split their last six games but felt good about their chances to go back to the Final Four for a third straight year. This season, especially, with the field so wide open, matchups were the key.

The rivals both received second seeds but were sent to different pods for their first two games. Duke, No. 2 in the Midwest Regional, went to Pittsburgh to face mid-majors Iona and Rhode Island, the No. 15 and No. 7 seeds, and blew them both out by a combined 47 points to reach Krzyzewski's 24th Sweet 16, the most ever by a coach and three more than Smith. As the No. 2 seed in the West Regional, Carolina drew the favorable pod in Charlotte, where a large contingent of Tar Heels fans sold out the Spectrum Center for their team's first two games, against 15th seeded Lipscomb and seventh-seeded Texas A&M, which defeated No. 10-seeded Providence in round one.

Carolina had a slow start against Lipscomb of the Atlantic Sun Conference but ran out to a 43–34 halftime lead and won going away 84–66 behind Pinson's 15 points, 10 rebounds, and seven assists. Before the Tar Heels played Texas A&M, Roy Williams called the Aggies "the biggest team I've ever seen." They started a front line of 6'9" Robert Williams, a future NBA first-round draft pick, 6'10" Tyler Davis, and 6'8" D. J. Hogg, with 6'10" Tonny Trocha-Morelos coming off the bench.

Unranked A&M, which finished seventh in the Southeastern

Conference with a 9–9 record, went into the game 287th in the country in 3-point shooting with a 32.9 percentage. The Aggies missed four of their first seven long shots and fell behind 20–13 after a short jumper by Sterling Manley with 11:37 left in the first half. Having opened the season 11–1 and ranked as high as No. 5, A&M lost 11 of its next 20 games and dropped out of the polls—and could not have seriously considered beating vaunted UNC in Charlotte at that point.

Had Carolina stretched the lead to double figures, the Tar Heels would have likely cruised into the West Regional in Los Angeles. But, instead, they went 6:12 without scoring and were on the wrong side of a 15–0 run to fall behind by eight points with 5:25 left in the first half. Now believing they could win, the Aggies outscored UNC 14–6 and led 42–28 at the break. It was a bad matchup and as bad a half as Carolina played all season, settling for 13 3-pointers over the A&M zone, missing 12, and getting outrebounded 25–18.

After A&M's T. J. Starks grabbed what he thought was the last rebound of the half and literally walked off the court without dribbling, the turnover gave the Tar Heels one more shot with two seconds left. Manley missed a bunny at the buzzer. Pinson, strangely, skipped down the court and into the runway, perhaps celebrating that the nightmarish half had ended. But the Aggies scored the first six points of the second half, and Carolina never cut the lead below 17 points.

For the game, A&M shot 51.7 percent from the field, 41.7 from 3-point range. UNC went out misfiring at 33.3 percent and hitting only six of 31 on 3-pointers for 19.4 percent.

The strange season, with peaks and valleys throughout, ended with the players and coaches having plenty of time to process the awful final 20 minutes. The noncompetitive Tar Heels went home with a 26–11 record and finished with a No. 10 ranking after splitting their last eight games.

"It's the most inadequate feeling I've ever felt," Roy Williams said. "I feel it all the time, last game of the year, but I think I felt it more today than any other time. I'm not ashamed to say I love these kids." He graciously said he was happy for Texas A&M coach Billy Kennedy, who continued on the job after being diagnosed with early-stage Parkinson's disease in 2011.

Berry's career ended with 21 points and eight misses on 10 3-point attempts, although two days before he moved past Michael Jordan into 13th place among Carolina's all-time leading scorers. He also joined Walter Davis as the only Tar Heel with 1,700 points, 400 rebounds, and 400 assists for his career. Luke Maye, who was one of fifteen finalists for the John Wooden Award (with Duke's Bagley) and made third-team All-American, turned in his 17th double-double of the season with 13 points and 11 rebounds. He earlier won the award for the ACC's top scholar athlete in men's basketball.

The same day Carolina lost as the No. 2 seed, the West Regional blew up when top seed Xavier was upset by Florida State. Third-seeded Michigan, the same team that had lost at UNC by 15 points back in November, kept some semblance of order by beating Houston by one point and advancing to the Sweet 16, where it crushed Texas A&M. But the upsets weren't over. No. 9 seed Florida State knocked off fourth-seeded Gonzaga and advanced to the regional championship game, won by Michigan for a trip to San Antonio and the Final Four.

For the second straight season, Duke faced a virtual road environment in the NCAA tournament at the Midwest Regional Sweet 16 in Omaha even though three ACC teams were there. The Blue Devils slipped past Syracuse, the No. 11 seed and the last team invited to the NCAA tournament. The Orange had survived a First Four game in Dayton against Bobby Hurley's Arizona State Sun Devils, then beaten sixth-seeded TCU and upset No. 3 seed Michigan State in the first two rounds.

With the 69–65 victory, Duke advanced to meet fourth-ranked Kansas, the No. 1 seed in the region. Thousands of KU fans had made the three-hour drive north from Lawrence to fill the CenturyLink Center, the home court of Creighton University in downtown Omaha. The Jayhawks had survived a comeback by fifth-seeded Clemson and reached their third straight Elite Eight game and their 10th in the twenty-first century.

Like the year before in Greenville, Blue Devils fans were heavily outnumbered by a hostile crowd, though their team was slightly favored by oddsmakers. Duke was trying to get back to a 17th Final Four, its first since 2015, and move Krzyzewski past John Wooden for the most Final Four appearances by any coach in NCAA history (they were tied with 12). Already joining Michigan in San Antonio were top-ranked Villanova and upstart Loyola of Chicago, a No. 11 seed that had knocked off ninth-seeded Kansas State earlier that day in the busted South Regional bracket.

Kansas and Duke played a tense, high-level game that went back and forth all evening, with the Jayhawks using their quickness and passing to penetrate the towering Blue Devils zone or get good looks over the top.

Once again, Duke's top two shooters were cold—Allen and Trent combined to make only 4-for-19 from the 3-point line. While the Blue Devils stifled Kansas star and Raleigh native Devonte' Graham, his backcourt mate Malik Newman torched the Duke defense for 32 points, including five 3-pointers. Surprisingly, the No. 6 rebounding team in the nation was beaten by the quicker Jayhawks 47–32 on the boards.

Yet, with under a minute left in regulation, Duke had a 72–69 lead and the ball after Allen made four straight free throws. Carter's missed jumper triggered a Kansas fast break and, with 27 seconds showing, Svi Mykhailiuk buried a 3-pointer from the top of the key to tie the score. The Blue Devils quickly set up for the final possession with

Allen controlling the ball. His short, lean-away jumper spun around the rim twice and fell off. The shot symbolized Allen's college career of ups and downs and indecisions. Instead of going hard to the hole with the score tied, Allen opted for an off-balance attempt in traffic.

Duke led by one in overtime when a controversial collision between a driving Newman and a defending Carter was called a block for Carter's fifth foul. Newman scored all 13 points in overtime for Kansas, which hung on for the 85–81 victory and its third Final Four trip under coach Bill Self since he succeeded Roy Williams at Kansas in 2003.

The Blue Devils should have won in regulation but let it slip away and ended with a 29–8 record, ranked ninth, after once being hailed as perhaps the greatest Duke team of all time. Allen, who burst into fame as a freshman on the 2015 national champions, could not get his team back to his second Final Four.

"I was trying to drive right, he cut me off. Went back left," he said of his last shot in regulation. "Their big stepped in to help. I had to get a shot up over him. I tried to bank it in and it about went in." Allen's only score in overtime was a meaningless 3-pointer with 0:03 remaining, closing his checkered career with 1,996 points, 450 rebounds, 432 assists, and 147 steals. Largely misunderstood by fans and media, Allen was an affable and respected teammate who graduated from Duke as a four-time academic All-ACC athlete. By staying all four years, instead of turning pro early, Allen left himself open to the foibles most one-and-dones avoided.

"It's kind of storybook," Krzyzewski said. "The eighth man on an eight-man team who scores eight straight points in the national championship game. Then he was an All-American the next year. And what he's gone through for the rest of his career. He's been the most scrutinized guy in all of sports. How do you handle that? How would *you* handle that? No one's gone through that."

According to Coach K, the media and fans "don't know about 90 percent" of what goes on inside a college basketball program. So he didn't care what people said about Allen, who he called the hardest worker on his team from the start. "I love the kid," Krzyzewski said. "He'd die for you."

For four years, Carolina had played and ended the season amidst controversy. Even before the academic scandal grew some teeth at UNC, suspended P. J. Hairston was the off-court story in 2013. Then the so-called paper or easy classes dogged the Tar Heels program and coach Roy Williams. The day they raised the 2017 national championship banner was the same day the NCAA announced it had found no reason to penalize the school, any coaches or athletes, which set up a reaction that the NCAA had let a cheater off the hook. College administrators and high-profile athletes weighed in. Former Navy All-American David Robinson, whose son Justin was a reserve on the 2017 and '18 Duke teams, said UNC not being punished for academic fraud was "maybe the most disappointing thing I've seen since I've been watching sports." His remarks made national news.

But throughout and after the 2018 season, Duke made almost as many headlines away from the court as it did with another one-and-done class going all the way to an NCAA regional championship game. It began late in the season when the *Oregonian* newspaper and website published a story questioning Marvin Bagley's amateur status because his father had allegedly received excessive money and benefits from Nike to coach his son's AAU teams, which were sponsored by the shoe and apparel giant headquartered outside Portland. Duke was quick to issue a statement saying the NCAA had approved Bagley's eligibility. But the *Oregonian* story revealed new information that, after filing for bankruptcy in Arizona, the Bagley family had moved to a gated community in Southern California, where Marvin finished high school.

"These kids sign things at every school, asking them if they took anything," Krzyzewski said in March 2018. "Our compliance works with them, trying to find out as much as you can. And if there was an incident, you take the proper steps with the NCAA before a kid would ever play for you. That's been done for my 38 years here. You do that. I'm comfortable with the way we handle that here."

The father of another freshman, Gary Trent Jr., questioned how his son was used at Duke, even though he had an outstanding season, averaging 14.5 points—including 97 3-pointers—and 4.2 rebounds. But he wasn't the spectacular player who recorded 31.8 points, 6.4 rebounds, and 3.8 assists per game as a senior at Prolific Prep in Napa, California, where he became a projected first-round NBA draft choice. His father, whom Krzyzewski said "coached Gary hard since he was three," claimed the Blue Devils' system of play stilted his son.

"You only saw my son do the speed limit," Gary Trent told the Raleigh *News & Observer*. "If you take a Bugatti and put it on a pedestrian street, you're only allowed to go 60 miles per hour. Just because the car is driven at 60, does that mean it cannot go 200 miles per hour? That's how I feel about my son's talent."

The parents of Wendell Carter Jr. felt similarly about their son's role at Duke.

After the season ended, Kylia and Wendell Carter said their son was "kicked to the curb" after Bagley reclassified from a junior to a senior in high school and joined Duke's latest recruiting class in August of 2017. "My initial reaction, I was pissed," Kylia Carter told NBA Sports. "And it wasn't because Marvin was coming. To be honest, I felt like that was information that was kept from us. It felt shady."

Wendell Carter Sr. was even stronger about how he believed his son was treated. "I was concerned because it felt like we were lied to," he said. "'Oh, Wendell's gonna be the man' and then the rug was pulled out from under us."

As the "other" post man for the Blue Devils, Carter averaged 13.5 points and 9.1 rebounds and led the team in blocked shots. He remained high on all of the NBA mock draft boards. Kylia Carter said she told Wendell Jr., "Everybody knows you can score. So let Marvin have all the damn points. They're throwing him the ball, the offense is geared around him. Defense is not the strong suit of this team. Fill that void."

Trevon Duval, the No. 1 point guard recruit in the country when he signed with Duke, had an inconsistent season with an early 8–1 assist-turnover ratio that shrank to 2–1. Duval led the team in giveaways and by far had the lowest 3-point percentage among the starters (29 percent). Duval was on several preseason mock NBA draft boards and was a projected second-round pick after the NBA Combine in May 2018.

Kylia Carter had already used her one year close to the Duke program as a rallying cry against the NCAA and its practices, and the NBA and its players association for setting the minimum age to enter the draft at nineteen. The former college basketball player at Mississippi said her son decided between Duke and Harvard and she recommended Harvard for its academic reputation and smaller focus on basketball.

Carter told the Knight Commission, supposedly the watchdog over college athletics: "The problem I see is not with the student-athletes, it's not with the coaches or the institutions of higher learning, but it's with the system . . . where the laborers are the only people that are not being compensated for the work that they do while those in charge receive mighty compensation.

"The only two systems where I've known that to be in place are slavery and the prison system. And now I see the NCAA as overseers of a system that is identical to that. So it's difficult for me to sit here and not say that there is a problem that is sickening."

She also said: "At the end of the day, the talent is being purchased, but the talented are not receiving any of the benefit. The colleges are only recruiting the talented kids for their talent. They're not recruiting them because they will excel academically at their institution. So [what] is the benefit of them going to that institution?"

Carter brought a parent's perspective to a longtime argument over how the NCAA and NBA defined eligibility: Were college athletes used to benefit their own futures or to win championships, and how much value did a college education have for athletes who made millions for their schools?

These were not new questions, but it was surprising that they came out of the Duke camp. And when Bagley, Carter, Duval, and Trent all declared for the NBA draft after their freshman season, it seemed like the shine had dulled on the Duke image.

Mike Krzyzewski wasn't deterred, at least to the point of not bringing in another five-star class that thought playing for Coach K, with his Olympic experience coaching pro players, was still the fastest and best way to the NBA. He had signed the No. 1, No. 2, and No. 5 prospects in the high school class of 2018, plus a point guard who could help them share the ball and win enough games that they would all stay in the gun sights of NBA scouts. And the 2018 draft bore out that optimism.

Bagley was the second overall pick by the Sacramento Kings and was guaranteed a two-year contract worth more than #15 million, plus $20 million more if the team picked up his third- and fourth-year options. Carter went No. 7 to the Chicago Bulls, who guaranteed him an estimated $9.6 million and another $13 million for years three and four. It was the third time (Jason Williams and Mike Dunleavy in 2002; Okafor and Justise Winslow in 2015) the Blue Devils had two players selected among the top 10 and the fifth time Duke had at least two lottery picks (top 14). For the eighth consecutive NBA draft, at least one Blue Devil went in the first round.

When Grayson Allen was picked No. 21 overall by the Utah Jazz, coached by long-ago Duke player Quin Snyder, it was also the third time that at least three Blue Devils went in the first round. Allen said he debated whether to attend the draft but decided to be at the Barclays Center in Brooklyn. His rookie contract was worth a guaranteed $4.5 million for two years and another $6.5 million if Allen was signed to his third- and fourth-year options by the Jazz.

Trent and Duval sweated out their selections. Somewhat justifying his father's criticism, Trent fell to the second round, the 37th overall pick, by Sacramento, where he was joining Bagley before his rights were traded to Portland. But Trent signed a guaranteed contract with the Trail Blazers for more money than six players drafted in the first round, three years totalling $3.9 million.

Duval slipped all the way out of the draft after an undisclosed lingering eyesight problem affected his shooting (42.8 percent overall and 29 percent from 3-point range). The first Duke one-and-done not to be drafted, Duval signed as a free agent with Houston to play in the NBA summer league and try to earn a spot on the Rockets' roster for the 2019 season.

Coach K increased his number of first-round draft picks to 38–18 in the last ten years—and nine more than Roy Williams' 29. That was a selling point Duke used in recruiting, but nothing compared to Krzyzewski's burgeoning brand as the millionaire-maker. His four players drafted off the 2018 team signed guaranteed contracts for $33.9 million; throw in all of the option years, and the deals were worth more than $73 million.

UNC seniors Joel Berry and Theo Pinson also were not drafted, as expected, but both quickly signed two-way free-agent contracts, Berry with the Lakers and Pinson with the Brooklyn Nets; how much money they made depended on the number of games they played in the NBA versus the G League. Berry had to prove he was quick and strong enough to score on and defend bigger NBA point guards. Pinson, an above-average defender and passer, was hurt by a 42.4 career shooting percentage in college that improved almost 60 points as a senior, when he was the first Tar Heel to average 10 points, 5 rebounds, and 5 assists in a season.

Luke Maye, who entered the NBA draft to get feedback from coaches, general managers, and scouts, worked out with the Charlotte Hornets, Atlanta Hawks, and Oklahoma City Thunder, but was not invited to try out at the NBA Combine. Like Justin Jackson had in 2016 and Wayne Ellington, Danny Green, and Ty Lawson did after the 2008 season, Maye returned to UNC for his senior year with more information about how to improve his game.

The players from both schools who had just finished their rookie seasons in the NBA, or playing for G League developmental teams, had mixed results.

Luke Kennard, drafted by the Detroit Pistons after his sophomore year at Duke, played 20 minutes a game—mostly behind starting guard and former UNC star Reggie Bullock—and averaged 7.6 points. Kennard also shot a respectable 41.5 percent from the longer NBA 3-point line. In his last two games of the season, Kennard scored 20 points against Toronto, with seven rebounds and two assists, and had 23 points, five rebounds, and five assists at Chicago.

Jayson Tatum, the third pick in the 2017 NBA draft, started 80 of the Boston Celtics' 82 games and made the NBA's All-Rookie team after averaging 13.9 points and five rebounds and making 43.4 percent of his 3-point shots in the regular season. The Celtics reached the

Eastern Conference finals, and Tatum was their star through the game seven loss to LeBron James and the Cleveland Cavaliers. The twenty-year-old Tatum, who was in high school two years earlier and signed a contract that with team options was worth more than $30 million, averaged 18.5 points in 19 playoff games, leading the Celtics in scoring and free throw shooting. In the Eastern Conference semifinals against Philadelphia, Tatum scored at least 20 points in all five games—28, 21, 24, 20, and 25—and made 52.6 percent of his field goal attempts.

Harry Giles never played in his first year in Sacramento. The Kings announced in January 2018 that he would "not be introduced to NBA game play during the 2018 season but focus on more vigorous practice activity and individual workouts tailored to continue developing overall strength and aid ACL injury prevention." Frank Jackson's rookie season with the New Orleans Pelicans also was postponed after he underwent three foot surgeries, dating back to spring of 2017.

Besides Tatum, Duke's biggest NBA story of 2018 was Quinn Cook, the undrafted senior from the 2015 NCAA championship team. After Cook played two seasons in the G League, his rights were purchased by Golden State. He was promoted from the Santa Cruz developmental team to the NBA Warriors to fill in for the injured Stephen Curry, and Cook played in 33 games, starting 18. He averaged 9.5 points and 2.7 assists and remained with the Warriors when Curry returned. Cook played in all 17 playoff games, averaging 4.8 points, and won a ring when the "Dubs" swept James and the Cavaliers in the 2018 NBA Finals.

The Tar Heels' NBA rookie class was also a mixed bag.

Justin Jackson's numbers with Sacramento weren't impressive—he averaged 6.7 points, 2.8 rebounds, and 22.1 minutes in 68 games—but his production increased in the latter stages of the season. Jackson's best overall performance came when he had 19 points, eight rebounds, and four assists against Phoenix. His top shooting performance was against Atlanta—seven of eight field goals, 4-for-4 on 3-pointers, and 2-for-2 free throws for a season-high 20 points. He also played six games for the Reno Bighorns in the G League.

Isaiah Hicks played in 18 games of the 2018 schedule for the New York Knicks, including the last eight, and scored 15 points against Cleveland in the season finale. He spent most of the season with the G League Westchester Knicks, averaging 15.6 points and 7.8 rebounds in 37 games. Kennedy Meeks, waived before the season by the Toronto Raptors, kept his NBA dream alive in the G League with the Raptors 905, which was coached by former UNC star Jerry Stackhouse. Meeks averaged 12.8 points and 9.6 rebounds in 45 regular-season games and 9.8 points and 9.2 rebounds in the playoffs, where his team reached the finals before losing to the Austin Spurs. In the one play-off game they faced each other, Hicks had 23 points and eight rebounds, Meeks 13 and 14.

Tony Bradley spent his rookie season going back and forth from the Utah Jazz to its minor league team in Salt Lake City, averaging 15.4 points and 10.2 rebounds in 24 games for the G League Stars and 3.2 minutes in nine games for the NBA Jazz. Bradley was a millionaire but, considering how his rookie year went and Carolina's quick ouster in the 2018 post season, Bradley's decision to turn pro as a freshman was still debated by Tar Heels fans and anyone else who cared.

The greatest players continued flowing through both programs, no matter how long they stayed. That had gone on at Duke from Vic Bubas to Bill Foster to Krzyzewski. The same at Carolina from Frank McGuire to Smith to Williams.

But the question grew louder each year: How long would the current caretakers of the Blue Blood rivalry stay on, and who would succeed them when they were ready to step down?

DUKE-CAROLINA COACHING TREES

(Current Head Coaches)

Who's Next at Duke?
Tom Amaker, Harvard
Mike Brey, Notre Dame
Jeff Capel, Pitt
Chris Collins, Northwestern
Jonny Dawkins, Central Florida

Bobby Hurley, Arizona State
Quin Snyder, Utah Jazz
Steve Wojciechowski, Marquette

Who's Next at UNC?
Jerod Haase, Stanford
C. B. McGrath, UNC-Wilmington
Wes Miller, UNC-Greensboro
King Rice, Monmouth
Jerry Stackhouse, Raptors 905/
Memphis Grizzlies

Wild Cards
Jon Scheyer
Brad Stevens
Mike White

Wild Cards
Hubert Davis
Billy Donovan
Kenny Smith
Brad Stevens

EPILOGUE

HOW LONG, WHO'S NEXT?

Jeff Capel III seemed to have everything in place to become the next head coach at Duke, if and when Mike Krzyzewski ever retired. He was a former Blue Devils player, went 175–110 as a head coach at two other major colleges, and was an integral part of Duke's recent recruiting windfalls, helping to lure and coach more than a dozen first-round NBA draft choices.

That Capel had turned down opportunities to take over at Georgia Tech and Arizona State in recent years gave credence to speculation that he was the heir apparent at Duke. It would not have been a reach for him to become the school's first African American head basketball coach; his father-in-law, Dan Blue, broke the same barrier as chair of the Duke Board of Trustees.

After seven years on the staff, the last four as associate head coach, Capel shocked much of the basketball world when he accepted Pitt's offer to rebuild its floundering program, which went 0–18 in the ACC in 2018. Speculation was rampant over what happened and why Capel left the second seat at Duke for a major reconstruction job. It also seemed to say Krzyzewski wasn't ready to retire at all.

Three factors were part of the most popular conjecture.

With the excitement of a new one-and-done recruiting class coming every year, the new players and older coach had a tacit agreement: They would all be there for at least one more season, which would overshadow speculation about Krzyzewski retiring. To some, that meant a lack of vision for the future of Duke basketball, but for most it meant looking ahead to another great Blue Devils team even though the names on the back of their jerseys were constantly changing.

Krzyzewski and the school were unwilling to name Capel, or anyone else, coach-in-waiting. If they were, Capel would have been the obvious choice. And if he wouldn't be the successor, he had few reasons to stay. At forty-three, Capel was at a prime age to land another head coaching job.

A third factor came from reports of disagreements between Coach K and Capel on how the program had been transformed from long-term stability to short-term success. This included the number of one-and-dones, who essentially were recruited to start ahead of players already in the program and waiting their turn, and the kind of quick-fix zone Duke played because man-to-man defense could not be taught successfully in one season. Krzyzewski admitted as much about the defense at the end of 2018.

Or perhaps this was all a smoke screen to keep retirement talk away from Coach K, who promoted Nate James and Jon Scheyer to associate head coaches and brought 2000 ACC Player of the Year Chris Carrawell back for his second stint on the Duke staff. With Nolan Smith elevated from special assistant to director of basketball operations, Krzyzewski was surrounded by former Duke players, but none of whom were ready to succeed him.

HOW LONG, WHO'S NEXT?

Dean Smith had been dogged over his last five years about how long he would coach. New England Patriots quarterback Tom Brady countered the banter over his retirement by saying he would play until his "midforties." Krzyzewski's latest contract ran through 2021, when he would be seventy-four. With those dates so far out, Brady and Krzyzewski could walk away at any time with no warning or potential victory lap season to endure.

It was far more likely that Krzyzewski planned to coach as long as he was healthy, which was another question completely. In 2016–17, Coach K had two ankle operations, a hernia procedure, lower back surgery, and both knees replaced. (That was on top of two hip replacements over the prior eighteen years.) But under care of the renowned Duke Medical Center, he was able to coach the U.S. national team at the 2016 Olympics in Rio and missed only a handful of Blue Devils games the last four seasons.

Clearly, nothing else on the horizon compared to the professional challenge and personal freedom he had at Duke. And, just as clearly, he was not ready to retire. Whenever close colleagues teased him about being the bionic man and the decades-old rumors that he dyed his hair, Krzyzewski had been known to smile and say, "I do what I can."

When they became opposing head coaches, Roy Williams and Krzyzewski were much closer in age than when Smith had 16 years and stature on Coach K, and they appeared much closer to winding down together. In fact, Williams could retire first. Besides being three years younger and in better health, he hadn't promised anyone anything. His latest contract extended through 2020, the year of his seventieth birthday.

Williams said he knew when it would be time to quit and that he had plenty of things he still wanted to do involving family and friends. Just as Krzyzewski was moved by the death of his former competitor and coaching colleague Jim Valvano in 1993, and Coach K's brother William in 2013, Williams had watched more close friends pass away in recent years.

Within six months of 2014–15, Williams lost his next-door neighbor and best friend Ted Seagroves, and coaching mentors Smith and Bill Guthridge after they all battled long illnesses. Woody Durham, the forty-year radio hall of fame voice of the Tar Heels and a former golfing buddy, died in early 2018. And Williams had his own cancer scare in 2012, when he promised, "I'm going to smell the roses a heck of a lot more every day."

Krzyzewski's decision to coach well into his fourth decade at Duke was more about enjoying and protecting his legacy than continuing to build it.

After all, what else could he accomplish? He had already coached at Duke two years more than Dean Smith had at Carolina, won more ACC championships than Smith and more games than any other coach in history. Krzyzewski was second in all-time national championships with five, and no matter what happened in his final seasons at Duke, he was destined to be considered at least the greatest college coach behind John Wooden, who won 10 NCAA titles.

But protecting the legacy so he could enjoy it may well have been paramount, more important than passing it on. No one likely amassed the power and money of Coach K without something he or she wouldn't want the public to know. His leash at Duke got longer until there was no leash, after he became the highest-paid employee and the face of the university. Just like some traced the academic scandal at UNC all the way back to Smith, who had similar power at Carolina, some lines probably were crossed somewhere. Even if Krzyzewski had nothing to do with, or no knowledge of, them.

Besides the guilt by association Williams suffered with the NCAA investigation at UNC, he did not welcome the scrutiny when he was at Kansas about the private deal for boosters to give gifts to players after their senior seasons. Smith was the master of confidentiality during his Carolina career, so much so that even his own family members claimed to know very little about the Tar Heels program or they were sworn to secrecy.

The Duke family was different from the Carolina family because it involved Coach K's personal family far more. His wife and three daughters were closely involved with the program since the little girls were gaga over the players, then on to their own marriages and nine grandchildren who became unofficial mascots for the team. The Krzyzewski home was always where the players went when they needed some TLC.

J. J. Redick said he considered quitting basketball after the Final Four loss in 2004, and vicious fans taunted his family on the road. Redick's self-admitted immaturity led him to believe he would be happier as a regular student, and the Duke family stepped in. The Krzyzewski women were the good cops, providing the comfort, while Coach K and his staff administered the tough love that Redick later said he needed badly.

They made Redick see a counselor and put him through grueling off-season workouts that began sometimes at 7:00 in the morning. Redick responded by getting into the best condition of his life and breaking the all-time Duke and ACC scoring records with two terrific seasons his junior and senior years. He reached the peak of a game he had learned on the outdoor court on his family farm.

"When I got to Duke, I knew how many points I needed each season to have a shot at Johnny Dawkins' record," Redick said. The Duke coaches still saw the real Redick, not the one who got lost and lonely halfway through.

Redick admitted that, during his lowest point, he stopped going to class. Duke and Krzyzewski didn't administer the kind of discipline that cost them games, and somehow the academics were taken care of like they were at most big-time athletic schools, as was documented at UNC. Thirteen years later, Coach K suspended Grayson Allen for one game for his flagrant fouling when national commentators, some with Duke ties, advocated for a stiffer penalty. At the end of their four-year careers, Redick and Allen said their coaches and their faith helped them make it.

Except for the nonstop scrutiny that made the magnifying glass bigger at Duke than at most schools, this went on in college athletics. Showcased prep stars went on to big-name colleges, some succeeding and some not. Highly touted recruits who washed out at Duke and transferred were fourfold what they were at UNC, where the spotlight was just as bright but the players seemed to live in a less stressful environment on and off a sprawling campus. Roy Williams continued the Smith tradition of keeping freshmen away from the media until the season started; Krzyzewski did it differently when he arrived at Duke.

In his early years, when he was known as "Mike" and not the revered "Coach K," Krzyzewski admitted feeling as much like an Army captain (which he had been) as he did a basketball coach because he was fighting for his professional life almost every day. His family was under siege in a city with more UNC alumni than Duke fans in the 1980s.

"The rivalry is there every day in our community," he said in 2012. "We've become one of the best programs in the country, but we're still a minority, which mystifies some people. North Carolina is the bigger school and a state school. So sometimes you have to learn to live with that when you're the Duke coach."

The epiphany came in 2004, when asked almost twenty years later to the day about the charge he made in 1984 that Smith and Carolina benefited from a double standard. The same claim was being leveled against Duke. Krzyzewski could have reacted harshly, defensively, or arrogantly to the question.

"I said it, and I believed it when I said it, but over the last 20 years I have learned to respect what Dean went through to get his program where it was," Coach K said in 2004. "Because we have gone through much of the same thing, and I understand his position much better now."

Krzyzewski had earned the same preeminent status as Smith but also coveted it more. Restricted far less by working at a private school, where his annual salary and bonuses exceeded $10 million and he became the highest paid nonprofit employee in the state of North Carolina, the celebrated Coach K had it like he never thought he would. It began to change after the back-to-back national championships in 1991 and '92, morphed into more of a corporate culture when he returned from missing most of the 1995 season because of back surgery and related exhaustion, and turned into a life of privilege in the twenty-first century, when his net worth was estimated at more than $25 million.

"My profession has stayed exciting because as my world expanded the core of that world is still coaching basketball," he said. "Basketball gives me a platform to do other things. I love the game of basketball, I'm not just using it, and as a result I get to do some really good things in other areas."

His life on and off the court has been managed by longtime associate Mike Cragg, who came to Duke in 1987 as assistant sports information director and went on to hold titles that read like he worked for a Fortune 500 company: senior administrator, Duke Basketball; co-founder of the Legacy Club, fund-raising arm of the basketball program; chief operating officer and deputy athletic director for operations. Others have been involved, as well.

Debbie K. Savarino, Krzyzewski's oldest daughter, served as an assistant director of athletics for special events and director of the Legacy

Fund. Even in formal meetings, she referred to her father as "Daddy." The younger daughters also worked somewhere for Duke before and while raising their children. Mickie Krzyzewski never held an official title but, some say, wielded the most influence over her husband's life.

They have all helped make Coach K a tightly scheduled recluse rarely seen in public and handled more like a brand. Bad hips forced him to give up racquet ball that he played regularly with certain Duke colleagues. Besides tending to his wine cellar and occasional gardening on the property around his private $2 million mansion only minutes from Duke, Krzyzewski and his wife spend whatever personal time he has with their extensive family there or at their beach home in North Carolina.

As far back as the 1990s, Krzyzewski started holding only four mid-week press conferences per season—one during the summer, one on the first day of practice, and one before each of the two regular-season games against Carolina. Once more abrupt in these meetings with mostly local media, the highly sought member of the Washington Speakers Bureau became entertaining, informative, and fun to be around.

"Since I was at Duke and we started winning, I have done speaking engagements at major companies and been around leaders in other fields," Krzyzewski said. "I get to study those companies and pick up things they do in leadership, and it's a bonus for me.

"In my sport, once you get to a certain level, people aren't going to share much with you. If you are the one who talks about basketball at clinics, where do you get your ideas from? How do you keep learning? So I have gone outside my field to keep learning from leaders in other fields."

Holding what's widely considered the best coaching job in America, he had coached pro players in the Olympics without having to run an NBA team and shared a bottle of wine with five-star generals, former U.S. presidents, and celebrities from the entertainment industry to financial moguls like Duke alumnus John Mack, former CEO and chairman of the board at Morgan Stanley. He flew his players and teams and family all over the country and across the world on private planes, an altitude unimagined for a poor kid from Chicago.

Television commentary, heading USA Basketball or the NCAA, commissioner of the NBA—any position posited—could never deliver the joie de vivre and the freedom he realized coaching an elite college basketball team of which he would always be the undisputed boss. That's why some believed he would coach at Duke until he physically no longer could.

Despite their mutual admiration, Roy Williams had written a much different story. The mountain man from outside Asheville, North Carolina, wanted to coach since he saw it as a way to go to college and escape the life of poverty he had as a kid. He never wanted to be more than a coach.

Williams did not hire an agent, like Krzyzewski had with David Falk, and that was probably why he earned less than half of Coach K's income for the first fifteen years they competed in the greatest rivalry in college basketball. His friends nudged him to get an agent who would negotiate more money, but Williams usually answered that whatever he made (estimated $4-plus million) was enough.

He had the assistant coaches and staff that NCAA rules allowed him to have, and Carolina, like Duke, had even more athletic department employees in support positions. Williams planned to continue working the same way he always did—full steam ahead, scouting, recruiting, and coaching, until he decided not to do it anymore. He remained much more visible in Chapel Hill than Coach K was in Durham, eating regularly at popular restaurants with Wanda, his wife of more than forty-five years.

Besides coaching basketball and building lifelong relationships with his players, Williams loved his family, a good golf game, and an occasional night at a casino in Las Vegas, the Bahamas, or on a cruise ship. He never seriously considered commercial endorsements like Krzyzewski had to pad his income, because Williams was never seriously approached about any. Most of his radio and TV spots were in support of his charity of choice, fighting cancer.

Williams hadn't had the physical setbacks of his rival at Duke, but his crisis in the summer of 2012 was worse than any ailment Krzyzewski had encountered. Doctors found spots on each of his kidneys and told him they were tumors that were likely malignant. "For 24 days, you think you have cancer," Williams said. "I don't care what the survival rate is. That scares you."

UNC planned to make veteran assistant Steve Robinson interim head coach if Williams stepped away for treatment. Meanwhile, he spent a couple of weeks at his beach home in South Carolina and then took his "foxhole" buddies on their annual golf trip. Williams came to the final hole of the four-day marathon and had a three-foot birdie putt.

"I've always said that I wanted to birdie the last hole I ever play," Williams said, shrugging. "God Almighty, what am I going to do now? I tried to make the sucker and I missed it, and it was almost the happiest thing I've ever done."

Three days later, Williams faced major surgery on his left kidney to remove the tumor. Despite a history of cancer in his family, the biopsy came back as a benign oncocytoma. A biopsy of the tumor on his right kidney yielded the same result. Williams was ready for practice and the 2013 season.

"It does change you," he said. "Anyone who says it doesn't is a lot stronger than I am."

That was when Williams had just turned sixty-two. Unlike Krzyzewski, who reset his priorities after sitting out most of the 1995 season, Williams didn't seem to slow down at all.

"My plan is what it was before; I hope to coach 6–10 more years," Williams said at the time. "As long as my health allows me to do that, I really do want to do it."

The 2018 season was his sixth since making that statement. And those closest to him insisted he wouldn't make it to the "10 more years," which would be after the 2022 season, when he would be four months shy of seventy-two.

Williams said he wanted to watch or coach his grandkids (three boys) in Little League, teach them to play golf, and have more time with Wanda, who had her own health problems in recent years. One of his longtime goals was to play as many as possible of the top 100 golf courses in the world, and he had played almost half of them while still coaching.

Williams' successor hadn't been decided, like it supposedly was when Smith retired and Guthridge held the job for three seasons. Williams was the school's choice after Guthridge retired, although it took him three more years to get to Chapel Hill. The days of automatically hiring from the Carolina family had ended at UNC. The next basketball coach might come from current or former assistants or players, but he would likely be the best coach available from the college or professional ranks—the right fit for the challenge and pressure, according to those making the decision.

UNC athletics director Bubba Cunningham, a non-alumnus who signed his own long-term contract, would likely collaborate with Williams and others on what would be another epic coaching hire for the Tar Heels. As at Duke, where athletics director Kevin White came from Notre Dame, a long line of internal and external candidates existed and probably would grow by the time Krzyzewski and Williams retired. Mentioning any of their names meant mentioning them all, which would be premature as the two Hall of Famers pressed on.

History has shown that the greatest athletic programs almost always slipped after iconic coaches retired, including UCLA and Wooden, Alabama and Bear Bryant, Tennessee and Pat Summitt. Duke dipped between Vic Bubas and Krzyzewski, as did Carolina between the Smith and Williams eras. How could they not?

Duke had won five national championships with Krzyzewski through 2018 and might cut down more nets before he leaves. Carolina had three NCAA titles with Williams and could add to its total of six sooner than later. Both programs were reloading for the 2019 season, when UNC's basketball team played its first game on the nearly christened Roy Williams Court at the Dean Smith Center. It was an overdue honor for the coach many believed to be the equal of his rival. Krzyzewski received a similar naming after his nineteenth year and two national championships at Duke, compared to Williams's three NCAA titles in fifteen seasons at Carolina.

The Blue Devils lost all five starters from the '18 team but had experienced reserves back, like junior center Marques Bolden, who Coach K was suddenly hyping as one of the best big men in the country, plus top five freshmen R. J. Barrett, Cam Reddish, and Zion Williamson scheduled to enroll in the fall. Duke's expected flows were outside shooting and which defense another new lineup could play most effectively.

The Tar Heels lost two starters but had three returning along with three big men who combined to play the minutes of a starter as freshmen. The team's most highly touted new freshmen were Nassir Little, Coby White, and Rechon Black; but who would take over for Joel Berry at point guard and replace Theo Pinson's intangibles were the pressing questions going into the season. The unknowns on both sides seemed to create even more interest.

HOW LONG, WHO'S NEXT?

So the Blue Bloods beat promised to go on indefinitely. Whenever Krzyzewski and Williams were no longer coaching, the rivalry could lose some national prominence for a time but not its ferocity. Alabama-Auburn football went on, as did Michigan–Ohio State. If the wrong coaches were hired to replace the icons, they wouldn't be there long. Bucky Waters lasted four years after Bubas, Matt Doherty three after Guthridge's three seasons.

With new coaches also come different philosophies as well as results. Clemson will eventually beat Carolina in Chapel Hill; Duke might not always bury the 3-pointer from the corner against the Tar Heels.

And if the biggest unforeseen change happened: After further conference realignment, Duke and/or UNC wound up in the Big Ten or Southeastern Conference, which in 2018 paid out to each of their member schools close to $50 million—almost twice as much in revenues as the ACC distributed?

And if, someday, the Blue Blood rivalry was not considered the greatest in college basketball? Would they cease playing at least twice a year? Would interest wane?

Hardly. Too many people would still want to watch. Too much would still be at stake.

And there would still be those eight miles of separation.

"It's easy for me to understand that," Krzyzewski said before his thirty-ninth season coaching one of the Blue Bloods. "If I was not with Duke or North Carolina, I would still want to watch Duke against North Carolina."

INDEX

INDEX

INDEX

INDEX

INDEX

INDEX